American Royalty

The Bush and Clinton Families and the Danger to the American Presidency

Matthew T. Corrigan

AMERICAN ROYALTY
Copyright © Matthew T. Corrigan, 2008.

All rights reserved. No part of this book may be used or reproduced in any manner whatsoever without written permission except in the case of brief quotations embodied in critical articles or reviews.

First published in 2008 by
PALGRAVE MACMILLAN™
175 Fifth Avenue, New York, N.Y. 10010 and
Houndmills, Basingstoke, Hampshire, England RG21 6XS
Companies and representatives throughout the world.

PALGRAVE MACMILLAN is the global academic imprint of the Palgrave Macmillan division of St. Martin's Press, LLC and of Palgrave Macmillan Ltd. Macmillan® is a registered trademark in the United States, United Kingdom and other countries. Palgrave is a registered trademark in the European Union and other countries.

ISBN-13: 978–1–4039–8416–6 paperback
ISBN-10: 1–4039–8416–6 paperback
ISBN-13: 978–1–4039–8415–9 hardcover
ISBN-10: 1–4039–8415–8 hardcover

Library of Congress Cataloging-in-Publication Data

Corrigan, Matthew T.
   American royalty : the Bush and Clinton families and the danger to the American presidency / Matthew T. Corrigan.
       p. cm.—(The evolving American presidency series)
   Includes bibliographical references and index.
       ISBN 1–4039–8416–6 (alk. paper)—ISBN 1–4039–8415–8 (alk. paper)
   1. Presidents—United States. 2. Bush family. 3. Clinton family.
   4. United States—Politics and government—1989– 5. Aristocracy (Political science)—United States—History. I. Title.

JK516.C618 2008
973.92092′2—dc22   2007035183

A catalogue record for this book is available from the British Library.

Design by Newgen Imaging Systems (P) Ltd., Chennai, India.

First edition: June 2008

10 9 8 7 6 5 4 3 2 1

Printed in the United States of America.

THE EVOLVING AMERICAN PRESIDENCY SERIES

Series Foreword:

The American Presidency touches virtually every aspect of American and world politics. And the presidency has become, for better or worse, the vital center of the American and global political systems. The Framers of the American government would be dismayed at such a result. As invented at the Philadelphia Constitutional Convention in 1787, the Presidency was to have been a part of a government with shared and overlapping powers, embedded within a separation-of-powers system. If there was a vital center, it was the Congress; the Presidency was to be a part, but by no means, the centerpiece of that system.

Over time, the presidency has evolved and grown in power, expectations, responsibilities, and authority. Wars, crises, depressions, industrialization, all served to add to the power of the presidency. And as the United States grew into a world power, presidential power also grew. As the United States became the world's leading superpower, the presidency rose in prominence and power, not only in the U.S., but on the world stage.

It is the clash between the presidency as invented and the presidency as it has developed that inspired this series. And it is the importance and power of the modern American presidency that makes understanding the office so vital. Like it or not, the American Presidency stands at the vortex of power both within the United States and across the globe.

This Palgrave series recognizes that the Presidency is and has been an evolving institution, going from the original constitutional design as a Chief Clerk, to today where the president is the center of the American political constellation. This has caused several key dilemmas in our political system, not the least of which is that presidents face high expectations with limited constitutional resources. This causes presidents to find extraconstitutional means of governing. Thus, presidents must find ways to bridge the expectations/power gap while operating within the confines of a separation-of-powers system designed to limit presidential authority. How presidents resolve these challenges and paradoxes is the central issue in modern governance. It is also the central theme of this book series.

Michael A. Genovese
Loyola Chair of Leadership
Loyola Marymount University
Palgrave's **The Evolving American Presidency**, Series Editor

The Second Term of George W. Bush
 edited by Robert Maranto, Douglas M. Brattebo, and Tom Lansford
The Presidency and the Challenge of Democracy
 edited by Michael A. Genovese and Lori Cox Han
Religion and the American Presidency
 edited by Mark J. Rozell and Gleaves Whitney

Religion and the Bush Presidency
    edited by Mark J. Rozell and Gleaves Whitney
Test by Fire: The War Presidency of George W. Bush
    by Robert Swansbrough
American Royalty: The Bush and Clinton Families and the Danger to the American Presidency
    by Matthew T. Corrigan

*This book is dedicated to my parents,
John and Patricia Corrigan for all
of their love and support.*

Contents

Preface ix
Acknowledgments xi

One   Introduction   1
Two   American Democracy and Family Presidencies   11
Three   Families Matter   29
Four   The Father Begins a Dynasty   55
Five   The Clintons Take Power   77
Six   The Bush Redemption   111
Seven   From First Lady to President?   153
Eight   The Prince in Waiting   179

Notes   195
Bibliography   209
Index   219

Preface

This book presents a normative argument that multiple presidencies within immediate families do not serve the nation or the presidency well. Chapter 1 will briefly present the two basic ideas that challenge the concept of family presidencies. First, family connections and name recognition give tremendous advantages to presidential relatives who seek the office. These advantages undermine the concerns of the founders about a concentration of too much power in the hands of the few. Moreover, for the modern presidency, family legacies dilute democratic maturation in the nation's politics. Second, family pressures and expectations can impact presidencies negatively especially in regards to policy outcomes.

Chapter 2 will examine the role of the office of the presidency as a representative institution. As political scientist James Barber states, "the presidency is different.... The one figure that draws people's hopes and fears for the political future." In our democratic republic, the president has a unique role. The office and the person who inhabits the office represent the entire nation. No legislator, governor, or appointee can make that claim. The background and family from which the president comes is important to how the president represents the entire nation. This chapter also will consider how the founders viewed a potential familial monarchy in the United States. The political domination of the Bush and Clinton families in recent years goes against many of the ideas and limits that the founders put in place. The modern presidency also offers a paradox for family presidencies. Family political networks aid presidential candidates tremendously, but family expectations and past failures can haunt presidencies. Moreover, how other nations view the prominence of these two political families in a time when the United States is trying export democracy will also be discussed.

Chapter 3 will show why family histories matter for presidents. Several examples of presidents and how their families impacted their presidencies will be discussed. The current standing of the Bushes and the Clintons will also be contrasted with other important historical, political families including the Adams, Roosevelts, and Kennedys.

The reciprocal nature of the Bush-Clinton political relationship will be highlighted starting with the emergence of George Herbert

Walker Bush in chapter 4. The rise of the first President Bush is as remarkable as the ascendancy of George W. Bush. This chapter will focus on some of the important events of George H. W. Bush's life and presidency and how they impacted both Bill Clinton's and George W. Bush's political prospects.

Chapter 5 will describe how a little-known Southern governor and his ambitious wife unseated the incumbent president of the United States. After a brilliant campaign, Bill Clinton attempted to consolidate power with his wife, Hillary Clinton, playing a major role. The chapter will also examine how the impeachment scandal, and the Clintons' unusual relationship impacted the presidency.

Chapter 6 will highlight the relationship between President Clinton's impeachment scandal and the rise of George W. Bush. Then the chapter will describe how the relationship between the first President Bush and the second President Bush helped him win the presidency but then has negatively impacted the policies of his administration and put an inexperienced son in the office of the presidency.

Chapter 7 will chronicle the transition of Hillary Clinton from first lady to senator and how her Senate win reestablished the Clinton family in elective politics. Her presidential campaign will be examined, and an argument will be presented that the first Clinton presidency may forecast problems for another Clinton campaign and potential presidency.

Chapter 8 will show how a second Bush son became a political giant in the fourth largest state in the nation. Jeb Bush's experiences in Florida will then be placed in context of possible presidential run in 2012 or 2016 and show the danger to the nation's democratic system involving the possibility of three Bush presidencies.

The individual chapters on the five political leaders examined are not meant to be complete biographies. The only events described here are those situations where the actions of the individuals may have impacted each other. Unlike other approaches, this book does not condemn these leaders, but instead makes an argument that presidential power is of such magnitude and complexity that it should not be shared among members of immediate families.

Acknowledgments

I would like to thank the staff at Palgrave Macmillan for making this book possible. In particular, Anthony Wahl has been a constructive supporter throughout the process. Professor Michael Genovese encouraged me to pursue this project from its inception. Michael has offered his support and advice regarding my scholarly work numerous times. I owe him a great debt for his interest in my career. I would also like to thank the Arts and Sciences Dean's Advisory Council at the University of North Florida (UNF) for a Faculty Fellowship. Academic Affairs at UNF also provided a semester sabbatical so my work could be completed. Jacci Dorey and Mark Swanhart of the Public Opinion Research Laboratory provided assistance in numerous ways. I owe a debt to the numerous presidential biographers listed in the book. Their research made this work possible. The anonymous reviewers offered helpful suggestions and insights. I thank them for their comments. Finally, thank you to my wife Mary for her patience and loving support, and to our son John (5) because I can finally say that, "Daddy is finished with his book."

Chapter One

Introduction

The year is 2012 or 2016, the presidential nominees from the two major political parties in the United States are about to debate on national television in the battleground state of Ohio. At the new Cleveland Convention Center, former First Lady Hillary Clinton, wife of former president Bill Clinton, is the Democratic nominee. Former governor of Florida Jeb Bush, son of the forty-first president of the United States, George H. W. Bush, and brother of the forty-third president, George W. Bush, is the Republican nominee. After three decades of dominating the political fortunes of the United States, the Bush and Clinton families battle again for the most powerful office in the world.

The above scenario is not a certainty, but it is a possibility. It should never happen. If it occurs, the ramifications on the nation's political system and the American presidency could be severe. Whatever the outcome of the 2008 presidential election, Jeb Bush and Hillary Clinton will remain leading candidates for the Democratic and Republican presidential nominations in the future. Hillary Clinton's difficulties in attempting to follow the Bush family dynasty in 2008 presidential campaign and George W. Bush's troubled presidency illustrate a basic premise: the American presidency and family legacies do not mix. This book will highlight the problems and the consequences of combining the most powerful political office in the world with family legacies and relationships and also serves as a warning for any future presidential family dynasties.

Why the concern? For the past twenty-eight years a Bush or a Clinton has been part of a presidential ticket. Moreover, a member of the Bush or Clinton family has been considered for the presidency or vice presidency since 1968, a span of forty years. Because of the importance of name recognition, political families are a central part of American politics. Yet, the presidency is the most powerful elected office in the world. For two families to be so prominent in regards to the office of the presidency for so long violates the basic concept of a true democratic republic. Executive political leadership based upon family connections and position belongs to the old monarchies of Europe and the current dictatorships of North Korea and Cuba, not the United States.

With a first look at the above scenario, these two candidates who are products of family political legacies seem qualified for political office. Hillary Clinton has been involved in the political world since the turbulent times of Watergate in the 1970s. She served as a congressional committee staff member during the Watergate scandal. She helped a young inexperienced law professor become attorney general of Arkansas and then governor. She played an active role in her husband's gubernatorial administration focusing on education and health care. One observer believes Mrs. Clinton was actually the most important executive administrator in Arkansas because her husband enjoyed campaigning more than governing.[1] When campaigning for Bill Clinton's presidential run in 1992, the Clintons promised "two for the price of one."[2] When her husband defeated the incumbent president George H.W. Bush, she was given an office in the West Wing and led several policy initiatives including the failed campaign to provide health-care insurance to all Americans. In 2000, she shocked the political establishment by running and winning a Senate seat from the state of New York, a state where she had never lived. She has enjoyed a successful term as Senator and won reelection overwhelmingly.

Governor Jeb Bush was seen by many to be the natural heir to the Bush political dynasty. He married early in life and left Texas for the state of Florida. In Miami, he went into business with a prominent Cuban-American developer, Armando Codino, and became a millionaire during the 1980s.[3] As a result of his important political name, he became secretary of commerce for the state of Florida at the age of thirty-four. Against the political wisdom of many in the state, he ran for governor in 1994 against a Florida political legend, incumbent Democratic governor Lawton Chiles. He almost pulled off a major upset in losing a close race 51–49 percent. After the loss, he regrouped and worked to reshape the Republican Party in Florida. In 1998, he won a resounding victory for governor over the sitting Democratic lieutenant governor. He quickly moved to consolidate power in the state. He overpowered the Florida legislature in his first term and started many policy initiatives including vouchers for public school students, limiting affirmative action programs, and overhauling higher education administration. He won another impressive victory in his reelection bid in 2002.

During his last year in office, he had approval ratings 20 percent higher than his brother, the sitting president. When he left the governor's office in January 2006, he was the undisputed political king in one of the most diverse and politically volatile states in the nation.

With these impressive political resumes, what is the concern about the Clinton and the Bush families again seeking the presidency? These personal and political stories have obscured a central reality. The Bush and Clinton families' pursuit of the American presidency is a danger to American democracy and the presidency itself. This book focuses on two major objections to this familial domination. First, the Bushes and Clintons could endanger the American presidency as a representative institution. The founders explicitly rejected a monarchy or any type of hereditary transfer of power. In fact, a major reason for the revolution by American colonists was the institution of a hereditary monarchy itself. The Declaration of Independence lists twenty-seven specific grievances against King George.[4] Moreover, the modern development of the presidency has also made the office and its occupant the number one national leader in the country's political structure. The chief executive of the government and its national representative should not be the exclusive domain of two families. The Adams and the Kennedy families attempted similar presidential dynasties with difficult and tragic results. Moreover, with the 2008 election the Clintons attempted to install two *consecutive* family presidential dynasties—a historical first.

Second, the Bushes and the Clintons have allowed personal family issues to dominate policymaking at a crucial time in American history. Because of their unique relationship, the marriage of Bill and Hillary Clinton became a major distraction throughout the Clinton presidency. The second impeachment of a president in our nation's history did not involve treason or neglect of duties; instead President Clinton was impeached for lying about a sexual affair with a White House intern. If President Clinton simply had told his wife the truth about the affair originally, he would not have perjured himself and the second term of the Clinton presidency could have been vastly different.

Similarly, the Bush presidencies show the importance of family relationships in determining policy outcomes. Some analysts believe that many decisions that George W. Bush makes as president are in response to the failures of his father's presidency.[5] George W. Bush's Iraq policy is a direct consequence of his father's decision not to invade Baghdad during the First Gulf War in 1991. President George W. Bush's most important advisor on the Iraq War, Vice President Dick Cheney, was a product of the first Bush administration. Cheney would go on to be George W. Bush's closest advisor.

President George W. Bush's burden of following his father as president is a crucial factor in any analysis of the forty-third president. Accordingly, the current struggles of the second Bush presidency should give pause to those Americans who are contemplating a second Clinton presidency or a third Bush presidency.

Beginnings of the Family Rivalry

The election year of 1980 was an unlikely place for the most competitive family political feud in recent American history to begin. After a business and political career of tremendous success, George Herbert Walker Bush became vice president of the United States in 1980. With his golden resume of World War II hero, congressman, head of the Republican Party, U.S. trade representative, and head of the CIA, Bush was selected over former president Gerald Ford to become Ronald Reagan's vice president. Conversely, Bill Clinton, the thirty-four-year-old governor of Arkansas, was losing his reelection bid. Clinton was running in a Southern state and was criticized for having a wife who would not take his last name, bringing in advisors from the Ivy League, and letting the state of Arkansas become overrun with Cuban refugees.[6] After the election of 1980, the Bushes were part of the popular Reagan revolution, and they were on the rise. The Clintons had lost the incumbency of a small Southern state, and he was being written off. There was no evidence at this point to suggest that for the next twenty-four years a Clinton or a Bush would be on a national presidential ticket. There was even less evidence to believe that George W. Bush and Hillary Clinton would pick up the respective political banners for their families and become major players in America politics in the early part of the twenty-first century.

In recent years former presidents Bill Clinton and George H. W. Bush have become friends and partners in several humanitarian causes.[7] These two leaders have much to celebrate and now much in common. They have placed their families at the center of American politics; their names are the most important brands in both the Republican and Democratic parties. In a nation founded on the idea of resistance against hereditary power, they have established family dynasties of their own.

This story of the political rise of the two families is fascinating. The winning tally for the Bush family thus far is two presidencies, a vice presidency, a U.S. House seat, and governorships of the two largest states in the Union. The Clintons have a two-term presidency, two terms as an activist first lady, a governorship of a Southern state, and a U.S. Senate seat from the state of the New York. These incredible elective and political accomplishments have given the press interesting and salacious stories to dissect. The Bushes have gone from crushing defeat in the 1992 presidential campaign to the "Bush Restoration."[8] The Clintons have provided an unlikely presidential win in 1992, a political comeback after the disastrous 1994 mid-term elections, personal scandals including the Whitewater scandal and Monica Lewinsky, an impeachment, and the first U.S. Senate election win by a sitting first lady in a state where she had never resided. What is more intriguing is that these two political families owe their continued political successes to each other. Bill Clinton rose to power by defeating the first President Bush by portraying him as an out-of-touch elitist who had damaged the economy. George W. Bush won the presidency in 2000 by claiming that he would "restore dignity" to the Oval Office.[9] This phrase was an obvious reference to Clinton's sex scandal that led to his impeachment. Bush won the office on character issues, and he and his staff carefully made the character of both Clinton and Vice President Gore the central issues of the campaign.[10] As the fortunes of the second Bush administration continued to deteriorate, Senator Clinton looked like a plausible alternative.

Danger to the American Presidency as a Democratic Institution

The strong American presidency of today almost did not exist. The debate at the Constitutional Convention in Philadelphia about the power of the executive was intense. The Articles of Confederation had been a miserable failure because no strong central authority existed in the confederated government. There was little question at the Constitutional Convention in 1787 that some type of national executive power was needed. Yet, a tremendous difference of opinion existed about what type of executive should govern. Many delegates to the convention believed that executive power should be a plural council that would only have powers that were given to it by Congress.[11] These delegates were concerned about their experience with the British monarchy and the danger that a powerful hereditary executive could become dictatorial. Another group led by James Wilson, a delegate from Pennsylvania, wanted a strong single executive. This executive would provide the leadership that a new nation would need to establish its place in the world. This executive would have a veto over legislation from Congress and the executive authority of the government would reside in this leader.[12] James Madison of Virginia and Gouverneur Morris of Rhode Island also argued for a strong executive. To get a resolution to support a single strong executive, the "presidentialists" had to assure the rest of the convention that there would be limits on this power.[13]

These limits included that Congress would have the power of the purse and could approve presidential appointments. George Washington, the consensus choice to head the new government, made it clear that he favored a strong executive with limits and rejected outright the idea of a monarchy based on family ties.[14] Washington believed that a monarchy would be "triumph for the advocates of despotism."[15] As the convention came around to the idea of a single powerful executive who would be elected every four years, the presidentialists argued that this new single executive would be a "man of the people" who could represent national interests while legislators represented local interests. Not all delegates were convinced. Virginian George Mason made this statement, "We are not indeed constituting a British Government but a more dangerous monarchy, an elective one."[16] This elective monarchy directly contradicts the meaning of the Constitution. The Bush and Clinton families are attempting to make George Mason's concerns a dangerous reality.

The Bush presidencies and the ambitions of the Clintons are a direct threat to these limits on presidential power. George Washington himself was concerned about too much power in the hands of one individual or one family. Washington, who could have been king, voluntarily agreed to give up the presidency after two terms. This voluntary two-term limit held through twenty-nine presidencies until Franklin Delano Roosevelt (FDR).

Moreover, the Twenty-Second Amendment, passed in 1951, explicitly limited presidencies to two terms. The idea behind this amendment was that no person should have control of the most powerful office on earth for more than two terms. Franklin Roosevelt had increased the power of the presidency to such an extent in the 1930s and 1940s that many congressional representatives thought he had gone too far. Roosevelt used the power of the federal government to regulate the stock market, establish banking reform, and proposed the beginnings of a welfare state. All these activities had the presidency at their core.[17] His successor Harry Truman also advocated an expanded presidency.

When Republicans took control of the Congress in 1947, they used the Twenty-Second Amendment as a way to limit this power. What the founders had established by tradition was now codified by law: presidential authority is temporal. Though the Twenty-Second Amendment was introduced in partisan circumstances, forty-one states ratified this amendment from all parts of the country. Its value has been justified by recent history.

Eisenhower did not have the health or energy for a third term. Johnson was physically and emotionally exhausted after five years in the presidency. Nixon exercised the "Imperial Presidency" in less than two terms and resigned in disgrace. A third term for Reagan would have placed a man with an unfortunate mental illness (Alzheimer's disease) back in the presidency. After Clinton's impeachment in the second term, his administration never fully recovered.

Relatives from the same family tend to have similar experiences, values, and worldviews. Family members are likely to have the same educational background, income status, and personal contacts. The presidency is the one national office that represents all of the United States. It should not be the domain of a few families in a country of 300 million people.

Family History and Relationships Impact Presidential Outcomes

A brief review of the personal history of recent presidents shows why the Bush and Clinton families' ambitions for multiple presidencies are dangerous anomalies. Presidents in the era since the Kennedy assassination have had many problems and reviews on their presidencies are mixed. Prominent political scientist Michael Genovese has even called this the failed era of presidential leadership with scandals, reelection losses, and massive deficits.[18] However, until George W. Bush, all presidents of this period shared a common trait; they all brought unique personal and political backgrounds to the job. These unique backgrounds also helped to shape their most important policy initiatives.

President Lyndon Johnson rose to politics from a poor area of Texas. This one-time schoolteacher saw the poverty of his home area and resolved to do something about it. His rise to president of the United States is a remarkable story. His experiences in Texas made him particularly sensitive to the needs of the poor and thus he launched his War on Poverty. The mixed success of this government effort does not diminish the fact that his life experiences and background were important factors in his concern about the poor in the United States.

Richard Nixon came from a lower middle-class family in California. He put together an impressive academic record that he was accepted to law school at Duke University. Using his legal background, he returned to California and launched his political career with particular emphasis on stopping Communism. He became Dwight Eisenhower's vice president in 1952. He lost a presidential race to John Kennedy in 1960 and a governor's race in 1962, but then made a momentous political comeback with the 1968 presidential contest. Even during the ongoing Watergate scandal that exposed his vast personal failings, he conducted an innovative foreign policy. His history of being a staunch anti-Communist allowed him to have political cover to pursue détente with the Soviet Union and an opening to China.

The next elected president was Jimmy Carter. This unlikely president was the owner of a peanut farm in Georgia who served as a Commander in the U.S. Navy. His upbringing in the rural South gave him special insight in the area of race relations. Carter relates the story of how his best friend growing up was an African-American. His rise to being elected governor of Georgia without acting as an outright segregationist helped to make major gains in race relations in Southern politics. He carried this concern to the White House where he appointed more African-Americans to positions in his administration than any previous president.[19] His presidency was viewed as a failure, but his unlikely win in 1976 made a statement about the democratic nature of the American presidency.

Ronald Reagan also took an unusual route to the presidency. Growing up in Dixon, Illinois, he launched his public career on the radio in the middle of the Great Depression. He moved to California and became a working actor. After World War II, he became the leader of the actors' union. With a momentous speech during the 1964 presidential campaign of Barry Goldwater, Reagan became a political force and was elected governor of California in 1966. When he won the presidency in 1980, he took his disgust of Communism with him. As a leader of the actors' union, Reagan confronted Communism and socialism for the first time. He became a firm believer in standing up to Communism, but he also has been criticized for helping to create an atmosphere of a witch hunt in Hollywood. With these strong views, Reagan was intent on managing and trying to win the Cold War. This confrontation with Communism became a central point of his presidency.

Each of these presidents brought different backgrounds and thus different policy interests to the White House. Accordingly, as the Bushes and the Clintons gain power, they bring their own family backgrounds and family relationships with them. These backgrounds and relationships ultimately impact decision making and policymaking. In a nation where so many diverse interests are present, different types of presidents are needed. This attempt by two families to dominate the presidency in the past fifteen years is unprecedented in U.S. history and violates the basic concern of the founders that the presidency should be powerful but temporary. The outcome of the 2008 election will show if the American voters accept or reject two consecutive presidential family dynasties.

Chapter Two

American Democracy and Family Presidencies

"One out of eight Americans is governed by a Bush."
—Barbara Bush in 1999.

"When you vote for Bill Clinton, you get two for the price of one."[1]
—Bill Clinton in 1992.

These two quotes show the depth of how power and family relationships have combined to promote both the Clinton and Bush families in recent years. The Bush quote came from former first lady Barbara Bush in 1999 about the fact that two of her sons now held the governor's office in two of the largest states in the nation. If the Bushes governed two states, why not the entire nation? This remark shows the incredible ambition of the Bushes to regain the presidency after the troubled presidency of George H. W. Bush. The Clinton quote took place in the middle of the presidential primary campaign of 1992. This quote highlights how politically connected Bill and Hillary Clinton were (and still are). For a candidate to seriously advance the proposition that his spouse would hold as much power in a presidency as he would is an obvious affront to the founders who explicitly rejected familial sharing of power. The presidency is not a monarchy handed off to a spouse or a son in a casual or automatic fashion.

Politics based upon familial relations is not new to the world or the United States. In places like Chicago, Illinois, voters have elected members of the Daley family as mayor for much of the past sixty years. In 2006, over fifty members of Congress were relatives of former members of Congress or governors.[2] The power of name recognition aids fund-raising and voter familiarity. Accordingly, family connections in American politics have been important in the past and will be important in the future. Familiar names offer important cues for voters who may lack information because of lack of time or effort.[3] This pattern will continue in the democratic republic that currently exists in the United States, and it is understandable that voters give an advantage to familiar names when making choices.

Yet, the presidency is of another magnitude. Having the presidency subjected to familial ties and strains is a critical difference from other elected offices in the United States. Family presidential dynasties will be examined in the next chapter; yet the problems that the Adams and the Kennedys experienced during their presidential campaigns and governments show that the office of the presidency is particularly ill-suited for family legacies.

Why the difference? In many ways, the office of the presidency saved the United States government. As mentioned before, the Articles of Confederation were a dismal failure because of the lack of centralized authority. The emerging nation needed centralized power after both economic and military threats jeopardized the postrevolutionary government. In Massachusetts, farmers engaged in open rebellion by attacking judicial courts and county sheriffs who were involved in foreclosures in a conflict known as Shay's Rebellion. This rebellion almost became a full-fledged insurgency. The federal government did not have the resources to quickly react to such circumstances.

Yet even with these governance problems, many of the first Americans were wary of any single powerful executive. The compromise that resulted was the office of the presidency. Constitutional Convention delegate James Wilson argued that the executive had to have energy and power.[4] Yet even with a vigorous single executive, this new executive would not be a king and would be subject to limitations on this power. As will be extensively discussed further on, the founders rejected outright leadership based upon family relationships. Moreover, as the office of the presidency has developed, the power of the office and its connection with American people has been enhanced. These modern developments in the office of presidency further highlight the need to reject hereditary and spousal relationships when the power of this office is transferred to another occupant.

Elected republican government is a relatively new development in modern world history. Until the American and French revolutions, the principle of hereditary monarchy was the guiding philosophy for human governance for most of recorded history. For most of this time, governments based upon family relationships have brought misery to their populations.[5] Government based upon family relations has led to "best documented record of inequality" in world history. European monarchies until the eighteenth century produced a decent standard of living to less than 2 percent of their populations. Moreover, over 80 percent of their populations lived on a subsistence level.[6] Beyond economic inequality, most familial governments have not advanced the cause of human rights and liberty.

In response to these abuses, philosophers and activists in the seventeenth and eighteenth century produced the ideas behind the Enlightenment that nurtured societal and political reform. The philosophers of this time argued that societies should be based upon reason. Equality should be the guiding principle over the traditional feudal and familial bases of political power. John Locke wrote his *Second Treatise of Government* in response to a book written defending family monarchies. Locke believed that installed aristocracies were "parasitical, decadent and out-of-touch with almost anything."[7] He argued that political power based only on traditional hereditary monarchies was unjust. Political power was in place to protect the rights of individuals; power was not the sole possession of certain families. Equality and absolute monarchies could not coexist.[8]

Adam Smith in the *Wealth of Nations* wrote that sovereigns have the responsibility to protect their subjects from injustice, but this is a responsibility most monarchs could not meet. Speaking of the governments of Europe, Smith wrote "the administration of justice appears for a long time to have been extremely corrupt; far from being quite equal and impartial even under the best monarchs, and altogether profligate under the worst."

Accordingly, the trend of the American electorate to consider multiple family presidencies runs against the ideas that these important political thinkers advanced; most civil societies in the world have moved beyond executive rule by families. Familial governments challenge the basic ideas of political equality and representation. The importance of the Bush and Clinton families represents a digression in the nation's political development.

American democracy has been far from perfect. Most of the founders had an elite bias that discouraged direct representation. Yet, the general trend in American history has been the expansion of the American democratic ideal. By the end of the Jacksonian era, almost every state in the Union chose their presidential electors by popular vote.[9] Barriers to eligibility for voting were gradually removed throughout American history. Most property owning requirements were removed in the 1830s; women's suffrage was granted in 1921; the civil rights movement culminated in the 1965 *Voting Rights Act*. Yet, this reliance on two families for political leadership at the beginning of the twenty-first century is a serious step backward for a nation that claims that it is the best example of a constitutional democracy for the entire world to see.

The founding fathers of the United States had serious reservations and an extensive debate about the presidency and a connection with a possible hereditary monarchy. A review of this debate below highlights how most of the founders would find the political power of Bushes and Clintons to be antithetical to basic principles of the Constitution.

Founders versus Family Executive Power

For American colonists to find themselves in the late 1700s rebelling against the King of England came as a substantial surprise. Even those colonists who led the movement to challenge the British monarchy in the 1760s believed that the American colonies and the British government would find a way to compromise. Yet as the colonists and the British government continued to clash, it became apparent that the ideas of liberty that the colonists were advancing would not be compatible with a hereditary monarchy. The genesis of this dispute between the colonists and the British government actually came from the impacts of a joint military victory. The Americans and the British government worked together to win the French and Indian War in the American colonies and Canada. Yet, the British government soon realized that victory in the war would lead to massive debts in the postwar period in the early 1760s.

In order to gain revenue to pay off its debts, the British government imposed several unpopular taxes on their colonists throughout the world. The *Stamp Act* of 1765 imposed a fee on all legal documents that would now require a stamp from the British government. This Act set off a large political disagreement between the colonies and the British government. The colonists did not argue that the tax was too high; they argued that the government of Britain had no authority to tax the colonies at all without political representation.[10] In a foreshadowing of events to come, the *Stamp Act* was repealed. However, the problem for the British Crown remained. To cut the debt from the French and Indian War, the British government instituted a series of taxes known as the *Townshend Duties*. These duties did not represent a huge increase in taxes, but they sparked a great debate within the American colonies. After the years of protests, the *Townshend Duties* were also repealed.

Yet the debate was not finished. The British Parliament and the monarchy wanted to reestablish the power of Britain over the colonies in matters of commerce. Thus in 1773, the *Tea Act* was passed. This Act reduced the import fees of tea coming into American harbors. American colonists were concerned that the British government would manipulate the American economy with fees and taxes. The famous

"Boston Tea Party" resulted from the passage of this Act. Thinly disguised colonists dressed as Mohawk Indians dumped tea into the Boston Harbor from a British ship. The protests of this time had one clear message: the American colonists wanted to protect their own economic and personal interests and limit the influence of the British Crown. As in most political disputes the important question centered on power.[11] What power would the British Crown exercise over the American colonists?

In 1776, the American colonists would give a clear answer to this question in the form of the Declaration of Independence. If one major common thought existed among rebelling colonists, it was that Americans did not want power in the hands of a single family. This aversion to the centralization of power would dominate American political thought for the next decade. In the Declaration of Independence, Thomas Jefferson advances the argument that all men are deserving of liberty and equality. Even though the British Parliament had been the most active British government entity to challenge the Americans, Jefferson saved most of his fire for King George III. In the document, he lists twenty-seven specific grievances against the king. Among these grievances are the denial of basic rights of due process, taxation without representation, and the sending of large amounts of troops to the American colonies without consultation. If Jefferson's message was not clear enough, he bluntly writes that the King "has plundered our seas, ravaged our coasts, burnt our towns, and destroyed the lives of our people."

Why did Jefferson make such a strong indictment of the king? The declaration was a political document. Jefferson went after a single monarch rather than to continually attack parliament. Jefferson's argument again was clear; power in the hands of a single individual who came to power by birth leads to tyranny. After the improbable American military victory in the Revolutionary War, the aversion of the centralization of power would dominate political thinking and political action.

The result of this aversion would be the Articles of Confederation. The Articles set up a form of government in which the former colonies retained a loose federation of autonomous and separate governments. By 1786, it was clear that the Articles had failed its new nation. In the United States, borders were not recognized; no money was coming into the federal treasury; the states were charging high tariffs applied to out-of-state citizens and products. The fear of centralizing power in the new U.S. government had paralyzed the nation. These problems would lead to calls for a convention that would rework American government, and it would be in this convention that the American presidency would be born. The challenge for the founders was to create an executive office that could be effective and respected but at the same time honor the ideas in the Declaration of Independence that argued strongly against an all-powerful monarchy. The spirit of this debate has seemingly been lost currently in the United States with the advancement of the Bush family and the Clinton family as seekers of the presidency. A review of the original debate is important to put into context why the current quest for power by the Bushes and Clintons goes against the core basic principle of the founding of the United States: too much power in the hands of a few is simply un-American.

Debate over the Presidency

The delegates to the Federal Convention in 1787 in Philadelphia had a large task on their hands in reference to the executive branch of government. In the Articles of Confederation, there had been no mention of an executive branch because of the fear of centralizing too much power. The depth of feeling about placing too much power in an executive was so great that the original government of the United States had *no executive* leadership. Thus a vigorous debate would ensue about what an American executive branch would look like. Would the executive consist of one person or be plural? How long would the executive serve? What powers would be designated to the executive? All of these questions had to be answered. The failure of the Articles of Confederation had shown that the need for executive leadership was vital in any government even a government that was born from a rebellion from a monarchy. As mentioned above, Delegate James Wilson from Pennsylvania argued for a single powerful executive. Wilson's vision of an American executive was one with "energy, dispatch and responsibility."[12] Delegates from Virginia including George Mason and Edmund Randolph strongly objected to a single executive. They saw a single executive as a pathway to an American monarch. Delegate Randolph referred to a single executive as a "fetus of monarchy."[13] Randolph went on to say that the people of the new nation would never have confidence in a one-person executive.[14]

During the debate at the convention, Wilson made it clear that the single executive would be totally different from a British system with a hereditary monarch. In order to get the idea of a single executive passed through the convention, enforceable limits on executive power would have to be in the Constitution. In fact, Wilson argued that a single-elected executive in a republican system would be the "best safeguard against tyranny" represented by a hereditary monarch.[15] Thus an implicit promise was made to the delegates who were concerned about family monarchies. In exchange for a single powerful executive, no hereditary transfer of executive power would be part of the America's future because the new executive would have limits.

These limits were few but meaningful. The Committee on Detail for the Convention proposed an executive that could be impeached by Congress; his appointees would have to be approved by Congress; an executive who could not spend money without authorization; and an executive who could not make laws.

However, the presidentialists carried the day with the approval of a single executive who had all of the executive power in the government. This new executive could also veto legislation from Congress. Most importantly, and in a complete reversal from the beginning of the convention, the new executive was granted the power of commander in chief of the armed forces. Even though the new nation did not have a national army, this executive civilian control of the military would prove to be a major contributor to presidential power.

Even with the assurances of the "presidentialists," the critics of this powerful new executive were still deeply concerned that this new leadership position would become a king.[16] Delegate George Mason in particular was shocked at the power given to this new single executive. Mason asked the convention "do gentlemen mean to pave the way to a hereditary monarchy."[17] Mason was so concerned about having too much power in the executive he proclaimed that the convention had exceeded its authority and eventually refused to sign the Constitution.

Mason's objections did not carry the convention. Yet his ideas were popular among many in the states and ratification of the Constitution was unsure. One anti-Federalist echoed Mason's concerns about this new powerful executive who could win reelection every four years without limit. This critic stated that a "four years President will be, in time, King for life, and after him his son."[18] Two hundred years after the convention, George H. W. Bush would win his presidency in 1988 and his son would win the same office in 2000.

The ratification debate would be a long, slow process. Conventions were held in each of the states to consider ratification. In order to answer these critics, Alexander Hamilton, James Madison, and John Jay wrote a series of articles now known as the *Federalist Papers* defending the new Constitution. In Federalist Paper 69, Alexander Hamilton gives a detailed list of contrasts between the American presidency and the British monarchy. Hamilton makes it clear that the new office is powerful but temporary. Of the presidency, he says "there is a total dissimilitude between him and the King of Great Britain, who is a hereditary monarch, possessing the crown as a patrimony descendible to his heirs forever."[19]

This new executive would require occupants that possess both strong leadership with an awareness of the limits of the office. The new executive was not a limited executive it was an executive with limits. As political scientist Charles Thach has written, the occupants of this office would have to define the office.[20] Article II of the Constitution is significantly shorter than Article I. In effect, the delegates left the presidency as an open book with many questions unanswered. Yet with all of this debate and revision, one clear principle remained from the Declaration of Independence all the way through to the Federalist Papers that defended the new Constitution. This principle was that family monarchies should not have the executive power in the United States. As stated above, someone from the Bush family has been considered for a national presidential ticket for the past forty years. With Hillary Clinton's candidacy, it is the first time in the nation's history that a spouse of a president sought the same office much like a royal queen taking the place of her king.

Washington versus the Bushes and the Clintons

The only way a concept of strong presidency passed the convention was because of the presence of George Washington. The delegates to the convention may not have written a Constitution that was clear in regards to the office of the president, but they knew what a president looked like. To paraphrase Supreme Court justice Potter Stewart, the founders may not have been able to define the presidency but they knew it when they saw it, and they saw it in George Washington. Washington's figure dominated the American political landscape before there was an American government. While the Continental Congress ruled the new nation in name after the Declaration of Independence, Washington had to make many decisions because the congressional committees could not. Historian James Flexner calls George Washington the "indispensable man."[21] After the victory in the Revolutionary War there came immediate calls for Washington to be king.

The young nation had difficult years immediately after the war. Alexander Hamilton wanted to see Washington emerge as the undisputed leader and ruler of the American people. When some of the veterans of the Revolutionary War wanted to take on the new government of the United States because of the lack of payment given to veterans and soldiers, Washington stopped a military coup in its tracks. Washington skillfully addressed the angry soldiers by pausing and pulling out his eyeglasses to read a letter. Most soldiers had never seen these glasses; Washington said; "permit me to put on spectacles for I have not only grown gray but almost blind in service to my country."[22] Washington walked the difficult line between providing leadership and knowing the proper boundaries to his power. As Jefferson would write "a moderation in virtue of a single character (Washington) probably prevented this revolution from being closed as most others have been by a subversion of that liberty."[23]

Washington never craved civilian leadership but he would be drawn to it as a result of his concern that the nation did not have a central government powerful enough to meet its needs. Because of this concern, he agreed to be president of the Constitutional Convention that would bring about the Constitution. As president of the convention he would not publicly debate the provisions of the new constitution, but again his character and presence were pervasive. A strong presidency that resulted from the convention would have never occurred without Washington's attendance. Flexner in his description of this phenomenon quoted one of the delegates who said Washington "shaped their ideas of the powers to be given to a President by their opinions of his virtues."[24]

As Washington assumed the presidency in 1789, he would begin addressing some of the gaps in the Constitution in regards to the presence of an executive. With a new system of government and a new nation searching for leadership, Washington could have amassed unquestioned power. Yet he recognized the need for strong central government, but he also recognized the need for humility and presidential restraint. Contrast Washington's political actions of the day with current American leadership. As president, Washington refused his salary even though he did not have the money to pay for the carriage ride to New York to take the Oath of Office. By contrast, the Bush and Clinton families have economically benefited from their presidencies and political offices. Both former presidents Bush and Clinton make millions of dollars a year in speaking fees. In order to keep the presidency open to all, Washington held office hours where any citizen could come in and talk to the president. Contrast this openness with the access to political leaders today. As a result of security concerns, no American president today could have complete open access to anyone, yet presidents and their families do control access. For the most part, the Bushes and the Clintons have used this access as reward for their close friends and big financial donors.[25] It is this relationship with financial donors that allow the Clinton and Bush political organizations to prosper and endure.

Washington did not want to run for president the first time and he certainly did not want to run again in 1793. In essence, Washington could have been elected leader for life. He turned this opportunity down in one of the most unselfish political acts in the history of the world. Washington voluntarily left the presidency after two terms. The president needed to be strong in Washington's view but also have limits. An important part of this limitation was to turn power over peacefully to the next leader chosen by the electoral college. After the Revolutionary War, Washington made it clear that he wanted to stay away from public life. Hamilton offered the simple proposition, "in a world of kings why should not George Washington also be a king?" Washington had a ready reply because he realized "the folly and madness of unbounded ambition."[26] Because he believed a strong national government was needed, he agreed to preside over the Constitutional Convention. By presiding over the convention, he was the obvious choice for the first new president of the United States.

After his first term, Washington again tried to remove himself from public life. Yet he agreed to serve in order to set a precedent of a peaceful transition from one presidential term to the next. Although there were serious disagreements within his government between Thomas Jefferson and Alexander Hamilton, Washington was still the most unifying figure in America. Even though his popularity had waned some in his second term, he was asked to run again, but he said no. In his farewell address, he warned against parochial interests and factionalism in politics and he pleaded for unity.

Contrast Washington's hesitancy to gain executive power with modern American politics. The Bush family has sought the presidency or the vice presidency in seven out of the past eight presidential elections. With the candidacy of Hillary Clinton, the Clintons are seeking the presidency for three out of the past five presidential elections. George H. W. Bush's ambitions for higher office were well known, dating back to the 1960s. Bill Clinton's presidential ambitions are legendary and best captured with the famous photograph of a young Bill Clinton as a high school student shaking hands with President John Kennedy.[27] Some of Senator Hillary Clinton's friends believed in the 1970s that she would be president.[28] George W. Bush said often in the 2000 campaign that he was not looking to be president.[29] These statements hide a strong political ambition. George W. Bush ran as a young unknown candidate in a congressional race in Texas in 1978. He stayed active politically throughout the 1980s assisting his father's presidential ambitions. In 1994 against the advice of his own mother, he ran for governor of Texas against the well-liked incumbent, Ann Richards.

There is nothing inherently wrong with ambition among public figures. In fact, ambition is a necessary characteristic in order to have the drive and the strength to be president in modern America. Yet it is important to contrast the thirst for political power that the Bushes and Clintons portray versus Washington's view of seeking the presidency. He sought the presidency out of public service not a personal desire for power.

Another major difference in approaching politics between Washington and the Bush and Clinton families is the ability to unify the nation. The reason Washington had two unanimous electoral college victories and became president is because he was a unifying figure. In his farewell address he pleaded with political leaders to refrain from moving into competing factions and parties. Washington's ideas about politics were naïve; in a new republic, debate and differences were going to emerge. Yet the current political process has taken this political debate to new extremes. A noted political scientist Gary Jacobsen has written a persuasive argument that George W. Bush may be our most polarizing president.[30] Bush has been able to win two presidential elections by expanding his political base and not reaching out to independents and Democrats. In 1992, the Clintons skillfully unified the Democratic Party in most circumstances but have been passionately rejected by most Republicans. The level of discourse and distrust in American politics has drawn criticism from many sources. This discourse has been led by the Bushes and the Clintons and their talented but hard-nosed political consultants. Even in a time of national tragedy reflected by the September 11, 2001 attacks on the World Trade Center and Washington, the nation remains divided politically. This division may be the worst legacy of the Bush/Clinton era in American politics.

Arguably a comparison between Washington and any other president is an unfair one because many historical figures look much better in the shadow of time. Moreover Washington was far from perfect. His presidency was marked by ceding much of his executive power to Alexander Hamilton. He also left many difficult issues for his successor, John Adams including possible wars with European powers. Yet for the purposes of this book, the comparison is necessary. Washington spent much of his public life making the point that too much power in the hands of too few could lead to tyranny. He also insisted that after his second term, the first peaceful transition of power in American history take place. Even though he could have had another term of office, he left the leadership of his government in the hands of the electoral college. Could Bill Clinton, George W. Bush, or Senator Hillary Clinton do the same? If they had a guaranteed term of office to be president of the United States, would they give that up? Washington wanted a strong presidency, but he wanted the power in that strong presidency to be transferred to new occupants on a regular basis. The attempted domination of presidential politics by the Bushes and Clintons do not respect Washington's ideals.

Family Executive Power and the Modern Presidency

For students entering college this year in the United States, the only two names associated with the presidency in their lifetimes are Bush and Clinton. What do these students think about the democratic process in the United States when the most important position in that democracy has belonged to two families during their entire lifetimes? Sen. Barack Obama's appeal to young voters is a reaction to this family domination. Above, we examined how family presidential legacies may violate the intentions of the founders. What about the development of the office since then? How do family legacies and the modern presidency mix?

The office of the presidency has changed dramatically since the founding of the nation. This book cannot examine all the changes that have occurred. Yet two important developments are necessary and relevant to this inquiry. These two developments are 1) the democratization of the presidency 2) increased powers and responsibilities of the presidency.

Presidency Becomes More Democratic and Powerful

The presidency has become increasingly dependent upon the American mass public since the founding. This relationship has developed through electoral changes and advances in mass communication.

Clearly, some of the founders had deep reservations about a close relationship between the American presidency and the American people. George Mason in particular was concerned that the public could not make an informed decision about the best candidate for president. Moreover, the small states were concerned that a popular election of a president would leave their citizens marginalized in a presidential election.[31] The electoral college was the result of these concerns. This college would be appointed by the state legislatures shielding the presidency from direct public input.

However, the presidency and the American people would not be kept apart. George Washington was a revered figure throughout the new nation. He was seen as the "guardian of the country."[32] As noted above, by the end of Andrew Jackson's presidency, all states but one chose their electors by popular vote. Jacksonian democracy advanced the proposition that America was the land of equality and that the presidency was the "tribune of the people."[33] Lincoln appealed directly to the public for support in the Civil War. Even with the rudimentary communication at the time, Lincoln claimed that nothing could be accomplished without public support. At the beginning of the twentieth century, Theodore Roosevelt used the bully pulpit to try to connect with American citizens. Woodrow Wilson as a scholar and a president also advocated heavy involvement by the American public in public policy.[34]

With the presidency of Franklin Delano Roosevelt, the degree of the relationship between the president and the people intensified. Along with this relationship the expectations of the office also expanded exponentially. The president was seen as the "steward of public welfare."[35] Political scientists Sydney Milkis and Michael Nelson have written that FDR "placed executive leadership at the heart of its approach to politics and government."[36] The presidency was the focal point of the nation's government and symbol of that government to the American people. The presidency took on the obligations of providing social welfare to American citizens along with military and foreign-policy leadership to the nation and the world. The economic depression had devastated American society to such a degree that the president was seen as the leader and rescuer of the American nation and American democracy. This combination of popular expectation and enormous responsibilities brought in the age of the modern presidency. Presidents since Franklin Roosevelt have had to deal with this legacy.

Moreover, the development of pervasive media technology intensified these trends and expectations of the presidency. With radio, television, and now the Internet, millions of Americans have access to information about their government on an instant basis. The president became the natural focus of most of this media attention. Attempting to cover 535 congressman is difficult; having one entity to focus upon is much more explainable to the viewing public.

In a review of media coverage, the president receives three times the amount of coverage as the Congress.[37] This increased attention often has made successful presidencies dependent upon their "personal leadership qualities."[38] For most Americans the president for better or worse is the embodiment of their government.

The increased media coverage of the president has also coincided with an intensification of the relationship with the American public. Civil rights advances have allowed women and African-Americans to participate fully as voters. The revamped presidential selection system has opened up the presidential nomination system to millions of new voters. The McGovern commission appointed after the 1968 disastrous Democratic convention in Chicago made changes to the nomination process that would ensure mass participation in the process.[39]

The Republican Party soon followed this example with a much greater dependence upon primaries and caucuses to select delegates for candidates for its nominating convention. Former presidents such as Jimmy Carter, Ronald Reagan, and Bill Clinton may not have been elected under the convention system that relied upon party leaders at the party conventions to make the presidential selection.

This intensification of this two-way relationship is not confined to elections. The president is the "psychological center" of most Americans political lives. The killing of President Kennedy was a national trauma that impacted many Americans.[40] Ronald Reagan lifted the mood of many Americans with his optimism and hope. Americans feel connected to their president on a personal level, and this connection can be positive or negative. Public opinion polling constantly tracks the popularity of the president; this approval rating is seen as vital indicator of the president's political standing.

The modern presidency combines the depth of the relationship between the American people and an office with increased powers and responsibilities of the job. In national security affairs, the president has the sober responsibility of being the commander in chief of the most deadly nuclear arsenal in the world.

Literally, one command by the president can end the world. More practically, the president can order troops into action at a moment's notice. Congress can reduce funding for military activities, but this decision may come months after the initial deployment of troops.

As President George W. Bush has shown, the American public and Congress give wide deference to the president with regard to initial military action. As Americans have tired of the Iraq conflict, these opinions have changed, but President Bush basically went unchallenged for the first two years of the Iraq conflict. Because of foreign aid and military might, the president is the main American actor on the international stage. Even with the challenges in foreign relations that the United States is currently experiencing, the president is a major world leader. Governments can fall and foreign armies can be challenged because of the judgment of one person.

Domestically, the president is more limited but still powerful. The president and his staff are given the responsibility of writing the 2 trillion dollar budget for the federal government. Congress will change this budget, but the presidency gets the first chance to set priorities. Clearly, the president is the chief agenda-setter for the federal government. The press, the public, and Congress look toward the president for guidance and leadership on major policy issues. These expectations and demands can ruin presidents, but these expectations are there and give the president a unique place at the center of American society. Although not all-powerful, the American president is the most powerful and influential person in the world. This elevated status of the presidency makes it even more imperative that the power of this office does not transfer from family member to family member.

With these developments, leadership by family legacy poses serious questions about American democracy. First, access to the leadership of the nation is severely limited. For the most part, the presidency has been the domain of white Protestant men. Yet, the occupants of the presidency have come from various backgrounds. As stated before these different backgrounds have produced different types of leaders. The idea that only a select few from a certain family lineage can aspire for the highest office in the land contradicts the wishes of the founders and subverts the concept of the modern presidency that has become a democratized institution.

George W. Bush and Hillary Clinton have many personal attributes to be admired. George W. Bush after a series of career failures turned his personal and professional life around when he turned forty. He worked on his father's successful 1988 presidential campaign and then became a managing partner in the Texas Rangers baseball organization. This involvement would net him a huge economic payoff before he began his political career. Senator Clinton gained a position on a Watergate Congressional Committee as counsel when she was twenty-four. She became a partner in an Arkansas law firm and became an important political and policy partner to her husband, the governor of Arkansas. Yet even with these solid achievements, it is difficult to imagine that either of these individuals would be considered for the presidency of the United States without being a son or a spouse of a former president. There are thousands of charming businessman from Texas. Likewise there are thousands of bright and successful lawyers in Arkansas and Washington, DC. Without these family connections, neither of these individuals would have been potential future presidents. This advancement by birth and marriage is a mark against American democracy. Those incoming college freshmen must wonder about the fairness and openness of the American political system when all they have seen are two families that have led their system for their entire lives. The 2008 election may break this family cycle of power.

Family Presidencies and World Opinion

This family domination also sends ambiguous messages to the rest of the world. Handing executive power to sons and spouses brings about images of colonialism and imperialism to the developing world. The rise of the Clintons and the Bushes at a time in which the United States is attempting to spread the ideas of democracy and freedom to the rest of the world undermines the credibility of U.S. foreign policy.

Imagine if you are a Jordanian freshman college student in 2008. The Arab press and many Arab governments have been condemning the United States since you were born. The criticism has been amplified in recent years because of the invasion of Iraq and America's support for Israel. Yet this student from Jordan wants to have a better understanding of democracy in the United States. What he has seen over the past two decades is an American political system seemingly created by King Henry VIII and not Jefferson. The first President Bush invaded Iraq after the Iraqi assault on Kuwait. The coalition triumphs but does not remove Saddam Hussein from power. After eight years of the rival Clinton administration, the Bush family sought the presidency again. In 2000, President Bush's son, George W. Bush, wins a disputed election over the vice president of the man who defeated the first President Bush. The election is decided in the state of Florida that is governed by another Bush relative.

After eight controversial and difficult years with the second Bush presidency and another Iraqi invasion, the American political system moves to elect another president. With all of the difficulties of the second Bush presidency, Americans again consider possible candidates for the presidency. In a nation of more than 300 million people the opposing party's leading candidate to repudiate the Bush family presidencies is the spouse of another former president? What would that Jordanian student think about American democracy?

Because of its wealth and military power, the United States will not be universally popular in the near future. Yet world opinion about the United States is still important. President George W. Bush has made the spread of democracy in the Middle East and in other parts of the world a top objective of his foreign policy. At his second inaugural address, he said "it is the policy of the United States to seek and support the growth of democratic movements and institutions in every nation and culture with the ultimate goal of ending to tyranny in our world." In his second inaugural, President Clinton made a similar point; "and the world's greatest democracy will lead a whole world of democracies" These bold statements make several assumptions. First, other nations seek American-style democracy. Second, the political system in the United States should be an example to others. It becomes difficult to make the argument that the United States has a free and open democratic system, when members of only two families have held the presidency over the past two decades. Moreover when the next president may be a relative of another former president, American democracy looks hollow.

United States cannot afford these negative images. The Pew Research Center has performed thousands of interviews with citizens from nations across the world. These important studies have a mixed message. For example citizens in most Muslim countries surveyed throughout the world want democracy and support democratic ideals. However, these citizens may support democracy but they do not support America. The negative image of the United States in the world is unprecedented.[41] At a time where the United States is trying to spread democracy, America does not appear to be very democratic when the highest executive office in the land is exchanged between two families.

Ironically, the United States is critical of many states that have hereditary or familial governments. Kim Jung Il, the dictator in North Korea, is a pariah to the U.S. government because of the misery he brings to his people. Syria's leader Assad, has been called one of the largest supporters of terrorism in the world. These tyrannical regimes have one common trait: power based upon family ties. As a result of their brutal behavior, Saddam Hussein's sons were killed by U.S. troops shortly after the Iraq War began.

Family presidencies can undermine the symbolism of democracy. Some regimes also have used the Bush family dynasty as a propaganda tool against the United States. In a huge political rally in Havana, Cuba, in January 2006, large billboards proclaimed that the Bush family governments have been governments of "mass murder."[42]

Even more confusing for observers of the United State is the support that it gives to the family monarchies of Kuwait and Saudi Arabia. How can the United States spread democracy when two of its strongest allies in the Middle East are monarchies who greatly restrict the liberties of women and political opponents? Is it hypocritical for the United States to push democracy on states like Saudi Arabia when it appears that presidential power in the United States is based upon family connections?

Chapter Three

Families Matter

> "I got Jack into politics, I was the one...he didn't want to. He felt he didn't have the ability."
>
> —Joseph Kennedy, father of John Kennedy.[1]

Families matter. Parents impact their children's behavior. The marriage relationship is the most consequential interaction most adults will have with another human being. Sibling rivalries and connections are also important in how people develop and behave. The cumulative impact of political pressure and familial pressure can be substantial. With a son of a former president sitting in the White House and a former first lady running for the presidency, these basic ideas deserve further investigation.

Sociologists have studied relationships between parents and their children. The impact of parents on their children in the context of their culture and surroundings is known as socialization. Strong family relationships involve parents providing both physical and emotional support. Children depend upon parents for basic survival needs such as food, shelter, clothing, and medical care. Yet emotional support is also viewed as critical; this emotional support includes love, nurturing, and the teaching of acceptable behavior.[2]

How these norms and values are taught to children may have important consequences for the child's adult life. For example the importance of fathers in a child's life has been the subject of much recent research. As sociologist Andrew Cherlin has summarized, fathers relate to children differently than mothers. Fathers tend to be more aggressive with children and their "influence is often indirect."[3] Since mothers spend more time with children in most families, the influence of the female parent may be greater. Yet this does not mean that fathers are not important to a child's development. How a father spends time with the child may be more important than the amount of time spent with the child.[4]

Similarly, the marriage relationship is the most important interpersonal relationship most adults experience. In American society, the institution of marriage has undergone fundamental changes. Cherlin makes the observation that marriage is an ongoing project between the husband and wife. Marriage now involves "a continuing effort to find a better personal life through an evolving relationship." Today, "there is a cultural imperative to keep changing and developing your identity throughout adulthood in order to maintain or…increase your personal fulfillment."[5] This fulfillment includes reaching a level of self-esteem and accomplishment. The relationship with the spouse is critical in developing this fulfillment. It represents a mixture of intense emotional and physical feelings combined with the pressures of societal status. Cherlin argues that this emphasis on improvement and fulfillment creates tremendous expectations of the modern marriage.[6] Of course, marriage has many benefits including security, intimacy, and companionship. Yet, the high expectations modern marriages are expected to meet can create serious pressures on both husband and wife. Divorce that impacts millions of American marriages is testament to these pressures.

Now imagine these important formative relationships occurring with public scrutiny in a punishing political atmosphere. In a democratic republic such as the United States, politicians must persuade eligible voters to support them. Instead of broad issue referendums, American electoral politics has relied tremendously upon candidates connecting with voters on a personal level.

The pull between political necessities and family obligations is substantial for elected leaders. Family and public life are intimately connected for elected leaders. Policy decisions can be impacted heavily by familial influences.

The Mixture of Family and Presidencies

Most historical biographers of presidents have acknowledged the importance of family relationships upon the public actions of presidents.

James Flexner in his brilliant work on George Washington highlights the disappointment that Washington felt after his father died when he was eleven. The early death of his father forced Washington to become the male leader in his family at an early age. This early responsibility provided the foundation for Washington's impeccable leadership qualities later in life. His older brother Lawrence became the dominant male figure in Washington's young life. Lawrence became a military officer with the British Army and young George wanted to emulate him. This is how the first great American general was truly made.

Washington found comfort and stability in a quiet widow named Martha Custis whom he married when he was a young soldier. Flexner is not convinced that this was the passionate love of George Washington's life. Yet he feels that the marriage had important consequences for him. "His marriage to Martha taught the rash and impetuous young husband a lesson that was deeply to influence the rest of his career; it taught him that in action, judgment was preferable to passion."[7] Martha was a steady influence for George. She did not seek a public life, and her hesitation in accepting a large public role influenced George to realize the limits of his appointed and elected offices. The marriage also provided Washington with large financial assets that he never had before. These assets allowed him the time and space to pursue a military and public life that would lead to the presidency.[8]

Historian Doris Kearns Goodwin has written about Abraham Lincoln and the substantial effects that his difficult upbringing had on his life and presidency.

While many politicians exaggerate the difficulties that their families faced when they were children, Lincoln's early life was truly harsh. His rise to the presidency is a remarkable example of democratic representation in the United States. His father, Thomas, was restless and frequently unemployed. His mother Nancy died when Lincoln was nine. This difficult circumstance was followed by a period of time when Lincoln's father left to find a new wife. Lincoln's sister Sarah, who was only twelve at the time, became responsible for young Abraham Lincoln. Goodwin describes Lincoln's life as a young child with the Lincoln children "living like animals."[9] To add further to Lincoln's family misery, his beloved sister died at a young age. Lincoln had no formal education and had to teach himself how to read. This difficult beginning in life helped to make Lincoln self-sufficient, ambitious, and strong. All of these traits would assist him in his presidency.

Lincoln's wife, the former Mary Todd, greatly impacted his political life. Mary Todd had many social and political contacts that Lincoln used to progress in his career. She also had a strong confidence in Lincoln's political ability and prospects. Lincoln's rival Stephen Douglas had courted Mary but she married Lincoln. She believed that Lincoln had "no equal in the United States."[10] This support greatly aided Lincoln in his unlikely quest for high political office. Yet Mary also struggled with mental illness and she would often descend into a rage. The Lincolns experienced the death of two of their children during their marriage. Neither Lincoln would ever recover fully from these tragic deaths. Between Mary's temperament and the death of two children, the Lincoln marriage was tumultuous.[11] Lincoln's inconsistent relationship with his wife added to his despair during many of the Civil War years. During the early Civil War years this despair may have contributed to some of the questionable military decisions made by Lincoln.

Observers who put great importance on presidential family history have also chronicled modern presidents. Famed presidential historian Robert Dallek constantly returns to this theme again and again in his important work *Lone Star Rising*. Dallek observed that Lyndon Johnson's tough surroundings in Texas gave him the strong ambition for political office. Dallek also observes that Johnson believed it was his birthright to be a leader. Even though Johnson grew up in near-poverty, his family had a strong interest in politics. In Dallek's view, Johnson used his childhood surroundings and his strong belief in his family as the emphasis for his rise to power. He brought his concern about Southern poverty to Washington when many Southern Democrats did not address the topic.[12]

His First Lady Claudia "Lady Bird" Johnson was instrumental in his rise to power. She overlooked his extramarital affairs that could have ruined his career. During his time in the military during World War II, she ran his congressional office so he would not have to give up his seat while he was in the military.[13] She also had an influence on his public policy. She made him eat dinner and rest when the Vietnam War led him to physical exhaustion. A highway beautification bill was initiated and passed during Johnson's presidency because the first lady wanted the bill. Johnson told his cabinet "I love that woman and she wants the Highway Beautification Act...By God we're going to get it for her."[14] When Johnson shocked most political observers and decided not to run for reelection, Lady Bird was not surprised. She had written him a memo "gently urging him to step down."[15]

Most historians and observers that have analyzed Richard Nixon's tragic presidency focus on his paranoia. Historian Stephen Ambrose wrote that Nixon felt alone in his own family and would remain alone for his entire life. Ambrose points to Nixon's feeling of isolation as the main reason for his distrust of others. It was this distrust that led to the abuses of power that occurred in Watergate.[16]

Sociologists, biographers, and other political observers seem to agree that the family background of presidents matter greatly. If presidents are impacted by their parents or spouses and siblings, it is logical to advance the simple point that presidents also affect their spouses and children to a great extent. In fact this impact may be far greater because of the considerable extra pressures that accompany family life under the shadow of the most powerful political position in the world. Having to conduct your family life in full public view creates considerable tensions and emotional stress. Franklin Roosevelt bluntly stated about his children: "one of the worst things in the world is to be a child of a President! What a terrible life they lead."[17]

Presidential Children

An adviser to President George H. W. Bush and Governor George W. Bush, Douglas Wead, wrote an important memo to George W. Bush after his father's 1988 presidential win. This memo detailed the lives of the children of presidents. This memo later became a book called *All the President's Children: Triumph and Tragedy in the Lives of America's First Families*. The book is an excellent summation of the impact that the presidency has had on the children of presidents.

The book has sobering conclusions. After examining all of the lives of presidential children throughout American history, Wead states "that being related to a president brought more problems than opportunities."[18] Wead found that there were "higher than average rates of divorce and alcoholism and even premature death" among presidential children.[19] Wead reveals that even George W. Bush (son of a president) himself was concerned about the effect the presidency might have on his daughters. Wead said that George W. Bush was unsure if he was going to run for president because of the age of his daughters. Wead reports that Bush said, "That they would be in college then and it (presidency) would ruin their lives."[20]

Examples of the difficulties that presidential children encounter are not difficult to find. George Washington's stepson John Custis tried to cheat his presidential father out of money and property. Andrew Jackson Jr., adopted son of the seventh president, accumulated massive debts and continually had to be financially rescued by his father. Buck Grant (Ulysses Grant Jr.) son of the Civil War hero Ulysses Grant got his presidential father involved in a stock firm that was dissolved because of financial wrongdoing. Both Ulysses Grant Sr. and Jr. were fortunate to avoid jail time.[21] The difficulties that presidential children face do not always translate into scandal. The simple fact of having a parent in the most public political position in the world can cause difficulties in the parent-child relationship. Franklin Roosevelt's children continually stated that they could not be close to their father. In fact, his sons had to get an appointment to see him.[22] Three of Ronald Reagan's children publicly commented during his presidency that their father was too far removed from them. Two of his children wrote books discussing this isolation.

Wead also notes that some presidential children succeed in their personal and professional lives. Of course, two presidential children, John Quincy Adams, and George W. Bush, have become presidents themselves. This book will examine their presidential experiences in-depth below. Other presidential children have been educators, legislators, industrialists, and noted authors.[23] Yet, most historians leave little doubt that presidential children face considerable obstacles.

This situation is not unique to only presidential children; however there is a critical difference between being a child of a high-achieving businessperson, medical doctor, or lawyer versus being a child of the president of the United States. Increasingly, a president is supposed to be "an ideal man with an ideal family."[24] Thus, children of presidents have to navigate family relations and tensions in a situation where their parent has perhaps the most stressful and high-profile job in the world. Although some presidential children have handled this difficult arrangement successfully, the pressures of being a presidential child are substantial.

In sum, parents of presidents heavily affect their children's presidencies. Children of presidents are also impacted heavily by their parent's position. Thus, when children of presidents seek to become presidents themselves, family history and relationships will be crucial to the second presidency within the immediate family. The presidency with its large expectations is difficult enough without the additional pressures of dealing with family legacies. Is a presidential child who seeks to be president, someone who continually tries to gain his father's approval? Or does the presidential child consciously or subconsciously try to rebel against their parent's presidency? Or is it some combination of both? Simply put, the presidency is difficult enough without adding not just family pressures but *presidential* family pressure. Interestingly, Wead concludes that George W. Bush can overcome the difficult history that many presidential children have encountered and be a successful president. This book takes a different interpretation. The demands and pressures of the presidency when mixed with internal family expectations and pressures are too many obstacles to overcome.

Siblings

Siblings of presidents also have difficult circumstances to overcome. Like most families, there are elements of sibling rivalries in their relationships. Several presidential brothers have been caught in difficult circumstances. Billy Carter, brother of Jimmy Carter, secured a lobbying contract with the country of Libya during his brother's presidency. Roger Clinton, brother of Bill Clinton, served time in prison for possession of cocaine. Sam Johnson, brother of Lyndon Johnson was famous for his partying ways with both alcohol and women. President Johnson resorted to having the Secret Service follow his brother to keep him out of trouble. James Monroe's brother Joseph literally abandoned his children at the White House and wanted President Monroe to raise and support them.[25]

Not all presidential siblings were such dramatic embarrassments. Of course, Robert Kennedy was a critical advisor to his brother John. Some observers have called him an "alter ego" to the president.[26] Jeb Bush was a successful governor of Florida and a possible contender for the presidency. Yet even these high-achievers had to operate in the shadow of their brothers. It is difficult to be a contemporary of a sibling who is the most powerful person in the world. Feelings of jealousy and insecurity are natural under the circumstances. No matter what a presidential sibling does in their life, their lives will always be compared to what their presidential sibling has done.

First Ladies

This dynamic of family pressure is also present with the first lady–president relationship. The role of first lady has received greater attention since the activist Eleanor Roosevelt was in the position. Yet the influence of the first lady on presidents is not confined to the post–New Deal age. Robert Watson, a prominent first lady scholar, writes that the importance of the first lady dates back to the presidency of George Washington. Watson believes this connection is so strong that the relationship between the first lady and the president should be called a presidential partnership.[27] The historical evidence that first ladies impact their husband's presidencies is strong. Even before Eleanor Roosevelt, various first ladies were important parts of their husband's administrations. Watson correctly points out that George Washington would never have been a general and president without the financial support of his wife.[28] Dolly Madison, James

Madison's wife, was a force in Washington, DC, and helped her husband win a second term.[29] Edith Wilson, Woodrow Wilson's second wife, essentially took over the duties of president after Wilson suffered a stroke in 1919. Wilson's condition was so bad that if it occurred today, the Twenty-Fifth Amendment could have been invoked and Wilson removed from office.

Eleanor Roosevelt showcased her influence and power in a much more public way. She traveled on the president's behalf. She held an important position in the administration concerning civil defense in the nation, and she openly advocated for more equality for women and blacks. Gil Troy, a political historian, believes that Eleanor Roosevelt started a new public role for the first lady.[30] The first ladies of the modern presidencies embarked on presidencies with their husbands. Troy does not believe that presidents and first ladies share equal status, but they do share the presidency.[31] Jacqueline Kennedy was more popular than her husband during most of his presidency. In many ways she was the cultural leader of the nation. Betty Ford spoke out on many issues including abortion and the Equal Rights Amendment. Ronald Reagan was criticized because his wife had major control over his schedule and public appearances. Hillary Clinton made it clear in the 1992 campaign that she and her husband would share the powers of a presidency.

Accordingly, little doubt remains that first ladies impact their husband's presidencies. However it must be remembered that this is a two-way relationship. Presidents and the presidency heavily impact presidential spouses. Many of these impacts bring up negative and difficult emotions.

Jack and Jacqueline Kennedy had problems during his presidency because of his numerous extramarital affairs.[32] Patricia Nixon was physically and mentally exhausted after the ordeal of Watergate. Betty Ford developed a serious drinking problem during Gerald Ford's presidency after two failed assassination attempts on her husband.[33] Nancy Reagan became so protective of her husband after his assassination attempt in 1981 that she limited his public appearances as much as possible. Her concern was so great that she consulted an astrologer about the president's travel schedule.[34] Hillary Clinton had to endure the embarrassing spectacle of her husband's affair being played out in front of the national media. This affair became the basis for only the second presidential impeachment in American history. These difficult emotional events affect presidential spouses. After dealing with these difficult emotional issues in a large public spotlight, could these spouses be effective presidents themselves? Would a

President Nancy Reagan who firmly protected her husband's public legacy try to enact policies that builds on that legacy whether the country needed these policies or not? Just as Bill Clinton attempted to share powers with his wife, will a President Hillary Clinton make her husband a copresident?

These questions are particularly relevant in light of the how the presidency has been transformed in the modern era. The presidency and the president have become (1) the center of the nation's politics, (2) the focal point of the nation's media, and (3) the leader in the nation's culture. "To talk politics in American is to talk of the president,"[35] historian Barbara Kellerman writes. The power the federal government acquired during the New Deal and World War II combined with the media saturation coverage of the Kennedy era has placed the president in a unique position as the central focus of the nation. Along with the attention on the president comes attention on the president's family. Troy writes that the nation's fascination with the president and the presidential spouse "sheds light on the growth of government, the epidemic of celebrity,...the ascendance of the mass media, (and) the vagaries of modern marriage."[36] Troy shows the combination of these factors produces intense attention and focus on the first family. "With the rise of the national media, the president has also become the nation's celebrity-in-chief as well. As the most famous man in America, his wife, his daughter,...become role models for the nation."[37]

With this intense attention placed upon the president and his family, can a family successfully endure two or multiple presidencies? More important for the nation, can the presidency be a vibrant and successful governing institution when members of the same family occupy the office? History provides some guidance to these questions. Below, two presidential family dynasties and one potential dynasty are examined: Adams, Roosevelts, and Kennedys. These presidential families can offer insight into the dynamics of presidential power based upon family legacies. The presidencies of William Henry Harrison and Benjamin Harrison are not examined below. William Henry Harrison died after a month in office, and his grandson Benjamin served only one term forty-eight eight years later.[38]

Each of these families examined highlights particular familial relationships that can be compared to the Bushes and the Clintons. The Adams dynasty just like the Bushes includes a son and a father who share the same name and also shared the presidency. Theodore and Franklin Roosevelt were distant cousins as presidential relatives, but Eleanor Roosevelt came from Theodore Roosevelt's side of the family.

Eleanor was Theodore's most important contribution to Franklin. Hillary Clinton based her activist approach to the office of first lady on Eleanor Roosevelt. Clinton's role as first lady propelled her to be a leading candidate in the 2008 presidential election cycle. Finally, the Kennedys showcased a potential presidential dynasty cut short by tragedy. This potential dynasty included a father with passionate ambitions for his children, and also a sibling relationship that resulted in Robert Kennedy seeking the presidency five years after his presidential brother was assassinated. As a result of this legacy, Senator Ted Kennedy also made an ill-fated run for the White House. Although the circumstances may be dramatically different, former governor Jeb Bush of Florida may seek the presidency in 2012 or 2016. In fact, George W. Bush has publicly stated that Jeb would make a great president.[39]

The stark lesson that can be drawn from earlier presidential dynasties is that combining the pressures of the office of the presidency with issues of family legacies is difficult and sometimes tragic. Undoubtedly, these intrafamily pressures also impacted presidential decision-making usually in a harmful way.

With a brief examination of these three historical families, the possible dangers of multiple Bush or Clinton presidencies can be examined more thoroughly.

Adams Family

If there was ever an American family that should have produced a successful presidential dynasty, the Adams family was it. This family record of important public service is almost unmatched in American history. Samuel Adams was a leader in Boston's independence movement before 1776. He was thirteen years older than his cousin John. He was a natural rebel who led with passion and encouraged the early believers in American independence.[40] His cousin John Adams did not come from a rich family in Boston, but used his intelligence and political drive to win the nation's first real competitive presidential election in 1796. John Quincy Adams, his son, also became a U.S. senator, representative, and president. Other members of the Adams family became congressmen, ambassadors, and the secretary of the navy.[41] Despite these achievements and service, the Adams presidencies were not successful. Both John and his son John Quincy were not reelected after one term in office. If these accomplished individuals could not fashion family presidencies that worked, then it is appropriate to ask the question, could any family?

John Adams started his political career with the Continental Congress in 1774. He'd been a successful attorney and taken several high-profile cases including one case where he actually defended a British general who fired upon a crowd in Boston. He became a strong voice in the Continental Congress for independence. He started an impressive diplomatic career as a representative of the United States in France in the middle of the Revolutionary War. After returning from France he authored the new Massachusetts State Constitution. As the war was drawing to a close, he was appointed by the Continental Congress as a representative to negotiate a peace treaty with Great Britain.[42] He did so successfully and also managed to negotiate foreign loans that helped to save the credit of the new United States.[43]

Adams' brilliant diplomatic performance cleared the way for his appointment as the first American ambassador to Great Britain. Adams would meet directly with King George III and have the difficult diplomatic task of representing a nation that had defeated the mighty British Military. The number one priority of the American government was to avoid another war with Great Britain over shipping and expansion interests.[44] Again, Adams managed all of these difficult issues and gave the new nation the necessary space to grow and develop.

As reward for this diplomatic service was a job that he did not like. He had the unenviable task of being George Washington's vice president. After the failures of the Articles Confederation, Washington was seen as the only public figure strong enough to lead the new government under the Constitution. For his first term, Washington was more appointed than elected. Adams came in a distant second to Washington in the electoral college and became vice president. He famously called the vice presidency "the most insignificant office known to man."[45]

The election of 1792 was a repeat of 1788. Although the government had a growing rift between Federalists and Anti-Federalists about the power of the central government, the nation's leaders again turned to Washington to head the government. Adams came in a distant second again. He was furious. He cursed the electors. Even though he was Washington's vice president, he saw himself as the natural leader of the nation. He waited eight long years to get his opportunity to be president.[46]

With all of his considerable experience, Adams presidency should have operated smoothly. Yet his time as president was anything but efficient. With Washington away from the scene, the unifying figure that held the government together was gone. Full-scale partisan politics broke open. Alexander Hamilton, Washington's secretary of the treasury led the Federalist Party, which sought more central government power and more authority for the National Bank. Jefferson had resigned from Washington's government back in 1793 because of his concern about Hamilton's authoritarian maneuvers. Jefferson led the anti-Federalists in their opposition to other Federalists in Washington's government. John Adams was caught in the middle. He was not a partisan figure but he was aligned with an administration of Federalists.[47]

Adams won a close election over the author of the Declaration of Independence, Thomas Jefferson, who became his vice president. Yet the fighting in his own government would make the Adams presidency a difficult one. Alexander Hamilton did not trust Adams and worked against his interests. Thus, many Federalists opposed Adams. During the threat of a war with France, Congress passed and Adams signed into law the *Alien and Sedition Acts of* 1798. These acts gave the president the power to expel any immigrant who looked "dangerous."[48] The acts also made it illegal to speak out against the government of the United States during wartime. The worst dreams of the anti-Federalists and Jefferson were coming true; the national government was acquiring more and more power even powers that directly contradicted the First Amendment. Adams was attacked as a monarchist and dictator in the partisan presses. Yet, he held the new U.S. government together during extremely turbulent times.

By the time the election of 1800 came around, the Federalists were seeking another candidate and even begged Washington to make another run before his death in 1799. During the 1800 campaign, Hamilton attacked Adams bitterly in a public letter. The Federalists were divided and Jefferson had a united anti-Federalist party behind him. When the electoral college met in late 1800, Adams incredibly was beaten by two challengers. As an incumbent president, this was a dismal performance. He finished third in the electoral college (one of the worst showings in American history for an incumbent). It was a jarring defeat for Adams and his family. Abigail Adams, his wife, said she was "sick of public life."[49] About her son John Quincy, Mrs. Adams said she would rather have him "thrown as a log on the fire than see him President of the United States."[50]

John Quincy Adams however did not heed this warning. He was raised in an atmosphere of accomplishment and expectation. His father had been a central figure in independence and securing America's place in the diplomatic world. He had inherited his father's brilliance and his love of diplomacy. When he was just thirteen, he served as an assistant to the American representative to Russia. He also assisted his father in diplomatic missions to Holland and with the peace treaty that brought an end to the Revolutionary War. He spoke multiple languages including Greek, Latin, Dutch, and French. During his diplomatic travels as a young man, he met and negotiated with some of the most important men in the world.

The other Adams children would not be so fortunate. Stephen Hess in his important work on political dynasties wrote that "it was almost unconscionably difficult to be an Adams and all who were so blest could not live up to their inheritance."[51] Alcoholism impacted two other sons of John Adams. His son Charles died an alcoholic. His other son Thomas also had a serious drinking problem. His daughter, Nabby, married a man who ran up large debts and tried to use the Adams named to his advantage. Also, Adams tried to name his son-in-law an adjutant general in the army to give him a meaningful job, but the Senate rejected his nomination. Adams remarked "my children give me more pain than all of my enemies."[52] He expected much from his children, and John Quincy was the only one who tried to fulfill his desires. The senior Adams told his son John Quincy "if you do not rise to the head... of your country it will be owing to your own laziness."[53]

As vice president, John Adams did not hesitate to support his son's appointment as ambassador to Holland in 1794 at the age of twenty-seven. This assignment would start a long and successful career in diplomacy. When John Adams assumed the presidency in 1796, Washington urged Adams to keep his son in the diplomatic corps. Washington thought John Quincy was an important representative of the United States abroad. When his father lost the presidency in 1800 John Quincy came back to the United States. The Massachusetts legislature soon appointed him a U.S. senator. However like his father he disagreed with many Federalists especially regarding relations with France. John Quincy Adams resigned from the Senate because of these disagreements. He resumed his diplomatic career as ambassador to Russia and worked on a peace treaty with Great Britain to end the War of 1812. He then became secretary of state under President James Monroe. This was an important position politically because in the early 1800s the office of secretary of state was seen as the major step to the presidency.[54]

The presidency was a prize that John Quincy Adams clearly wanted. Yet, like his father, he would not campaign for the position. The Adams family did not believe in partisan politics and they did not believe in campaigning for the office. Even with John Quincy's sterling qualifications he would have a serious fight for the presidency. The election of 1824 came down to Adams and Andrew Jackson, the military hero of the battle of New Orleans, and Henry Clay, the speaker of the House from Kentucky. Jackson won the electoral vote and the popular vote but he did not gain a majority, and thus the election was thrown into the House of Representatives. Adams had finished a strong second and so the kingmaker for the next presidency would be Speaker Henry Clay. Clay thought that Adams was a superior man. He was not as impressed with Jackson's credentials. Clay stated "that killing 2500 Englishmen at New Orleans" did not qualify Jackson to be president.[55] Clay gave his support to Adams and with it the election of 1824. When Adams was notified that he had won the presidency, he quickly contacted his father. His father rejoiced at the news and told his son "never did I feel so much solemnity as upon this occasion."[56] The Adams presidential dynasty had come to fruition. Two of the most intelligent and diplomatically skilled Americans had become president.

Yet, the way John Quincy Adams won the presidency would come back to haunt the Adams family. John Quincy Adams did not anticipate that one of his first actions as president-elect would lead to his downfall. He appointed Henry Clay as secretary of state. Andrew Jackson and his supporters cried foul. They believed the office of the secretary of state was used as a bargaining chip for the presidency. The 1824 election was quickly labeled as "the corrupt bargain." No real evidence of this trade has surfaced, but Jackson had an issue to take to the people. He charged that the will of the people had been ignored. Jackson told a friend that Clay was "Judas of the West" and asked if "was there ever such a bare-faced corruption in any country before."[57]

Jackson used the corruption issue to immediately begin campaigning for the next presidential election. The Tennessee legislature was so upset at the 1824 election that it committed its presidential electors to Jackson for the 1828 election a full three years before it was held. Jackson used this dispute to signal his allies in Congress to block John Quincy Adams' agenda. Adams envisioned internal transportation improvements and new diplomatic initiatives. Jackson's allies made sure these initiatives never passed. Jackson's newspapers continually painted Adams as an elitist New Englander. Some of these attacks included the name "King John II."[58]

The 1828 election was a foregone conclusion. Adams won New England, but Jackson carried Pennsylvania, the West, and the South. Supporters of Adams were concerned that his victory represented a victory for the mob. Adam's intelligence was used against him while Jackson's common sense was highlighted. Jackson and his forces clearly had an organizational advantage over Adams. Although Adams refused to engage in campaign politics, supporters of Jackson collected money, assembled voter lists, printed pamphlets, and even wrote campaign songs.[59] Jackson won by nearly 100 electoral votes. John Adams died in 1826 and did not have to see a second Adams lose the presidency as an incumbent. John Quincy Adams had made his father proud by rising to the presidency, but he ignored his mother's warnings about the heartache the office can bring.

After his presidency, John Quincy Adams went on to be elected to the House of Representatives, the only former president to take this path. He also became a prominent abolitionist and warned the country about the perils of slavery. He had served his nation as a diplomat and as leader in the debate about the most important human rights issue the young nation had ever faced. He was a great American and a bad president. With all of his talents and his impeccable resume, John Quincy Adams only failed at two things in his life: being president and being a father.

John Quincy Adams transferred his father's ambitions to his own sons. They were expected to be leaders of their nation and their professions. His children knew what was expected. He boldly named his firstborn son George Washington Adams. George Washington Adams' early life fulfilled some of these expectations. He was a brilliant student at Harvard and he was elected to the Massachusetts legislature at a young age. However the expectations of his family and his own problems soon combined to bring a tragic end. He committed suicide by throwing himself off a steamboat and leaving a note for his family.[60] John Quincy's second son, John, also tried to live up to these expectations. He embarrassed his father by being expelled from Harvard; he attempted to run the family business but it soon failed. He died at a young age as a result of alcoholism.[61] John Quincy's only daughter Luisa tragically died as a baby when John Quincy was on one of his diplomatic missions in Russia. His third son Charles found more success than his siblings. He married well and was elected to the House of Representatives. Like his father he also became a skilled diplomat and helped to keep Great Britain from supporting the Confederacy during the Civil War.[62]

Yet, the Adams presidential dynasty would end with John Quincy. The family gave the nation so much, but could not deliver a successful presidency. The only other family to have two of its immediate members become president is the Bush family. There are other similarities between the two families. John Adams and George H. W. Bush both used their diplomatic career as preparation for their presidencies. Both served two terms as vice presidents under immensely popular presidents, George Washington and Ronald Reagan.

They both had impeccable resumes but they lacked political charisma. They both were defeated after one presidential term becoming the first and last incumbent presidents to lose reelection. Disloyalty by their own party members played major roles in the reelection defeats of both men. Alexander Hamilton and many Federalists abandoned John Adams in 1800 while conservative Pat Buchanan and other conservatives directly challenged George H. W. Bush in 1992.

However, they treated their sons much differently. John Quincy Adams was a diplomatic secretary by the age of thirteen and by his own admission, George W. Bush did not find himself professionally until the age of forty. John Adams always expected his son to be president. George H. W. Bush thought his second son Jeb would be the politician. George W. Bush had an inconsistent relationship with his father's legacy. Like his father, he attended Yale University, went into the oil business, and then launched his career in Texas politics. He clearly struggled with following his father and finding a life of his own.

John Quincy Adams had the diplomatic and political career that emulated his father's life. He was a diplomatic prodigy, a U.S. senator, and secretary of state before he entered the presidency. George W. Bush failed in the oil business, lost a race for the U.S. House from Texas, and struggled with alcohol dependency. He overcame these setbacks to become governor of Texas before he assumed the presidency. A brief comparison of the two families advances this important question. If the Adams family, one of the most prestigious families in American history cannot produce a successful presidential family dynasty, is any family capable of such a feat?

Roosevelts

Even though the Roosevelt name covers two important and successful presidencies, they are not an authentic family presidential dynasty. Theodore and Franklin Roosevelt were distant cousins. The young Franklin clearly admired his cousin Theodore. Theodore's bold public successes as a military leader, president, and explorer inspired Franklin politically.[63] Franklin also deftly used the Roosevelt name to his advantage in social and political situations. Yet the reality of their relationship is that he was Theodore's fifth cousin. Franklin advanced his political career in a political party different from that of his cousin Theodore. When Franklin Roosevelt ran for vice president in 1920, he took a position sharply different from the family of Theodore Roosevelt on the most important issue of the day: the ratification of the League of Nations. Theodore Roosevelt had died a year earlier. However Theodore's family was so upset with Franklin's support of the League that Theodore Roosevelt Jr, wounded veteran of World War I, denounced Franklin Roosevelt and said "He does not have the brand of our family."[64] This would produce a feud between the Oyster Bay Roosevelts (Theodore) and the Hyde Park Roosevelts (Franklin) and most of Theodore Roosevelt's family would never again support Franklin Roosevelt.

Yet, Theodore Roosevelt's side of the family had given Franklin Roosevelt his most important political partner: Eleanor Roosevelt. Eleanor and Franklin were also distant cousins when they married. Franklin could never have guessed the central role that Eleanor would play in his political life. Hillary Clinton clearly modeled her time as first lady on the example of Eleanor Roosevelt. As Senator Clinton has entered presidential politics, it is instructive to revisit Eleanor Roosevelt's time as first lady and her post-presidential achievements.

A biographer called Eleanor Roosevelt "the most important public woman of the twentieth century."[65] This imposing title would not have seemed possible in 1905 when Eleanor married Franklin. Eleanor Roosevelt was shy and reserved as a result of the early death of both of her parents. She offered Franklin Roosevelt stability, and he offered her excitement. After their marriage, she settled down and began a long period of raising a family of six children. Her life changed dramatically when she found out that her husband was having an affair with social secretary Lucy Mercer. The Roosevelts nearly divorced. With the intervention of Franklin's mother Sara, Eleanor and Franklin came to an understanding. There would be no more intimacy in the marriage, but they would stay together for their children and Franklin's political career. This decision helped Franklin to save his political future and helped Eleanor to pursue other interests. She became active in the League of Women Voters and the Women's Trade Union.[66] She no longer would be a dutiful housewife; she became a political activist.

When Franklin Roosevelt contracted polio in 1922; Eleanor Roosevelt traveled on behalf of her husband and kept his name in front of the public while he adjusted to his new physical limitations. Franklin Roosevelt was elected governor of New York and she became a passionate advocate for women's issues. Although once she wrote, "wives of great men may keep her own opinions, but she must keep them to herself," she became a stronger political presence as her husband's political profile increased.[67] When Franklin Roosevelt was elected president in 1932, Eleanor Roosevelt was an important part of his political team and a growing liberal voice in the nation.

She transformed the role of the president's wife. She held weekly press conferences; she traveled extensively without her husband. Franklin Roosevelt, with the combination of new technologies and the growing role of the federal government, made the presidency the central hub of power in the federal government. This increased power gave more attention and influence to the presidential first family especially the first lady. During the years of Depression, she acted as the guardian of the poor and dispossessed in the nation. She worked on issues regarding women, blacks, and labor. When World War II came, her human rights concerns turned to the entire world. All these concerns she relayed to President Roosevelt through a constant stream of memos. She was intensely involved in public policy. She was a "policy adviser, policy implementer and policy evaluator."[68]

Yet, Eleanor Roosevelt's influence did have it limits, she differed with some of her husband's policies especially his reluctance to push meaningful civil rights legislation through Congress.[69] Eleanor lost a very public and bitter fight with her husband about keeping Henry Wallace as the Democratic vice presidential candidate in 1944. As President Roosevelt's health declined, he relied on his daughter Anna more than his own wife.

After Franklin Roosevelt's death in 1944, Eleanor Roosevelt was at a crossroads. She was no longer the dutiful wife of thirty years earlier; she was a national and world figure. With widespread sympathy for the Roosevelt family across the nation after the president's death, she could have won elective office.

Harold Ickes Sr., an important advisor to Franklin Roosevelt, wanted her to be a candidate because she would be "unbeatable."[70] His son Harold Ickes Jr. would later advise First Lady Hillary Clinton to run for the U.S. Senate.

Eleanor Roosevelt flatly refused these suggestions about elected office. She became an even more important voice in international affairs and Democratic politics. Harry Truman appointed her as part of the American delegation to the London Conference that organized the United Nations (UN). She soon became the de facto leader of the delegation where she carried her commitment to human rights to a wider audience. She won an important victory at the UN regarding displaced refugees.[71] Her most important accomplishment was leading the commission that drafted the Universal Declaration of Human Rights (UDHR) at the UN. Never before had so many nations agreed on a document that stated that all citizens of the world should have basic human rights. This was a stunning accomplishment. It helped Eleanor Roosevelt earn the title "First Lady of the World."[72]

She resigned her UN post when President Eisenhower was elected in 1952. She began an astonishing last decade of her life. She traveled the world spreading the gospel on human rights. At home, she challenged Senator Joseph McCarthy when few other Americans would. She increased her advocacy of civil rights by joining the National Association for the Advancement of Colored People (NAACP) and engaging in nonviolent protests. She constantly prodded the Democratic Party to engage in social justice issues. She was the most important public woman of her time. When she died in 1962, President Kennedy and former presidents Truman and Eisenhower attended the ceremony.

Hillary Clinton has declared that Eleanor Roosevelt was a role model; this declaration masks serious differences between their political development and growth. When Eleanor Roosevelt married Franklin she had no interest in politics. In fact, she didn't think that women should be allowed to vote. In contrast, Hillary Clinton came to her marriage with Bill Clinton with strong career ambitions. She was the breadwinner of the family for many years. She served as a major advisor to her husband during his time as governor. Moreover, when Bill Clinton ran for president, the Clintons promised "two for the price of one." Hillary Clinton also made her intentions known that she would be a dominant force in her husband's administration by requesting a West Wing office close to the Oval Office. Eleanor Roosevelt also was heavily involved in the politics and policy of her husband's administration. Yet her influence had limits. If President Roosevelt disagreed with her, he simply ignored her advice and publicly stated his opposition.

Most importantly, a comparison shows dramatically different paths after their husbands' presidencies. After her husband's death, Eleanor was approached by important party leaders to run for elected office. She refused these entreaties several times through the 1940s and 1950s. Instead, she put together a remarkable diplomatic and political career outside the presidency. She was known as the conscience of the Democratic Party and a world leader in her own right. Conversely, Hillary Clinton moved aggressively to seek elected office even while her husband's presidency was continuing. More boldly, she attempted to run for Senate from a state which she never had lived. In many ways, Eleanor Roosevelt was free to pursue her passions about social issues when she left the presidency and the White House. She put together a remarkable legacy outside the White House. In contrast, Hillary Clinton seeks to define her legacy by winning the White House in her own right.

The Kennedys

When most observers think of a presidential family dynasty, one family immediately comes to the forefront: the Kennedys of Massachusetts. Ironically they are not a presidential family dynasty. As a result of tragedy and political defeats, the Kennedy family has one shortened presidency to show for all of its political activity. They have certainly been a political family dynasty, but the family's pursuit of the presidency provides a stark historical example of the problems of mixing family legacies with the American presidency.

Clearly, the Kennedys were the family in American history with the most direct plan to occupy the American presidency. This urge to dominate American politics came directly from the patriarch of the family, Joseph P. Kennedy. His father Patrick had reluctantly entered politics through his business interests as a bar owner and a bank investor. His son Joseph was a business prodigy with undeniable ambition. Joseph was a bank president by the age of twenty-five and a millionaire by the age of thirty-five. He expanded his business empire to include the stock market, Hollywood movies, and real estate.[73] When a friend once asked Joseph Kennedy what he wanted in life, Kennedy replied "everything."[74]

Everything for Joseph Kennedy included the American presidency. His own political career benefited from his relationship with Franklin Roosevelt. He was a major contributor to the Roosevelt's 1932 presidential campaign. Franklin Roosevelt kept a wary eye on Joe Kennedy as a possible competitor, but he also rewarded his work with several government posts including the chair of the Securities and Exchange Commission (SEC), the head of the Maritime Commission and an ambassador to Great Britain. Joseph Kennedy's political career ended with his support for isolation from the world and negotiation with Nazi Germany before World War II. The sons would have to carry on the political legacy. His oldest son Joseph Kennedy Jr. would be the obvious heir to his father's desire for political power.

The sons understood this expectation very well. John Kennedy stated, "Joe was supposed to be the politician. When he died, I took his place. If anything happens to me, Bobby would take my place. If something happened to Bobby, Teddy would take his place."[75] This expectation would dominate the lives of Joseph Kennedy's children and grandchildren, and in many ways the political life of the United States for twenty-five years.

World War II would change the fate of the Kennedy political machine. In 1943 in the Pacific Ocean, John Kennedy commanded a Patrol Torpedo (PT) boat. His boat was attacked by a Japanese destroyer and the ship was disabled. He somehow managed to keep his men alive by swimming to a nearby island. The crew was rescued three days later. The PT 109 incident became national news. Instead of being identified with appeasement, the Kennedy name was now known for war heroics. When Joseph Kennedy Jr. heard about John Kennedy's bravery, he was privately tormented because his brother was a war hero, and he was not. Joseph Kennedy Jr. knew that a political career was his destiny after the war and he could not be outdone by his younger brother.[76] The expectations on Joseph Kennedy Jr. were so pervasive that he volunteered for a dangerous mission. He volunteered to fly a large airplane loaded with 10 tons of TNT to take out German missile sites. Some military observers believe the mission was doomed from the beginning. The plane exploded in midair and the heir to the Kennedy political throne was killed.[77] This tragic incident was the beginning of a terrible price the family would pay for the pursuit of political power.

John Kennedy knew what was expected of him after his brother's death. Two biographers called John Kennedy the "stand in."[78] In many ways John Kennedy was not the ideal candidate to take up the political banner. Unlike his brother Joe, he was skinny and slight in appearance. He did not show the interest in pursuing political office that his brother Joe demonstrated. Yet his fate was sealed. He knew that his father would demand a political career.[79] John Kennedy told a friend in referring to his deceased brother "I'm shadowboxing in a match the shadow is always going to win."[80]

Thus John Kennedy began a legendary political career. This career was very much a family political operation. Joseph Kennedy made the bold statement that he was going to sell Jack "like soapflakes."[81] In both his House campaign and Senate campaign, John Kennedy was sold as a product. Using the Kennedy name and the new medium of television, John Kennedy was sold as a good-looking, patriotic American. Polling and advertising techniques were successfully introduced to American voters via the Kennedy campaigns. The Kennedy money would allow John Kennedy to compete anywhere. The marketing campaign was such a success that Kennedy won the Democratic nomination for president in 1960 on the first ballot and won the general election against Vice President Richard Nixon. Joseph Kennedy's dreams were now a reality.

Yet, Joseph Kennedy wanted more. He advised John to appoint his brother Robert Kennedy as attorney general. Robert Kennedy had been the hard-charging campaign manager behind the Kennedy victory in 1960, yet his qualifications for attorney general were weak. Yet both John and Joseph Kennedy realized that the new president needed a family member close by. This presidency would be a family enterprise.

Joseph Kennedy Sr. wanted more. Two years later, the youngest Kennedy brother, Ted, would run for John Kennedy's vacated Senate seat from Massachusetts. Teddy was only thirty at the time he ran for office. Joseph Kennedy simply stated a year before the election "look I spent a lot of money for that Senate seat. It belongs in the family."[82] Teddy had struggled in college and was suspended from Harvard for cheating on an exam. He had an undistinguished law school education at the University of Virginia. He was a district attorney in Massachusetts for a brief period and then he ran for U.S. Senate. By the time the Senate campaign came around in 1962, the Kennedy political machine was at its zenith. He won the Senate seat but did not impress many people in the campaign. The *New York Times* called his election "demeaning to the dignity of the Senate and the democratic process."[83] He won because he was a Kennedy and that was enough.

By 1962, the Kennedy family was dominating American politics. Although John Kennedy's legislative agenda was stalled in Congress, the Kennedys had the attention of the American public. After a foreign-policy disaster with the Bay of Pigs, John and Robert Kennedy showed leadership and savvy in negotiating a peaceful end to the Cuban missile crisis. As John Kennedy's presidency matured, Robert Kennedy took a larger role in advising his brother. Joseph Kennedy had suffered a stroke in late 1961, and could no longer be of counsel. President Kennedy had always been wary of appearing to be too dependent upon his father even before the stroke. Thus, Robert became his most trusted friend and aide. As noted previously, Robert Kennedy was known as the alter ego of the president.[84]

When President Kennedy was assassinated in 1963, the world and the nation all looked to Robert to take up the fight. Yet Robert was emotionally and physically devastated after the assassination. Besides his potent name, he was also an unlikely candidate. He was somewhat awkward in his public appearances and did not have the grace and charm of his older brother.[85] He was immediately considered for vice president, but he and President Johnson saw each other as rivals. He instead decided to run for the U.S. Senate from New York. Again the Kennedy name gave him special privileges. He was not from New York, and he ran an inconsistent campaign. He prevailed with the help of President Johnson's landslide in 1964. Yet he was still lost about his purpose in politics and in life. He found the Senate boring and continually looked for other outlets to find himself.[86] He traveled extensively and even climbed a mountain named Mt. Kennedy in Canada. The problems with the Vietnam War confounded him, and he was unsure of his next political step.

Yet after Eugene McCarthy drew strong support in the Democratic New Hampshire primary in 1968, Robert Kennedy decided to run for president. Not surprisingly, some of his family members were not initially supportive. His parents were wary that Robert was exposing himself to danger.[87] Joseph Kennedy could not stop the political machine that he had started so enthusiastically years before. To showcase the idea that Robert was finishing his brother John's work, he announced his candidacy from the same Senate room from which John Kennedy had announced his campaign. His family mobilized to support Robert but they were also reserved. Robert Kennedy was torn between following his brother John and staking out his own identity. A Kennedy friend stated, "Bobby felt he was in Jack's shadow."[88] He found his voice in the 1968 campaign advocating for civil rights for blacks and help for the needy. Yet in the tragic year of 1968, he became the third Kennedy brother to be killed; he was assassinated on the night of the California primary on June 5, 1968.

In the 1920s when Joseph Kennedy Sr. set his goal of obtaining the presidency for his family, he could not have imagined the personal cost for his family and the nation. By 1968, the Kennedys had lost three brothers in the pursuit of their political ambitions. Joseph Kennedy Jr. volunteered for an impossible military mission in order to keep up with his brother. Two assassins helped to end the first Kennedy presidency and prevent the second.

With only one surviving brother remaining, the Kennedys had given enough in the pursuit of a presidential family dynasty. Yet expectations and pressures immediately were directed toward Ted Kennedy after Robert's assassination.

Teddy Kennedy had used his energy since his 1962 election to become familiar with the Senate rules and procedures. He was becoming an effective senator and a liberal icon in Democratic circles. His life changed dramatically after the 1968 Kennedy assassination. The "crushing weight of the Kennedy Legacy" was now on Teddy.[89] After a period of withdrawal from the public, he made his first major speech since the assassination right before the Democratic Convention in 1968. On cue concerning his family legacy he said:

> Like my three brothers before me, I pick up a fallen standard...I shall try to carry forward that special commitment to justice, to excellence, to courage that distinguished their lives.[90]

Not surprisingly, he could not live up to the high expectations and pressures of being the last Kennedy brother. He could not fully embrace the expectations placed upon him. He actually could have made a late run at the presidency at the 1968 Democratic Convention in Chicago. The split convention may have rallied around the Kennedy name. Yet even Ted Kennedy knew it was too much for him, but he also knew that 1968 was perhaps his best opportunity to be president.[91]

After he declined to put his name in nomination, his personal and political life went into turmoil. In 1969, he took a trip to Alaska to examine the plight of Alaska's Indians. On the return flight from that trip, many reporters and friends on the plane noticed how drunk he had become. He told a reporter "they're going to shoot my ass off the way they shot Bobby."[92] Later in that same year, Ted Kennedy drove his car off a bridge at Chappaquiddick and his female companion drowned in the accident. Ted Kennedy did not report the accident until the next day. He gave conflicting statements about his actions that night and showed callous disregard for the fate of his companion, Mary Jo Kopechne. Ted Kennedy stumbled to give a public response to this accident. The fact that the last Kennedy brother had been in accident that killed a woman was thought to have ended Ted Kennedy's chance of the presidency.

Historian Garry Wills wrote that the Kennedy legacy had "imprisoned" Ted Kennedy.[93] This imprisonment would again compel Ted Kennedy to seek the presidency even after Chappaquidick, his failing marriage, and other personal troubles. In 1980, Ted Kennedy sought to challenge a weakened incumbent president Jimmy Carter for the Democratic nomination. Kennedy led Carter in the early polls, but the incumbent president won the Iowa caucus and the New Hampshire primary decisively. Kennedy would go on to lose most of the primaries and the nomination. He was listless on the campaign stump and seemed befuddled in the presidential campaign. His personal problems would help to doom his campaign. Wills who was covering the Kennedy campaign said, "Kennedy (Ted) was forced every day to demonstrate that he was not as good as his brothers."[94] Ted Kennedy gave the speech of his life at the 1980 Democratic Convention when he ended his campaign for president. He said the "dream would never die." Since his failed presidential run, he has become a powerful force in the U.S. Senate. He is an icon of Democratic Party, and he is both detested and feared by conservatives, but he will never be president.

Not surprisingly, this Kennedy imprisonment has had some of its most damaging personal impacts on the next Kennedy generation. Many of the thirty Kennedy grandchildren of Joseph Kennedy have experienced a series of personal and political problems trying to grow up in the Kennedy shadow. John Kennedy Jr. would die in plane crash after he showed questionable judgment in trying to land a plane on the small island of Hyannis Port. Robert Kennedy's son David died of a drug overdose after being a drug addict for many years. Ted Kennedy's son Patrick would also struggle with drug abuse. As an elected congressman from Rhode Island, he rammed his car into a U.S. Capitol police station. He says he did not remember the accident. These are only a few of the examples of the difficulties that the young Kennedy generation has faced. Torn between the crushing legacy of Joseph Kennedy and the realities of present-day America, many of these Kennedy children have found little peace.

If Joseph Kennedy Sr. could have looked into the future and seen the fruits of his presidential dynastic ambitions, he may have never pursued them. His presidential ambitions for his family cost him the lives of three of his sons and left a second generation of Kennedys struggling to cope with their family legacy. The Kennedy story is the starkest example of the problems of combining a family legacy with the American presidency.

Is the Kennedy example relevant for the examination of current family presidential legacies? With a father and a son who have attained the presidency and another one who may seek it, the Bushes are the most appropriate contemporary comparison. Unlike Joseph Kennedy, neither Prescott nor George H. W. Bush demanded that their sons pursue a political career. In fact in his autobiography, George W. Bush scoffs at the notion that that his father was planning a family political dynasty. "I think they envision the Bush family growing up, gathered at my father's knee, discussing America's role in the world...as dad would put it. 'Didn't happen.'"[95] Yet while there may have been no grand plan for the Bushes to take over American politics, the family has put together one of the most potent political machines in the nation's history. The Bushes are also not immune from the considerable family pressures that the Kennedys experienced. George W. Bush himself has talked about his problem with alcohol. Neil Bush, President George H. W. Bush's third son also had a series of personal and business problems. Like Robert Kennedy, Jeb Bush would have to follow an older brother on his path to the presidency. No matter how independent former governor Jeb Bush would like to be, if he pursues the presidency, he will inevitably be compared to his brother George. The Bushes have not provided the Shakespearean drama that the Kennedy family has offered the American public. Yet the Kennedy experience presents an important warning to all families who may pursue presidential ambitions. When you attempt to win the most powerful political office in the world more than once, you cannot escape your family.

Chapter Four

The Father Begins a Dynasty

> "For George (W), everywhere he went, his father was there: Andover, Yale, Texas...George Bush the father was like the Tiger Woods in a golfing community...As a young man how do you compete with that?."
>
> —John Ellis Bush, cousin of George W.[1]

George W. Bush had to live under the shadow of a prominent and politically powerful father. At the end of his political career in 1992, George H. W. Bush would leave his sons with two important legacies that would shape their political careers. The first legacy was the unresolved ideological battle in American politics among liberals, moderates, and conservatives. In 1964, George H. W. Bush was called too conservative. In 1970, he was called too moderate and not a real Texan. When he ran for president in 1980, conservatives in his party abandoned him for Ronald Reagan. After serving eight loyal years as Reagan's vice president, he won the presidency on his own, but then was constantly attacked from the Right and lost his reelection. His sons learned from his political defeats. The Bush sons would never be called moderate or liberal.

The second legacy offered to his political sons was the ability to access a modern national political machine. The new politics of the latter half of the twentieth century were not based upon the urban political machines of New York and Chicago that had patronage and immigration at their core. The politics of the modern era required a large fund-raising network, media saturation, and loyal partisanship. Modern politics has given rise to a new era of family dynasties, and in the Republican Party, the Bush family has dominated this era.

The fact that George W. Bush in the year 2000 had eliminated almost all of the opposition for the Republican nomination by the time the caucuses and primaries began in January 2000 is a testament to the power of the Bush political name. Senator John McCain of Arizona offered difficult competition in New Hampshire and a few other states, but most of the other competition was eliminated much earlier because of a lack of fund-raising. The thousands of financial supporters that George H. W. Bush had cultivated throughout the country during his twenty-six years in politics had morphed into a national political network. In some ways, this national network exceeded anything that the Kennedys ever put together. The core of the Bush network was other people who would contribute and get their friends to contribute to the campaigns of the Bushes. The Kennedys had to fund most of their political activities on their own.

From Connecticut to Texas

George W. would have to confront his father's accomplishments and defeats, but he would also benefit from his political organization. This was not a new phenomenon for the Bush family. Prescott Bush, George H. W. Bush's father was a successful investor and U.S. senator. His grandfather Samuel Bush was a successful business leader in the railroad industry. Ironically, Samuel Bush was a Democrat, but his strong support of business and corporations foreshadowed the political leanings of his descendents.[2] Prescott Bush followed his father's example and turned his professional attention to business.

Before he started his career as an investment banker on Wall Street, Samuel Bush provided a good education for his son. Prescott Bush attended a prominent boarding school and then was accepted to Yale where his own son and grandson would eventually attend. At Yale, he joined the Connecticut National Guard and volunteered to join the fight against Pancho Villa in Mexico in 1916. The Yale president asked the military not to send Yale students to Mexico, and they were returned to campus. Prescott Bush's affiliation with the Guard however would put him in line for a stint in the army during World War I and he saw action on the front lines in France.[3]

As a businessman, Prescott Bush experienced tremendous success. He went from a management position in the flooring industry to an investment house broker on Wall Street. Prescott Bush's commitment to his career in the Northeast after World War II would have an important impact on his family's political future. The Bushes of the 1930s, 1940s, and 1950s would be Northeastern Republicans who lived in Connecticut. Prescott Bush excelled on Wall Street during the boom years of the 1920s and the Depression years of the 1930s. With Democratic president Franklin Roosevelt pursuing heavy regulation of the stock industry, Prescott Bush's political affiliation was clear: he was a pro-business Republican. After his business successes, he would start a late political career. His accomplishments and setbacks were prominent in George H. W. Bush's own career plans. A prominent Bush biographer, Herbert Parmet wrote that Prescott was such a large and important figure that George H. W. Bush could "never get out from under."[4]

George H. W. Bush found a way to make his mark in early adulthood. Although he was accepted to Yale, he immediately volunteered for the U.S. Navy at the onset of World War II. He became one of the youngest aviators in the navy. While the Bush family has been controversial because of its involvement in politics, George H. W. Bush's military career is above reproach.

Before his twenty-first birthday, George H. W. Bush flew fifty-eight combat missions and made 126 landings on an aircraft carrier. Moreover, his plane was shot down twice during his war service. He received the Distinguished Flying Cross for his wartime activities.[5] George H. W. Bush was a genuine war hero. This record would be the beginning of a large shadow that he would cast on his own sons.

After World War II, George H. W. Bush returned to Yale and resumed his studies. He had married Barbara Pierce, daughter of a publishing executive from Connecticut, just before he was released from the military. George W. Bush was their first child; he was born in 1946 when they lived in student housing in Connecticut. Instead of taking a job on Wall Street and following in his father's path, George H. W. Bush decided to go into the oil business and move to Texas in 1948. George H. W. Bush "did not want to ride on...(his) father's coattails."[6] George H. W. Bush and Barbara wanted to move away from their parents and strike out on their own. Amazingly, this simple career decision from a young couple in their 20s would help remake American politics in the late twentieth century. The Bushes in Texas would eventually launch an unlikely political dynasty.

Texas was a whole world away from the Republicanism of Connecticut. It was a Solid South Democratic State that that was extremely conservative. Below the presidential level, Texas Democrats dominated politics. This move to Texas would later lead to George H. W. Bush's efforts to build the Republican Party infrastructure in one of the largest states in the South. This type of Southern Republicanism would put him in conflict with his own father's career and would leave stark impressions on his sons as they began their political careers.

After a successful business career and active civic involvement in the city of Greenwich, Prescott Bush ran for the U.S. Senate from Connecticut in 1950. He ran as a progressive Republican who was a fiscal conservative and an internationalist. He advocated a UN Army to combat Communism; he argued that the Truman administration had been slow on implementing civil rights legislation, and said that the current Democratic administration was corrupt.[7] He had a well-funded campaign that was on the verge of success. The weekend before the election, a radio ad targeting Catholics claimed that Prescott Bush supported the "Birth Control League." Birth control was illegal at the time and the support of birth control was seen as an affront to Catholics in Connecticut. Prescott Bush had supported some of the efforts of Planned Parenthood and the issue came back to haunt his senatorial campaign. He lost the election by 1,100 votes.[8] The Bushes learned a tough political lesson. Fiscal conservatism may be responsible but social conservatism can offer wedge issues that win elections. Social and cultural issues would force two generations of the Bush family to separate themselves from their own father's ideology.

Prescott Bush would not be denied his seat in the U.S. Senate. Just two years later, the elder Bush would win a close race for a vacant U.S. Senate seat in Connecticut. Prescott Bush was a Rockefeller Republican from the Northeast. He was a fiscal conservative but moderate to liberal on social issues. He advocated for increased welfare payments for the poor. He was a leader on the issue of civil rights in his party and in the Senate. He argued that aid should be denied to states that were not conforming to desegregation of public schools. This bold position put him in direct confrontation with senators from the Southern states—the very region where his son, George H. W. had taken up residence. He praised President Kennedy's support of aid for the unemployed but questioned his spending on the space program.[9]

In the late 1950s and early 1960s, the Republican Party was in the middle of a burgeoning ideological debate. Conservatives led by Senator Barry Goldwater from Arizona wanted the Republican Party to be more conservative. This conservative stance included a much stronger states' rights position that would appeal to Southern whites who favored racial segregation. The other side of the party was led by Nelson Rockefeller, the governor of New York. Rockefeller wanted the party to strongly advocate for civil rights in the tradition of Abraham Lincoln. He also believed in a more internationalist approach in dealing with the cold war and the Soviet Union. Ironically, Prescott and his son George would take up different sides in this struggle. To represent Connecticut, Prescott Bush was a solid Rockefeller Republican. To begin his political career in the Southern state of Texas, George H. W. Bush would have to be a Goldwater Republican.

The Bushes of Texas

When George H. W. Bush moved to Texas in the 1940s, he and Barbara soon got a lesson in the political dynamics of Texas. While in Odessa, Texas, they invited a local African-American National Association for the Advancement of Colored People (NAACP) staff member into their home. The invitation was not accepted, and the invitation became public knowledge. The Bushes were told by a local resident that inviting a black man into their house could lead to violence against the Bushes and any black visitor.[10]

After over a decade in Texas, George H. W. Bush had succeeded in building a successful oil business. He had been aided by investments from his family members including his Uncle Herbie. His company was an innovator in building oil platforms and seeking international trading partners.[11] When his father Prescott retired from the Senate in 1962, George H. W. Bush was ready for the political world because he had enough financial resources to take care of his family.

George and Barbara Bush moved to Houston in 1960. By this time they had three other sons Jeb, Neil, and Marvin and a daughter, Dorothy. A young daughter, Robin, had tragically died of leukemia in 1953 at the age of three. By 1962, George H. W. Bush was running for the party chairmanship of Harris County in Houston. Texas was an eclectic nexus of Southern conservative Democrats, John Birch conservatives, and entrepreneurial Republicans who were not native to Texas. Houston was in the midst of this ideological struggle on the Right. Bush rejected the conspiracy theories of the Birch Society members, but he also realized he was not in New England anymore.[12] He would have to balance competing interests and appeal to all segments of the new Republican Party in Texas. He was especially criticized for placating the John Birchers. The Birchers were vehemently anti-Communist and believed in almost no role for the federal government in American society. They also had a wide belief of a socialist conspiracy to take over the world. The son of a Northeastern Republican did not rebuff the John Birchers; he preached unity in the party and was able to hold the party together during his tenure as chair. This would not be the only conservative faction that would dog George H. W. Bush during his political career.

When he took chairmanship of the local party, he began the remnants of a family political machine that would come to dominate American politics. As a chair, Bush would intimately learn the basics of political organization by building a new party. With his business experience, he was excellent as an organizer in the nascent party. He organized more than 200 precincts in the town and raised a record amount of money in a short period of time. He also learned the basics of modern political campaigning. He moved the party headquarters to a new building with better phone lines and equipment.[13] His experience and his contacts would aid him greatly in the future.

The 1964 political season would transform the nation's politics, and George H. W. Bush would be part of this transformation. In 1963 when George H. W. Bush announced his intention to run for the U.S. Senate from Texas, he seemed a good bet to defeat a liberal populist incumbent Democrat Ralph Yarborough. Yarborough, who took the brave position as a Southern senator of supporting civil rights, was seen as vulnerable in the conservative state of Texas. George H. W. Bush showcased his immense political ambition by deciding to run for the U.S. Senate as his first elected office.

The political ground shifted under George H. W.'s feet when two months after he announced his run for the Senate, President John Kennedy was assassinated in Dallas, Texas. Texan Lyndon Johnson was now elevated to the presidency. This Democratic political legend would not let both of the Senate seats from Texas fall to the Republicans. The other Senate seat was occupied by Republican John Tower who would become an important figure in the Bushes' political future. As a result of the sympathy for the Democratic Party from the Kennedy assassination and with a Democratic Texan at the top of the presidential ticket in 1964, George H. W. Bush's electoral chances evaporated.

He was also saddled with a controversial Republican presidential nominee, Barry Goldwater. Barry Goldwater's political appeal was based on his opposition to the 1964 *Civil Rights Act* and his confrontational approach to foreign policy. Goldwater even defended "extremism" for the sake of liberty in his 1964 acceptance speech. Goldwater's losing campaign highlighted an important dynamic for the Bush family. The Bush political fortunes were not in Connecticut anymore. The retired Prescott Bush would have quickly rejected Goldwater's approach. Yet his son, George H. W. Bush, had to embrace Goldwater. George H. W. Bush even made a direct private call to his father and urged him to keep his silence about his opposition to Goldwater.[14]

Bush had taken most of Goldwater's positions. The future ambassador to the UN denounced the organization in 1964. He also opposed a nuclear test ban treaty. In a move that would help his sons much later in Florida politics, he also advocated more direct confrontation with Fidel Castro's Cuba after the Bay of Pigs fiasco in 1961.[15]

Yet the centerpiece of the 1964 Republican campaign was opposition to the *Civil Rights Act*. The 1964 act banned racial discrimination in government agencies and in public accommodations such as restaurants. Many Southern whites saw this act as an intrusion of federal power and encouraged resistance. Supporters of the act argued that the federal government was the only force in society that could end segregation and discrimination.

The act was a watershed for many African-Americans in the country because it was the most sweeping civil rights legislation since Reconstruction. Lyndon Johnson's leadership on this bill made the Democratic Party the civil rights party even though many Southern Democrats supported segregation. It also made the Republican Party the sanctuary of Southern whites who opposed the act. This important piece of legislation was a litmus test for supporters of civil rights. Bush's opposition to the 1964 act drastically hurt his reputation among African-American groups in his state. Bush later supported open housing legislation in 1968 to limit discrimination, but it was too late for many blacks. In many ways his negative reputation among African-Americans was transferred to his sons. George H. W. Bush would receive little support among blacks in his 1966 congressional race. His sons have not done much better in Texas and in Florida. Although in 2004, an increase in George W. Bush's black vote in Ohio may have secured the presidential election for him.[16]

Goldwater's opposition to civil rights paid huge dividends in the once solid Democratic South. When he signed the legislation, President Lyndon Johnson was heard to say "there goes the South," and away the South went. Goldwater won five Southern states; many of these states had not voted for a Republican presidential candidate since 1928 when Catholic Al Smith ran on the Democratic ticket.[17]

Yet, Texas was a different story. With Johnson at the top of the ticket, any Republican would have had a difficult time winning the U.S. Senate seat from the state. In addition to Johnson's presence and Goldwater's problems, George H. W. Bush had other challenges. His opponent Ralph Yarborough could not get to the Right of George Bush in Texas, but he could get to the "South" of him. Bush had to prove that he was not an "intruder" in the state.[18] Yarborough would not let him. He went after Bush's Connecticut upbringing and his international business contacts. In the campaign, Yarborough said that Bush was a "carpetbagger from Connecticut who is drilling oil for the sheik of Kuwait to help keep the harem going."[19] This statement is fascinating considering that the future president George H. W. Bush would launch a major war to defend Kuwait in 1991. In 1964 being a native Southerner who was Democrat was still crucial in Texas, and Yarborough made the point everywhere he went that George Bush was not a Texan. Watching all of these attacks on his father was eighteen-year-old George W. Bush. As in any family, these personal attacks hurt George H. W. Bush's wife and children. George W. Bush would learn from the campaign of 1964 that he better establish political roots in Texas or face political attack. On election night in November 1964, George H. W. Bush lost the election by more than half-a-million votes. His sons George W. Bush and Jeb Bush were beside him on election night and they cried.[20] The Bush sons knew from their father's experience that losing a political campaign was a personally devastating experience. The sons would lose close campaigns of their own, but they would never be outworked because they knew the pain of running and losing. These early political defeats would help make Jeb and George Bush two of most competitive and stubborn individuals in modern American politics.

The Bushes Go to Washington

Although George H. W. Bush clearly lost the 1964 election, he learned many important lessons about political organization. Many of the Texas precincts had no local Republican Party structure. Traveling throughout the state he met thousands of citizens and many financial supporters. He received the most votes of any Republican in state history. He also recognized that he had misread the public. Bush made this comment to his minister in Houston about the 1964 election, "I took some far right positions to get elected I hope I never do it again. I regret it."[21] Bush had come a long way from Connecticut. This pull between New England Republicanism and Southern Republicanism would be a constant in George H. W. Bush's political life. His sons would learn the lessons from the father and do everything they could to cast their lot with Southern Republicans. Prescott Bush left a large shadow for his family, but the Republicanism that his two grandsons would come to practice is a Republicanism that he would not recognize.

For someone who lost a U.S. Senate race by a decisive margin, George H. W. Bush was in good political standing after 1964. His aggressive stance as Harris County Republican chairman paid off. He had sued the state of Texas as chairman of the Republican Party by arguing that the legislative districts were drawn unfairly. A court ordered a new legislative district map be drawn, and one of these congressional districts was in Houston. Having just run a tough political race in 1964, Bush easily won the Republican nomination in 1966 for a U.S. House seat. His Democratic opponent ran as a Southern conservative Democrat. This opponent, picking up where Ralph Yarborough had left off, called George H. W. Bush a "carpetbagger."[22] Yet the Democrats misjudged the district. Unlike the whole state of Texas, the congressional district in Houston was full of newly arrived Texans. Bush easily won the race and became a U.S. representative from Texas. Bush's campaign was aided tremendously by a visit from former vice president Richard Nixon. Nixon had been fond of Bush's father and immediately recognized the younger Bush as a politician on the rise. This friendship would play a pivotal role in Bush's political future.

Bush would have a brief congressional career, yet his congressional experience showed the divisions in the Republican Party. Bush's voting record was clearly moderate compared to other Southern conservatives. He was not governing as a Goldwater Republican. Bush was a fiscal conservative and supported the Democratic president on the Vietnam War. Yet on social and cultural issues, he took a different path. He voted for open housing legislation that prohibited discrimination based upon race. His support for the *Civil Rights Act* of 1968 earned him much criticism from conservatives in Texas. He also supported parts of Johnson's War on Poverty.[23]

Population control around the world became a crucial issue in the late 1960s. George H. W. Bush took to the issue intensely. He believed that an important way to control poverty was through birth control. A prominent Democratic congressman jokingly called Bush "Rubbers" for his devotion to the topic. George H. W. Bush also had sympathy with the position of Planned Parenthood on the issue of abortion. Bush advocated for choice in the abortion debate because of his concerns about abortions being performed by unlicensed doctors.[24] His positions on birth control and abortion would put him far to the Left of many social conservatives. Yet in the late 1960s, the religious conservative movement had not yet been launched and *Roe v. Wade* did not become law until 1973. With these issues, George Bush was in the center of his party in 1968. With the same positions in 1980 when he ran for president, he would be Left of his party and its new conservative leader Ronald Reagan.

George H. W. Bush's relationship with Richard Nixon would strengthen during Bush's congressional career. When Nixon won the White House in 1968, he immediately had plans for George H. W. Bush. Nixon wanted more Republican support in the Congress so he asked Bush to run for the U.S. Senate from Texas again. Bush would be forced to give up a safe U.S. House seat and try to win a Senate seat in the still Democratic-heavy Texas. Bush's prospects again appeared solid when liberal Democrat Ralph Yarborough was the expected opponent. Again the political ground shifted on George Bush. As a conservative Democrat, Lloyd Bentsen won the primary and would be the Democratic nominee from Texas. Bush's campaign plan would have to be revamped. He had planned on running from the Right as a real Texas conservative. With Bentsen in the race, Bush faced an opponent with better Texas credentials who was more conservative. Bush was forced to move to the center to try to attract minorities and Democrats. In a surreal repeat of 1964, Bush was labeled a "liberal Ivy League carpetbagger" who favored gun-control.[25] Nixon's White House staff wanted Bush to hit back at Bentsen with personal attacks. Bush refused to go after Bentsen negatively.[26] Even two visits by President Richard Nixon could not save Bush's campaign. Again Bush ran well but he could not beat a conservative Democratic Texan. Once more, his family joined him for election night. Again George W. and Jeb shed tears after the loss.[27]

The 1970 U.S. Senate race loss was devastating for Bush and his family. As a member of the U.S. House in the mid-1960s, George H. W. Bush was seen as a Republican version of Jack Kennedy. He was good-looking, telegenic, and an excellent political organizer. In 1968, he was even mentioned by some close to Nixon as a possible vice presidential running mate.[28] After his second statewide loss in Texas, his once bright career seemed doomed. He had moved his young family from New England; he started a successful oil business in Texas; and he ran as a Goldwater Republican in 1964. With all of these conservative Texas credentials, he was still painted as an elitist New Englander.

George H. W. Bush's 1970 loss would have important impacts on his sons. As they pursued their own political careers in two Southern states later in life, they took the lessons of the 1970 campaign with them. (1) Avoid being associated with New England and Ivy League schools. (2) In the South, the word "liberal" is fatal in political campaigns. (3) Do not let your opponent outflank you on important social issues such as gun-control. (4) Hit your opponent with everything you have or your opponent will define you. The Bush sons had to watch the father they adored learn these difficult lessons in a very public way. They would not forget these lessons, and their political careers would be shaped by these early campaign experiences. These difficult experiences gave them the drive and tenacity to take on the political process later in their lives.

Nixon Saves George H. W. Bush

George H. W. Bush had one ace left in his political career and that was Richard Nixon. Nixon promised Bush that if he ran for the U.S. Senate from Texas and lost, Nixon would find an administration job for him. This relationship with Nixon would take George H. W. Bush on an unlikely odyssey from UN ambassador to political operative to foreign-policy diplomat and CIA Director. Without Richard Nixon, Bush's political aspirations would have ended in 1970. After Nixon tapped him as the UN ambassador in 1970, George H. W. Bush would be a central figure in American politics for the next twenty-two years.

This time at the UN was invaluable for Bush's foreign-policy experience. Bush was criticized as a political appointment with little diplomatic background, but he used the opportunity to make important political contacts both in the United States and abroad.[29] He would use many of these contacts during his presidency to establish a coalition in the Gulf War in 1991. As UN ambassador with a suite in the Waldorf Astoria in New York, he was able to host many functions and network with many important people. His time at the UN was short, but the UN position began his political comeback. George H. W. Bush was no longer a two-time U.S. Senate race loser, he was ambassador to the UN.

After a landslide win in the 1972 election, Nixon called on Bush to remake the Republican Party as the chair of the Republican National Committee. Bush agreed to Nixon's request even though it meant something of a demotion from the job of ambassador. Bush would be entering a political situation that would rapidly begin to deteriorate under the Watergate investigation. Bush had to hold the party together during the Watergate crisis and the resulting Nixon resignation. Bush was one of the first party leaders to tell the president that he needed to resign.[30] He was in an impossible situation of trying to defend the president while simultaneously protecting the party. His time as chair was tremendously stressful, but again he complemented his knowledge of the basics of political organization. He became the only national political party chair to ever be elected president. He knew the importance of contacts, relationships, and fund-raising. These skills would bolster his political career and the political careers of his sons.

After Nixon's resignation, Bush, the loyal party man, was considered for the open slot of vice president. In just four years after his defeat in Texas, George H. W. Bush almost became the vice president.

The Republican Party was in the midst of a crisis. Nixon's election in 1968 had tempered the division between conservatives and moderates, but with the Watergate scandal, these divisions reappeared. Gerald Ford turned to Nelson Rockefeller, patron saint of Northeastern Republicans, to be his vice president. George H. W. Bush was definitely in the running and came close to being nominated. Bush had strong support among many Republican lawmakers, but Ford chose the party's establishment figure.[31]

Bush was given the job of a U.S. representative to China. Nixon's bold stroke to engage China during his second term was redefining the relationship between the two large nations. While diplomatic relations had not yet been established, putting a U.S. representative in China signaled a new era in U.S.-Chinese relations. This was an important assignment that added to Bush's foreign-policy resume.

In his short presidency, Ford would call on Bush again for another important assignment. Bush took the helm of the CIA during its difficult post-Watergate time. He appeared before Congress numerous times to defend the agency as its director.[32] His move to the CIA also eliminated him as a possible vice presidential nominee and President Ford's running mate in 1976. Responding to pressures from conservatives, Vice President Nelson Rockefeller declined to run again. Bush was seen as a likely choice, but he could not serve as CIA director and political candidate at the same time. Gerald Ford acknowledged this and made a public statement declaring that George H. W. Bush would not be considered as a vice presidential nominee in 1976. Bush was disappointed that he again was passed over but he worked hard for restore the integrity of the agency and further supplemented his national security credentials.[33]

In the span of six years after his devastating loss in 1970, George H. W. Bush had emerged from defeat to hold three important political and policy positions on the national level. He also was considered for the vice presidency on three different occasions. After Ford's loss to Carter in 1976, there only remained two real political stars in the Republican Party—Ronald Reagan and George H. W. Bush. With Nixon as his mentor and Ford as his superior, George H. W. Bush was identified with the moderates in his political party. Four years later Ronald Reagan would make Bush pay for his affiliations with moderates. After serving the party faithfully, Bush thought it was his turn. After finishing second to Ford at the Republican Convention in the 1976, Reagan felt he had earned his nomination for 1980.

Bush Goes for the Presidency

After Ford's loss to Carter in 1976, Bush was removed as director of the CIA. He took up several business ventures to provide again for his family. Bush even declined a job offer from fellow Texan Ross Perot. After coming close to the vice presidential slot three times in the last eight years, Bush set his sights on the presidency.[34] He traveled the country and supported Republican candidates in 1978 and continued to build a network of friends and supporters. Although Ronald Reagan had come extremely close to winning the Republican nomination in 1976, Bush would not concede the nomination to him. Bush and other Republican candidates battled with Reagan for the Republican nomination in 1980. Reagan was in strong position. He had been running since he lost in 1976, and he also had a large group of activists across the country. He was seen as the true conservative in the race at a time when the Republican Party was looking for a conservative.

With Reagan appearing as the front-runner, the Bush campaign knew that the early Iowa caucuses would be important. Reagan's campaign took the state for granted, and he made just a few appearances. The Bush campaign organized many Iowa counties and did the grassroots work that was necessary in a caucus state.[35] Caucuses require voters to show up for several hours of debate and then publicly proclaim their allegiance for a candidate. The process takes time and political passion. Organization is everything in a caucus state, and the Bush campaign outworked Reagan's campaign. Bush won the Iowa cauces and was proclaimed the only real threat to Reagan in 1980.

Bush's challenge to Reagan represented a crossroads for the Republican Party in 1980. The Republicans could choose a moderate candidate in the form of Richard Nixon and Gerald Ford or they could go with the heir to the Goldwater legacy, Ronald Reagan. Conservatives had waited nearly two decades for their moment, and they did not let it pass them by. Bush with his New England connections believed he could win the New Hampshire primary. At the time, New Hampshire had a strong conservative faction within the state Republican Party.

This faction firmly rejected George H. W. Bush. After two debates in which Reagan proved to be the clear winner, Bush lost the New Hampshire primary by 26 points to Ronald Reagan. The loss was the beginning of the end for George H. W. Bush in 1980 as a presidential candidate. Bush would win several Midwestern states, but he could not appeal to the conservative base of the party. He fared badly in the

Southern states. Conservative activists resented Bush for challenging Reagan and also criticized him for his lack of conservative values. To distinguish himself from Reagan, Bush called Reagan's economic plan based upon massive tax cuts "voodoo economics."[36] Bush was also heavily criticized for his more moderate positions on abortion and his support for the Equal Rights Amendment.

The Bush campaign also underestimated Reagan's appeal to Christian evangelicals. Many of these evangelicals supported Jimmy Carter in 1976. Reagan had strenuously courted these Christian conservatives for his run in 1980. Bush's moderate position on abortion and other social issues gave the Reagan plenty of material to attack the Bush candidacy. In the state of Florida, conservative activists labeled Bush a "liberal."[37] The culmination of these attacks eroded Bush's political position. Bush even lost his adopted home state of Texas, a personally embarrassing defeat.

His family suffered this presidential loss with George H. W. Bush. Jeb Bush would move his family back to Houston to help his father in the 1980 campaign. He would work to organize Florida and help his father wherever he needed it.[38] Jeb Bush worked tirelessly on the campaign and would take the loss badly. George W. Bush would not be an important factor in this race since he had just lost a congressional race in Texas in 1978. Barbara Bush traveled across the country and campaigned for her husband.[39] Again, the two future political sons in the family learned from their father's defeat. In the Republican Party of the late twentieth century, candidates would have to be known conservatives.

The word liberal had now become a devastating political attack on an opponent. Both Jeb and George W. Bush would both paint their future opponents as liberal and out-of-touch elitists. George H. W. Bush's loss in 1980 would show his two sons how to win in the 1990s.

All the Bushes again would gather for George H. W. Bush to announce the end of his presidential campaign. It was another crippling defeat. George H. W. Bush with all of his background and experience still had not won a political campaign since 1968. He had served as chair of the Republican Party and taken other political positions to help Republican presidents. Yet, he had been defined as an outsider to the base of his own party. His political career was in real jeopardy of being finished.

In a surprise move that would help shape politics in America for the next twenty years, Ronald Reagan chose George H. W. Bush as his vice presidential nominee. Reagan needed to make a gesture to the center of the party, and Bush was the logical choice. This choice came as a surprise though because former president Gerald Ford had shown interest in being offered the vice presidential slot. Negotiations between the Fords and the Reagans broke down at the Republican Convention in Detroit. The Reagan team quickly turned to Bush as an alternative. Bush had to agree to the platform of the convention.

This conservative platform supported Reagan's tax cuts and a strong antiabortion position.[40] Bush would have to leave all remnants of his father's Republicanism behind to be the running mate of the most conservative Republican candidate since Barry Goldwater. The Bush family was now aligned with a popular conservative president. George W. and Jeb Bush would eventually run for office and govern more like Reagan conservatives than their own father.

To achieve his ultimate goal of the presidency, George H. W. Bush would have to serve eight years as a loyal vice president. Conservatives in the Reagan administration still distrusted him, but he never disagreed with the president in public[41] Bush served as a quiet and solid vice president. He maintained his composure during the assassination attempt on President Reagan in 1981. He campaigned tirelessly for Republican candidates during election years. After the difficult midterm elections of 1982, Reagan's popularity soared and with this popularity, George Bush's presidential ambitions also increased. Unlike 1980, he would be the clear establishment front-runner for the Republican presidential nomination in 1988.

Bush almost lost this strong political position during the Iran-Contra scandal of 1986 and 1987. The Reagan administration had been caught trading arms for hostages in Beirut and funding anti-Communist groups in Nicaragua. The funding of the anti-Communists groups in Nicaragua was expressly forbidden by law. The president and his staff could not provide plausible explanations for these events. Vice President Bush gave differing accounts about his role in the scandal.[42] Yet the scandal did pass, and Bush headed into the 1988 presidential race as a clear favorite.

In the fall of 1987 Bush began his presidential campaign. This presidential campaign was twenty years in the making and would be a culmination of George H. W.'s political life. On the very day he was set to announce his intentions, *Newsweek* magazine came out with a cover story on Bush entitled "Fighting the Wimp Factor." The story went on to summarize how some political observers viewed Bush as a nice man who was a weak leader.[43] The impact of this story on the Bushes cannot be underestimated. George H. W. Bush was furious at the insinuation. This provocative cover story also must have impacted Bush's family. They had been through too much to let this attack go by. Their husband and father George H. W. Bush had been through a political grinder over the past twenty-five years. In 1964, George Bush was not "Texan" enough for the voters. In 1970 he was cast as an "Ivy League liberal" and lost another Texas Senate race. He served his party in important positions during the Watergate years, but he was denied the vice presidency at least three times from the period of 1968–1976. When he ran for president in 1980, he was not conservative enough. A New Hampshire newspaper editorial called him an "incompetent liberal."[44] Finally, he was Ronald Reagan's second choice as a vice presidential nominee. During all of these volatile political fights, George H. W. Bush kept going. His dogged perseverance of the presidency was evident. Thus, in 1988 as the party favorite for the presidency, it should have been his time. For a national magazine to run a cover story with word "wimp" on the cover was the ultimate insult.

George W. Bush and Jeb Bush would be active participants in the election effort. They had followed their father through the defeats and victories of his long political career. They were determined that the 1988 Bush campaign would be tough and efficient. Lee Atwater and Roger Ailes, two skilled campaign consultants working for the Bush campaign, deeply believed in attack politics.

In the future, George W. Bush and Jeb Bush would both run aggressive and confrontational campaigns, and they would govern in a similar fashion. This aggressive approach would have obvious political benefits but would also cause serious problems for the Bush sons in Texas and Florida.

After an embarrassing loss in the Iowa caucuses, the Bush campaign recovered in the 1988 New Hampshire primary. The campaign ran a tough political ad accusing their chief Republican rival, Senator Robert Dole, of being indecisive on the most important issues facing the nation. In particular they attacked Dole's record on raising taxes. The strategy worked and Bush won the New Hampshire primary and went on to decisively win the Republican nomination. Bush also vowed never to raise taxes in his administration.

The 1988 general election campaign would be another important legacy moment for the Bush family. The vice president was actually trailing the Democratic nominee Governor Michael Dukakis of Massachusetts in most polls going into the general election. With the economy going well and the Cold War winding down, there were no major issues that dominated the campaign. Yet the background of Governor Dukakis provided the perfect opportunity to practice attack politics. The Bush campaign doggedly turned the attention of the media away from issues and toward character. George H. W. Bush, a native northeasterner, was able to portray Dukakis as a Northeastern liberal who did not understand the nation's values. The Bush campaign hammered Dukakis with TV commercials charging that he had (1) released murderers on weekend passes, (2) vetoed a bill that would require the Pledge of Allegiance to be recited in classrooms in Massachusetts, and (3) had no understanding of military issues. In other words, Dukakis was the embodiment of the word that had been used against George H. W. Bush in his previous campaigns: Dukakis was a liberal.[45] An independent conservative group also ran the infamous "Willie Horton" commercial that highlighted the case of an African-American murderer who had been given a weekend pass in Massachusetts and then committed another murder. Civil rights groups protested the racial inference of a commercial, but the media gave the commercial wide coverage.

The 1988 campaign that had been called "Trivial Pursuit" by some observers for its lack of substance would result in a landslide win for George H. W. Bush.[46] After twenty-four years of pursuing the presidency, George H. W. Bush finally reached his goal. Just as important for the Bushes, his sons watched as he achieved victory. He did not run as a gentleman from the Northeast. He ran a tough political campaign that relied on Southern voters, and he devastated his opponent with personal attacks. Six years later, two Bush sons would pick up the political standard and run similar aggressive campaigns. The Bush sons would never be called wimps as governor or as president.

George H. W. Bush had a tremendous misfortune of following a political and cultural icon. Ronald Reagan finished his second term as the most popular two-term president since FDR. More problematic for Bush is that Reagan was extremely popular among the conservative base of the party. This conservative base again never fully trusted George H. W. Bush and his Northeastern roots. Like John Adams following George Washington, George H. W. Bush had expectations that he could not meet.

The First Bush Presidency

The Bush campaign of 1988 was aggressive and personal. No one issue or trend captured the electorate and thus George H. W. Bush had no mandate for domestic policy. Bush also had to deal with the legacy of the Reagan economic program. Tax cuts and the expanding economy were welcome news for the nation, but the resulting deficit warned of economic trouble to come. Unlike Reagan's first six years in office, Bush had to deal with a Democratic majority in both houses of Congress. He also had to address the huge deficits left over from the Reagan tax cuts and defense buildup of the 1980s. In the campaign Bush promised "no new taxes" so he could appeal to the conservative base of the Republican Party. With large deficits and no way to raise additional revenue, Bush had no money to start new bold policy initiatives.

Moreover, Congress challenged his pick for defense secretary. John Tower, Bush's friend from Texas politics, was denied confirmation by the U.S. Senate. Tower was attacked for his active social life that included drinking and the pursuit of different female companions. Tower's confirmation battle was Bush's first major setback in the new Congress. More importantly this battle also left a critical legacy appointment to his son George W. Bush. Tower's replacement was Representative Dick Cheney from Wyoming. Without the Tower scandal, Dick Cheney would never have been defense secretary for George H. W. Bush and arguably would not have been vice president for George W. Bush. Dick Cheney is a dominant figure in George W. Bush's presidency. Supporters and detractors alike have called Cheney the most powerful vice president in American history. Cheney was the driving force behind the invasion of Iraq in 2003, and is the strongest voice on rebuilding Iraq after the invasion.[47] George W. Bush's presidency would have been drastically different without Dick Cheney, and Dick Cheney came directly from George H. W. Bush's political orbit.

In his first 100 days, George H. W. Bush was criticized heavily as having no domestic agenda.[48] This lack of a comprehensive vision is a criticism that would stay with the administration until its end. In January 1991 with two years left in his presidency, George H. W. Bush's chief of staff John Sununu was asked what was remaining on the president's domestic agenda for the rest of the term. Sununu quickly replied "not that much."[49] Because of fiscal realities, George H. W. Bush would have to renege on his no new taxes promise. He agreed with the Democratic Congress that some new taxes would be necessary to control the deficit. This reversal on his taxes pledge would haunt George H. W. Bush. Many conservatives would never forgive him. His lack of a domestic agenda gave an opening to his critics and the Bush administration lost control of the debate. Again his sons watched these developments in Texas and Florida. They would not make the mistakes of their father in the domestic arena. When elected to the executive positions of governor and president, Jeb and

George W. Bush would control the agenda. Many would not agree with their ideas, but no one would have doubts about who was leading Florida and Texas. This aggressive leadership from Jeb and George W. Bush would be obvious, but this type of leadership would also lead to a damaging overconfidence and arrogance that would have serious policy impacts.

In contrast, George H. W. Bush did not have to put forth a foreign-policy agenda, the crises and the agenda would come to him. In 1989, many states in the Eastern Soviet bloc began deteriorating highlighted by the breaching of the Berlin Wall in late 1989. The collapse of the entire Soviet bloc took place over the next two years. Bush did not overreact and did not make bold public statements about these historical events. He did not want to give ammunition to Soviet hardliners to strike back. Bush was criticized for not showing more emotion and braggadocio.[50] He felt the events were going in the U.S. direction and he did not want to inflame the situation. This type of diplomatic nuance would evade his sons. George W. Bush in particular made his emotions and opinions clear during foreign crises. George W. Bush would never be accused of humility and understatement in foreign affairs.

The First Bush and Iraq

The signature foreign-policy crisis of George H. W. Bush's presidency was the Gulf War with Iraq. In a stark example of the large impact one family presidency may have on another, this military action not only dominated George H. W.'s presidency, but the impacts of the First Gulf War would also dominate his son's presidency twelve years later.

The seminal events of the first Bush presidency would come as a surprise. The United States had been a wary ally of Iraq in the 1980s. Saddam Hussein and Iraq acted as a counterweight to the influence of the Islamic Republic of Iran.

When Saddam Hussein invaded Kuwait, he took much of the Bush administration by surprise. From this initial shock, George H. W. Bush would do the best strategic and diplomatic work of his presidency. Bush's first concern was defending Saudi Arabia from an Iraqi attack. Yet he soon moved from a defensive strategy of defending Saudi Arabia to an offensive strategy of expelling Iraq from Kuwait.

Bush used his experience as a former diplomat and CIA Director to put together a diplomatic and military coalition that would challenge

Saddam Hussein. In order to put together the strategy for the maintaining the coalition, Bush relied heavily on his foreign-policy team. Two central figures for President Bush were Colin Powell, the chairman of the Joint Chiefs of Staff, and Dick Cheney, secretary of defense. Other important figures included Condoleezza Rice, an aide on the National Security Council, and Robert Gates who also served on the National Security Council. All these individuals would go on to serve President Bush's son George W. during the next Republican presidency. The most important part of the elder Bush's legacy to his son George W. are the individuals who made up his foreign-policy team.

Yet for George H. W., this team was executing a foreign policy that would be far different from the ideological foreign policy of George W. Bush. The first Bush administration understood that any military action in the Middle East could set off a strong anti-American reaction. Thus the Bush team worked extremely hard to consult and negotiate with allies in the region. As secretary of defense, Dick Cheney in 1991 had the delicate task of convincing Saudi Arabia to allow American soldiers on to Saudi soil. The Bush administration even courted Syria to join the anti-Iraq coalition. Colin Powell wanted the president's assurances that he would be given the overwhelming military manpower and firepower to combat Saddam Hussein. Secretary of State James Baker worked the diplomatic channels to ensure the UN would pass a resolution condemning Iraq and setting a deadline for withdrawal from Kuwait. Bush's diplomatic team even managed to keep Israel out of the fight.[51]

Bush also asked the U.S. Congress for a resolution approving the use of force against Iraq. In a foreshadowing of his son's war with Iraq twelve years later, the congressional resolution cited Iraq's capability including chemical, biological, and nuclear weapons.[52] With congressional approval, Bush gave the order to attack Iraq. After over a month of aerial bombardment, the coalition army moved into Kuwait. The ground campaign worked better than anyone could have expected. Within three days, the Iraqi Army was in full retreat back to Iraq. This presented President Bush with a difficult dilemma. Should the coalition take the fight all the way to Baghdad or should Bush be content with driving Saddam Hussein's army from Kuwait? The UN resolution that the coalition was operating under gave no authority beyond expelling the Iraqis from Kuwait. The Iraqi Army was overwhelmed and overmatched. George H. W. Bush did not want the rest of the Arab world to see coalition forces destroying retreating soldiers. He asked his advisers about ending hostilities with a cease-fire.

General Powell and Dick Cheney all agreed with the president that it was time to cease hostilities.[53]

This decision to end hostilities after only four days of ground combat has been heavily criticized since 1991. Several generals on the ground during that time including Major General Barry McCaffery disagreed with the decision. McCaffrey believed that too much of Saddam's Republican Guard remained intact for the war to end.[54] Some other generals shared the same concern. Saddam Hussein used the remnants of his army to put down revolts by the Shiites in the South and the Kurds in the north. Saddam's forces were cruel to the Iraqis who were in revolt. At times, Saddam's forces would taunt nearby American Forces who could not respond with military firepower because of the cease-fire. Kurdish refugees were trapped between Iraqi Forces and the Turkish border. Up to 50,000 Kurds were trapped in the mountains along the Turkish border without food or water.[55]

Desperate pleas came from the revolting Iraqis for American military assistance, but the American forces respected the original cease-fire. President Bush had urged Iraqi citizens to rise up and overthrow the government, but he would not use the American military to aid this revolution.[56] The clear triumph of the American military was tarnished as a result of the messy aftermath of the Gulf War.

Even with these terrible circumstances, the Bush administration did not have a real option to attack Baghdad and occupy the country. The United States' closest Arab allies, Egypt and Saudi Arabia, did not want to encourage a Shiite State in Iraq.[57] The UN resolution was clear about the limits imposed upon the coalition. Moreover, the U.S. military, who had prepared brilliantly for the air and ground assault against the Iraqi Army, had few strategic plans and little experience in maintaining long occupations of large countries.

Even though he wanted to see Saddam overthrown, Bush would "live with" an end to the war that allowed Saddam Hussein to remain as leader of Iraq.[58] However the Bush family would not be finished with Saddam Hussein.

Even with the controversial end to the war, George H. W. Bush could highlight an amazing military and diplomatic success. He had put together a broad coalition of nations including many Arab countries to expel Saddam Hussein from Kuwait. The Bush's administration diplomacy was so good that the administration convinced Israel to stay out of the war even after Iraqi missiles attacked Israeli cities. He had done all this with approval from the UN. The American military had performed brilliantly and George Bush could point to a

"New World Order." He was also seen as politically invincible. His approval ratings went up to an astounding 90 percent. He playfully asked the media, "do you think the American people are going to turn to a Democrat now."[59]

This confidence would be President Bush's undoing. In a development that would be difficult to imagine in 1991, his foreign-policy triumph in the Gulf War would also leave another important legacy to his son George W. Bush. George W. Bush would view his father's war as unfinished business. Finishing Saddam Hussein would consume the presidency of George W. Bush. Moreover, George H. W. Bush's lack of a domestic agenda would give an opportunity for an unknown governor with a tremendous amount of personal baggage to challenge him for the presidency. The shortened presidency of George H. W. Bush would give rise to the next two presidents: Bill Clinton and his own son George W. Bush.

Chapter Five

The Clintons Take Power

"Bill and I are going to run."[1]

—Hillary Clinton in 1991.

This statement from Hillary Rodham Clinton was made to a fellow member of the Children's Defense Fund Board in 1991. When few other political professionals thought that George H. W. Bush, the hero of the First Gulf War, could be beaten in the 1992 presidential race, Hillary Clinton thought differently. She's sensed Bush's weakness on the economy and felt that his approval ratings were inflated.[2] The use of the plural pronoun "we" also shows the closeness of the Clintons' political relationship. This would be a joint project and in some ways, a joint presidency.

Later in 1991, Bill Clinton made the comment "If she would run, I would withdraw."[3] It was meant as a joke at the time, but the public and private lives of Bill and Hillary Clinton reveal that the statement may have had a ring of truth to it when spoken. As two leaders of the baby boom generation, they came together in marriage and formed a powerful political partnership. This unusual marriage has continually sustained Bill Clinton's roller-coaster political career. Their personal and political lives are so closely intertwined that their respective political careers are inseparable. Senator Hillary Clinton's candidacy for president has placed this political partnership front and center in American politics once again. This partnership also highlights the connection between family and political power in the United States. Without this partnership, Bill Clinton may have never become president, but Senator Clinton definitively would not have been a viable candidate for the presidency in 2008. This dynastic political family of early twenty-first century puts forth troubling questions about American democracy and the presidency.

Beginnings

At first inspection, the term dynasty connected with Bill Clinton's name makes little sense. His mother referred to the young Bill Clinton as "Bubba."[4] His early family life was unstable and difficult. His father, William Blythe, had served in World War II and spent little time with his mother Virginia during their marriage. After returning from the war, William Blythe took a job in Chicago as a traveling salesman. Before Bill Clinton was born, his father was killed in an automobile accident in 1946. In order to support her newborn son, his mother left Bill Clinton with her parents in Arkansas and attended nursing school in New Orleans. Bill Clinton was separated from his mother through most of his first three years. When his mother returned to Arkansas from nursing school, she quickly married a car salesman named Roger Clinton. Young Bill would take his stepfather's last name, but they were not close. Roger Clinton was an alcoholic who cheated on his mother and also physically abused her.

As Bill Clinton grew up, he assumed the role of the most responsible man in the house. As a teenager, he had to physically confront his stepfather and demand that he never hit his mother again.[5] His mother divorced Roger Clinton in the early 1960s, and much to the disappointment of Bill Clinton agreed to remarry him a short time later.

For this child of an abusive home to rise from one of the poorest states in the country to become president of United States is a considerable achievement. Moreover, it demonstrates the opportunity American democracy can present. Clinton's family was not of the social status of the Rockefellers, the Kennedys, or even the Bushes. From these humble beginnings, he managed to graduate from Georgetown University, become a Rhodes Scholar, and attend Yale Law School. He then was elected to statewide office in Arkansas six times. He beat an incumbent president who had recently won a war in the Middle East. Even with his well-reported personal failings and problems, the story of Bill Clinton's rise in American politics is truly remarkable.

How Bill Clinton's life and political career become connected to a family political machine is through his relationship with Hillary Rodham. This relationship helped to save his presidential candidacy but almost ruined his presidency. He met Hillary Rodham at Yale Law School in the early 1970s. They were drawn to each other because of their intellect and mutual social concerns. Clinton biographer David Maraniss describes how they complemented each other: "her focused intellect was also a perfect counterpoint to his restless diffuse mind;" Bill Clinton offered charm, a wide curiosity, and broad vision. Hillary Rodham offered strong discipline and an inner toughness.[6] Hillary Rodham liked him because he was the unusual male "who did not seem afraid of her."[7] Bill Clinton was so impressed with

Hillary Rodham that he made sure that his housemates at Yale would be on their best behavior when she visited.[8]

They both shared an unquenchable political ambition. When Hillary Rodham went to Washington to work in the summer of 1974, she told her coworkers that her new boyfriend would be the president of the United States one day. She told a law school friend "the more I see him, the more I discover new things about him."[9] She also told this friend that Bill Clinton's ambition "to do something with his life" was what her life was about as well.[10] Even with their turbulent marital history, they both believed that they shared an important political future. Their relationship would never only be about personal feelings and romance; it would also be about political destiny. In 2007, Bill Clinton addressed a crowd at a fund-raiser for his wife's presidential run by telling them when they met he thought "she was the best leader of her generation and she is 'still the best.'"[11]

Thus, when they were married, the Clintons did not see themselves as a young couple beginning their careers; they viewed themselves as young leaders of their generation. This bold thinking would have a profound impact on their marriage and highlights a major premise of this book. Their relationship and marriage are inexorably tied to their political life. All elected leaders have to balance their private lives with their public duties. Yet, the Clintons are different; politics are such an important part of their relationship that it can be difficult to see where the marriage begins and the political partnership ends. This intense relationship would also heavily impact a Hillary Clinton presidency.

This close political relationship does not mean they do not share general affection even with Bill Clinton's infidelities. Many of their friends from the 1970s have commented how close they were when they met and fell in love. In both of their autobiographies, they relate their mutual love for each other. Yet, this emotional attachment is also accompanied by a shared desire to become political players. At many important junctures in Bill Clinton's political career, his wife played a central role. As noted in chapter 3, many first ladies have important effects on their husbands' presidencies. Yet the Clinton relationship is strikingly different from other presidential marriages. Next to her husband, Hillary Clinton was the most dominant figure in the Clinton presidency. Their marriage was the central drama in Bill Clinton's presidency and may be the same for a Hillary Clinton presidency.

While Hillary Rodham Clinton was critical in Bill's political rise, it would be incorrect to assume that Bill Clinton would have never been successful in politics without her. As a child and a teenager emerging from a difficult family life, Bill Clinton was a leader very early in his life. He was junior-class president in his high school and a leader in a civic education program called Boys State. Boys State allowed high-school students to learn about their state government. It was through this program that Bill Clinton went to Washington as a teenager and shook the hand of President John F. Kennedy in 1963. Footage of this moment would be played twenty-nine years later at the Democratic Convention when Bill Clinton was nominated for president. Through his high-school record, he gained admission to Georgetown University.

At Georgetown he became a student leader and was elected freshman-class president. In the mid-1960s, he focused his attention on Arkansas politics for the first time. Even then he had a keen understanding of what truly was important in learning the game of politics. In 1966, he volunteered to work on the gubernatorial campaign for a Democratic judge named Frank Holt. Instead of asking for more glamorous duties, Clinton volunteered to be a driver for Judge Holt's family. In this way, Clinton was able to accompany the Democratic candidate throughout most of the small towns of Arkansas. Clinton's biographer David Maraniss thought this first real political experience was invaluable. Clinton met most of the important political people throughout Arkansas in the local courthouses and diners. He also was exposed to the grinding poverty of black Southerners through trips to towns throughout the Delta region of Arkansas. Clinton in a letter to his college girlfriend said "I couldn't believe my eyes when I saw a restrooms and waiting rooms still marked in Colored and White. It made me so sick to my stomach."[12]

A segregationist candidate would beat Frank Holt in Bill Clinton's first political campaign. Clinton learned another important lesson with this outcome. The daughter of the candidate told Bill Clinton "When you lose an election, it's like a death."[13] Clinton understood the stakes of political campaigns; his strong political competitiveness was partially born out of this first experience. He went on to work on other Arkansas campaigns including being the driver and aide for Democratic Senator William Fulbright.

Another critical point in Bill Clinton's early political development was his anguish over the Vietnam War and the draft. Through his attempts to get into the ROTC at the University of Arkansas and also drawing a high lottery number, Bill Clinton managed to avoid military service in Vietnam. Yet, he was not ready to declare himself a conscientious objector. In a letter that surfaced in his 1992 presidential campaign, he thanked the University of Arkansas ROTC instructor for "saving him from the draft" during the Vietnam War. In the letter dated December 1969, he wrote to his instructor that he could not be a conscientious objector because he wanted to "maintain my political viability within the system. For years, I have worked to prepare myself for a political life characterized by the practical political ability and concern for rapid social progress."[14] For a man in his early 20s to openly declare that he had been preparing himself for political life for years shows Bill Clinton's considerable ambition. To also declare that he wanted to balance political reality with rapid social progress foreshadows some of his future political struggles. He wanted to change American politics from within the system but maintain his political popularity at the same time. This balancing act would become more difficult as the nation's politics became more partisan. A young Bill Clinton had a clear political design for his life, and when he met Hillary Rodham he found someone else who shared this ambitious vision.

Likewise, to argue that Hillary Rodham Clinton owes all of her political standing to Bill Clinton would be an overstatement. At the beginning of their relationship, she was seen as the more important political figure. At her undergraduate school of Wellesley, one of her professors called her a "forceful presence on campus."[15] In the mid 1960s, she was conflicted politically. She had been a Goldwater girl in 1964 supporting the most conservative candidate to run for American presidency in the twentieth century. At her undergraduate college of Wellesley, she served as the president of the Young Republicans for a short time. She even attended the Republican National Convention in 1968 in an effort to draft a more moderate Nelson Rockefeller instead of Richard Nixon. Yet during the same tumultuous year, she also met and interviewed Saul Alinsky, a Chicago community organizer who believed in radical change to the capitalistic system.[16] Other activities at Wellesley showed her strong movement toward social liberalism. As opposition to the Vietnam War increased throughout the nation, Hillary Rodham supported student strikes to protest the Tet offensive in 1968.[17]

When she was named the first student graduation speaker in Wellesley history, her political ideas seemed to solidify. U.S. senator Edward Brooke, a black Republican from Massachusetts, also spoke at graduation that day. Brooke emphasized the importance of protests remaining peaceful and he offered a hopeful outlook for the students and the nation.

When Hillary Rodham heard his words, she altered her prepared speech. She thought that the senator was defending Richard Nixon and minimizing the dissension that students felt. She directly criticized the Senator and complained that political leaders were far too hesitant to engage in substantive change including ending the Vietnam War. She also questioned the typical goals and directions that most graduates attempt to attain, "some things we feel, feelings that our prevailing acquisitive and competitive corporate life...is not the way for us. We're searching for more immediate ecstatic and penetrating modes of living. And so our questions about institutions, about our colleges, about our churches and about our government continue."[18] As her future husband began his political rise, Hillary Rodham would have to move away from these ideas that challenged the basics institutions of American society to retain their political viability.

However, confronting a U.S. senator directly brought tremendous notice to Hillary Rodham. *Life* magazine did a story on the speech complete with a picture of Hillary Rodham with long hair and big glasses. The one-time president of the Young Republicans at Wellesley was now viewed as an important young leader of a liberal and socially active generation.

All of these considerable achievements for Hillary Rodham present a searing question. Why did she stake her political future on Bill Clinton? She chose Yale Law School because of its reputation for social activism. When she arrived on campus she was already viewed as an important student leader. Michael Medved, now a conservative commentator, told a newspaper reporter in 1992 that "at Yale Law School, Hillary Clinton was a 'star.'"[19] She was invited to address a national convention of the League of Women Voters; she soon went to work for a Congressional subcommittee and began a very close special relationship with Marian Edelman the founder of the Children's Defense Fund. A roommate of Bill Clinton's put it very simply about his arrival on campus; "Bill Clinton was a relatively unknown quantity compared to Hillary Rodham."[20]

However, progressive politics were popular politics in the late 1960s; in the late 1970s and the 1980s, the nation's political spectrum would move back to the Right. Bill Clinton would be one of the first Democrats to recognize this shift. If Hillary Rodham was to continue to be a national figure, she would need to join Bill Clinton in a move toward the political center. Without Bill Clinton, Hillary Rodham may have made it to the U.S. House or even the U.S. Senate. Yet, even with her resume, a female liberal social activist from the late 1960s would have a difficult path to the presidency on her own in the more conservative post-Reagan period in American life. The Clintons close political relationship and personal relationship would eventually set her on her own course to the White House.

First Couple of Arkansas

As Bill Clinton and Hillary Rodham completed Yale Law School in 1973, the time had come where they would have to make a decision on their mutual future. After their graduation in the spring of 1973, Bill Clinton and Hillary Rodham took a trip to Europe. On this trip, Bill Clinton proposed to Hillary Rodham for the first time. In her autobiography, Hillary Rodham detailed her answer. She told him no although said she was "desperately in love with him but utterly confused about my life and future."[21] This would be a natural reaction since Bill Clinton was clear on what he was going to do with his future. He would return to his native Arkansas and run for political office.[22] If Hillary Rodham was going to be part of Bill Clinton's life, she would have to move to Arkansas.

This would be a monumental choice for Hillary Rodham. Coming from Wellesley College, she was already a well-known figure. She did well at Yale Law School and increased her contacts among politically active attorneys in Washington. She was viewed by her women friends as an important leader in the fight for women's equality. Immediately after law school she went to work for the Children's Defense Fund, an organization that advocated for children's rights. She did fail the District of Columbia bar exam, but her opportunities were still numerous.[23] During 1974, she was offered a tremendous opportunity to work as a staff member of the House Judiciary Committee in Washington. This committee was investigating the possible impeachment of Richard Nixon. In an ironic twist of history, Hillary Rodham would become an expert on the seldom-used Congressional impeachment power. Twenty-four years later, she would watch in agony as another Congress would use this power to impeach her husband for perjury involving an affair with a young intern in the White House.

In short, Hillary Rodham's career was off to a brilliant start. She had gained national notice with her graduation speech from Wellesley. In a time when liberal social activism was seen as a plus, she was heavily involved in several important progressive causes. She became a protégé of Marian Wright, an authority on child welfare issues. She also played a supporting role in an investigation that led to the resignation of the president of the United States. Her opportunities were wide and diverse. Bill Clinton was asking her not only to marry him but also to subjugate her career ambitions to his. If Hillary Rodham agreed to marry Bill Clinton and move to Arkansas, it would not only be a personal decision but a political one as well.

Many observers who have chronicled Hillary's Clinton's life agree that the decision to go back to Arkansas with Bill Clinton was the most important decision of her life. Gail Sheehy entitled her book on Hillary Clinton as *Hillary's Choice*. David Brock, a one time severe Clinton critic, wrote a generally sympathetic biography called *the Seduction of Hillary Rodham*. Stanley Renshon, an expert in political psychology who wrote a book about the Clinton presidency identified the chapter about Hillary Clinton as *a Life's Choice*.

These observers are making a critical point. Once Hillary Rodham decided to go back to Arkansas to be with Bill Clinton, both their personal lives and their political careers would become tightly intertwined.

Sensing the possible tensions and trouble between these two ambitious people, friends and relatives generally discouraged the relationship. Bill Clinton's mother in particular was concerned that the two were not a good match. She saw Hillary Rodham as an unlikely political wife in Arkansas.[24] Hillary's friends were also seriously concerned about her future with Bill Clinton. Her friend and roommate Sarah Uhrman put it bluntly to Hillary, "are you out of your mind. Why on earth would you throw away your future."[25] Hillary Clinton wrote in her autobiography, that "I chose my heart instead of my head. I was moving to Arkansas."[26] She would go to Arkansas and teach at the University of Arkansas Law School. With this decision, Hillary Rodham would become part of every important political decision that Bill Clinton would make.

The move to one of the most conservative states in the nation for a liberal social activist in the early 1970s would present daunting career challenges. She was making a large sacrifice to be with Bill Clinton. His political successes and failings would be her successes and failures. For the purposes of this book, this decision is monumental. A strong combination of personal feelings and career ambitions would put the Clinton-Rodham relationship at the center of Bill Clinton's political life. The importance of this relationship would be so substantial that it would come to dominate a presidential campaign in 1992 and also dominate the Clinton presidency itself. The relationship would also serve as a springboard for another presidential candidacy; the candidacy of Hillary Rodham Clinton. The intensity of the family relationship and the intensity of the American presidency would become linked. This linkage would have important consequences for American democracy and the American presidency.

Run for Governor

The impact of Hillary Rodham's decision to move back to Arkansas in 1974 would be readily apparent both in Clinton's campaign and his personal life.

In 1974, Bill Clinton launched an improbable challenge to a sitting congressional Republican incumbent in Arkansas. Clinton gathered together a group of young aggressive campaign aides and traveled throughout Arkansas seeking votes and money. In the year of Watergate and the resignation of Richard Nixon, it was a good year to be a Democrat. Clinton won the Democratic primary and was ready to face off with the Republican incumbent. After the Nixon resignation of 1974, Hillary Rodham moved to Arkansas to help her boyfriend. She immediately took a leadership position in the campaign and alienated Bill Clinton's campaign manager and other aides.[27]

Hillary Rodham would have more to be concerned about than just campaign strategy. She had given up a career option of being with the Washington elites and invested everything in Bill Clinton. A terrible reality for Hillary Rodham would be that she would have to continually compete for Bill Clinton's attention and affections. When she came to Arkansas in 1974, Bill Clinton reportedly was in the midst of a relationship with the student from the University of Arkansas and had several other relationships with other women in Arkansas.[28] Clinton and Rodham were not married at the time so his opponents could not label him as an adulterer but womanizing rumors were abundant. Yet, the campaign of 1974 was an indication of "the central fact" of their relationship and future marriage.[29] Bill Clinton's reckless interest in other women would continually endanger his marriage and his political career. Rumors of his continuous infidelity also gave Hillary Rodham an unhappy power over him. Bill Clinton's reported infidelities clearly hurt Hillary Rodham as they would any girlfriend or wife.[30] Clinton's habits also gave Hillary Clinton a veto power over Bill Clinton's political life. If he strayed too far away from her, she could reveal his secret life with other women and wreak havoc on his political career. His political hero John Kennedy could get away with such activities with a compliant press in the early 1960s. Yet, the post-Watergate media and the hunger for public gossip by the late 1970s should have made Bill Clinton realize that the rules would be different for him.

Bill Clinton and Hillary Rodham lost their first political campaign in an extremely close race. Yet, he had impressed the political establishment of Arkansas by coming very close to unseating an incumbent member of Congress. He was seen as a politician on the rise and would have many other opportunities in Arkansas politics to gain public office. In the year following his political loss in 1974, Hillary Rodham and Bill Clinton officially got married. Much to the disappointment of Bill Clinton's mother, Hillary decided to keep her name and remain Hillary Rodham. With his new bride, Bill Clinton soon announced his intention to run for attorney general of Arkansas in 1976. Due to his favorable reviews of his 1974 congressional race, he easily won the race for attorney general at the age of twenty-nine.

Clinton would use the attorney general's office as a launching pad for the next governor's race. In 1978, a competitive U.S. Senate race in Arkansas left the field for the governor's office barren. Clinton moved in to fill the void. Smartly he used his connections as attorney general to solidify his run for governor. Local county courthouses in Arkansas were the centers of political power. Knowing the county clerk and the sheriff was especially important in rural areas of Arkansas. Clinton capitalized on these connections from his 1974 and 1976 races. His opponents attacked his wife for not taking his name and even for her legal career. One opponent also made an issue of his draft avoidance.[31] None of these charges made much impact with the voters. At the age of thirty-one, Bill Clinton won the governorship of Arkansas with an astounding 63 percent of the vote.

At his inauguration, friends of both Bill and Hillary Clinton came from across the country. Through their connections at Yale Law School, the Washington legal community, women's rights advocates, and Democrats looking for new and exciting prospects, Bill Clinton and Hillary Rodham had a formidable list of supporters from across the nation. This core of supporters would be the beginnings of a national political structure that would carry them to the White House in 1992. Biographer David Maraniss entitled his chapter on Bill Clinton's first gubernatorial term as "Great Expectations." Bill Clinton certainly had these expectations, but his first term quickly became a disaster. He installed young aggressive aides who did not have good relations with the Arkansas legislature. He presented a laundry list of ideas including the creation of new government departments, a reform of the health-care system, and a new education system. This aggressive agenda overwhelmed the old Southern political system of the

Arkansas legislature. Viewing the need for a new road system throughout Arkansas, he also asked for a new car license fee. The fee turned out to be wildly unpopular.[32]

The Clinton administration was a victim of bad luck as well. During 1980, Cuban refugees from the Mariel boat lift in Florida were assigned to be housed at Fort Chafee Arkansas because South Florida was being inundated with refugees. Rioting soon broke out and Clinton had to call in the National Guard to retain order. The Carter administration broke a promise not to bring any more refugees to Arkansas. When word of the new refugees reached Arkansas voters, Clinton's political standing collapsed. In his 1980 reelection race against Republican Frank White, he was portrayed as betraying the state of Arkansas for his political friends in Washington. A series of negative campaign ads severely hurt Clinton's chances of reelection. Unlike his savvy campaigns of the future, Clinton did not respond and lost his reelection.[33]

The loss in 1980 brought both Hillary Rodham and Bill Clinton to an important crossroads. Bill Clinton became the youngest ex-governor in American history.[34] He had lost to a little-known Republican and would now have to return to the private sector where he called himself a "fish out of water."[35] Hillary Rodham also faced a difficult path. She had given up the glamour of a Washington legal career so Bill Clinton could pursue his political career in Arkansas. She had to move to a conservative Southern state where women attorneys were scarce and drew little respect. She was heavily criticized by the press and others in Arkansas for not taking the name of her husband and for her frumpy appearance. She also had to endure rumors about her husband's infidelities. All these challenges came when she was beginning a corporate law career with the Rose Law firm in Little Rock and also becoming a mother in 1980 with the birth of her daughter Chelsea. Either Bill Clinton would right his political ship or Hillary Rodham might be stuck in Arkansas forever as a corporate attorney supporting an unhappy husband. After his loss in 1980, Bill Clinton was emotionally devastated. It fell to Hillary Rodham to plan his next campaign and his next career moves.

Hillary Rodham would also have to give up part of her social activist identity. Mack McLarty a good friend of Bill Clinton and his future chief of staff, believed that Hillary's inability to take Bill Clinton's last name had cost him the election in 1980.[36] Other observers also approached Hillary and suggested the change. Hillary Rodham took the advice to heart and changed her name and her appearance. She lost weight; she exchanged her glasses for contacts; and she lightened her hair. These were important transformations for Hillary Clinton.[37] At Wellesley and Yale Law School, she was viewed as a leader for women's rights, but she knew that she had cast her lot with a Southern politician from a conservative traditional state. The stakes were higher for the Clintons in the gubernatorial election of 1982. If Bill Clinton lost this race, his political career was over. Hillary Clinton knew this better than anyone. She knew it so well that she agreed to change her name and her appearance even though it conflicted with her cherished ideals of women's independence. She received rave reviews from the Arkansas press for her changes and her name conversion to being Mrs. Clinton.[38]

She also led the organization of the 1982 comeback campaign. She made sure to bring in Dick Morris, the tough political consultant from New York. His opponent in 1980, Frank White had attacked Bill Clinton over the airwaves in 1980 without a response from the Clinton campaign. The Clintons learned their lesson. When attacked, they respond. In both the primary and general election campaign for governor in 1982, the Clinton campaign filled the airwaves with negative attacks on their opponents. Bill Clinton apologized early in the campaign for his failures as governor. Through this apology, the attacks by his opponents in 1982 fell short. When the incumbent Republican Frank White, refused to debate with Bill Clinton, the new Mrs. Clinton asserted herself and publicly attacked White for ducking the debates.[39] Betsey Wright, the campaign organizer brought back to Arkansas by the Clintons, put together a tremendous voter database from which the Clintons could target voters directly. This combination of toughness and organization gave Bill Clinton his redemption. He won the election in 1982 and saved his political career. To a great extent, he had his wife to thank for the victory.

Bill Clinton knew he wouldn't get another chance to lose in Arkansas politics again. He had to make the most of his opportunity to govern so he took on the major issue of education reform in his second term as governor. He quickly turned to his most capable campaign organizer, Hillary Rodham Clinton to lead the education reform effort. Education reform was a brilliant combination of politics and policy in the South. Helping to improve the schools was good for students and their parents; it also could help businesses that needed an educated workforce. Clinton's early recognition of the issue brought his administration national notice. For his most important policy priority, he turned to his wife to lead the effort.

Hillary Clinton wanted to be heavily involved in her husband's second term in office. Being a partner in the Rose Law firm in

Arkansas was not fulfilling her need to be socially involved. Moreover she had helped rescue her husband from political oblivion and wanted to make sure that he did not repeat the same mistakes.[40] This commitment to Bill Clinton's government in Arkansas was an important transition for the Clinton family and their political fortunes. Her successful efforts in passing education reform in Arkansas in the 1980s would convince the Clintons that they could replicate this type of political partnership in the White House in the 1990s.

Hillary Clinton was named head of the Education Standards Committee in Arkansas and she delved into her work. The committee held meetings throughout Arkansas to get input from teachers, students, and parents. She committed to memory all the different requirements of each school district in Arkansas.[41] She put together a comprehensive list of reforms including mandatory kindergarten, the testing of students, and lower class sizes. Her most controversial proposal was to test teachers for their competencies. There was a tremendous backlash among Arkansas teachers to this proposal. However in order to implement all of these proposals, a tax increase was needed.[42] She and her advisors concluded the tax increase would never be approved without the requirement of teacher testing.

She testified before the Arkansas legislature to sell the program. In a surreal scene, Bill Clinton attended one of his wife's presentations to a legislative committee. She was delivering a strong performance so Bill Clinton left the proceedings. After she was done one of the legislators announced, "Well fellas it looks like we might have elected the wrong Clinton."[43] The education package eventually passed and Bill Clinton had an important policy accomplishment from which he could launch his national ambitions. As of this writing, little evidence exists that education in Arkansas improved tremendously, but the passage of the reforms were important politically.[44]

Hillary Rodham Clinton played such a critical role in its accomplishment that some observers believe that she was the real executive running the state of Arkansas. Biographer Gail Sheehy wrote that from 1982 to 1986, Hillary "exercised the ruling power in Bill Clinton's kingdom."[45] Bill Clinton's chief of staff in Arkansas, Betsey Wright, said that Mrs. Clinton was critical to Bill Clinton's government, "Hillary made herself absolutely indispensable."[46]

The 1982 campaign and the education reform effort showed Bill Clinton that his wife was his most important political partner. These events also demonstrate that the Clintons' relationship was far different from a typical political marriage. Although most political spouses offer advice to their partner, Hillary Clinton was Bill Clinton's most important policy and political adviser. Moreover on some important issues she seemed to be the actual decision-maker.

Why is it important to examine this unusually close political relationship between husband and wife? As stated in chapter 2, the overriding concern of many of the founding fathers was too much power in the hands of too few people. The presidency was a compromise. The nation needed executive leadership but did not want to install a king. Hereditary or spousal succession was rejected by the founders. For the modern presidency, the Twenty-Second Amendment was approved by over three-fourths of the states in 1951. This amendment explicitly limited a presidency to two terms. The idea behind this amendment was to limit power that one individual could have over the nation. The closeness of the Clintons' political partnership brings into question whether a Hillary Rodham Clinton presidency would violate the intent of that amendment. The centrality of the Clinton relationship and their political lives makes this issue important to examine.

The central role of Hillary Rodham Clinton in her husband's government would be extraordinary even with a typical marriage as its foundation. The Clinton marriage by all accounts could not be described as typical. The volatility of their marriage makes it an uncertain bedrock from which their political relationship works. Thus, the instability in their marriage translates into instability in their governance and politics.

The Clintons Go for the Presidency

Bill Clinton's decision not to run for the presidency in 1988 illustrates this troubling collusion between personal relationships and political outcomes. In 1987, no strong Democrat was emerging to take the presidential nomination. This fact was a mixed blessing for Bill Clinton because one of the strongest possible nominees was Senator Gary Hart of Colorado. Hart had suspended his political campaign in May 1987 when he was caught being unfaithful to his wife by a newspaper reporter. Although Hart would reenter the race, his political stock was severely diminished because of his adultery.

In other circumstances a possible rival would have welcomed these developments. Yet for Bill Clinton, rumors about his own adultery also could damage his political prospects. When he was about to announce his campaign for president in 1987, he met with his Chief of Staff Betsey Wright. According to biographer David Maraniss,

Wright warned Clinton that numerous women might come forward to the press and reveal their alleged relationships with Clinton.[47] She advised him not to get into the race because it would harm both his wife and his seven-year-old child.

Citing family concerns, Bill Clinton withdrew his name from consideration for the 1988 presidential race. He had once again put his wife Hillary in a terrible position. She had saved her husband's political career by managing his campaign in 1982. She then helped him to achieve national prominence by getting his education reform measure passed in Arkansas. The Democratic field for president was wide-open especially for a Democratic governor from the South. Yet the Clintons would be denied their chance at the presidency in 1988 because of his personal behavior. This episode highlights the destructive interchange between the personal life of the Clintons and political decisions. It also foreshadowed an issue that would haunt them for the next decade.

After Clinton withdrew from the 1988 race, both Clintons faced a series of difficulties. Bill Clinton had been given a tremendous opportunity to give a nominating speech at the 1988 Democratic National Convention in Atlanta, Georgia. The convention hall was noisy and distracted when Clinton attempted to give the speech. The speech went on for more than 30 minutes and delegates were booing and asking Clinton to get off the stage. It was a difficult moment for Bill Clinton because he prided himself on his speaking abilities. He was ridiculed by national news anchors. However he deftly recovered a couple nights later when he appeared on the *Tonight Show* with Johnny Carson and made fun of himself. The 1988 presidential campaign went no better. Clinton strongly supported Michael Dukakis of Massachusetts. Yet he was disappointed that the Dukakis campaign did not strike back at George H. W. Bush when the Bush campaign attacked him. Clinton had learned this lesson in his 1980 gubernatorial campaign; when you get hit, hit back hard.[48]

After the strange political year of 1988, the Clintons again were at a critical juncture. The one time new and young governor from Arkansas was now serving his fourth term in the office. His administration had been successful with their education reform and several economic develop development initiatives, but it seemed to be running on empty by 1990. He had to make a decision whether to run for governor of Arkansas again in 1990 or attempt to seek the presidency without being a current officeholder. Indecisiveness on the issue prompted Hillary Rodham Clinton to consider running for governor of Arkansas herself. The Clinton's political consultant and pollster

Dick Morris later claimed that Mrs. Clinton asked him to run a poll about her own political prospects in Arkansas. The poll showed that few in Arkansas could separate her contributions from the administration of her husband.[49] Whether she liked it or not, she was politically tied to her husband.

Bill Clinton finally decided to seek the governorship in Arkansas in 1990 by promising that he would not run for the presidency in 1992. A liberal Democrat Tom McRae challenged him in the Democratic primary. McRae argued that Arkansas had had enough of the Clintons. At his own press conference McRae attacked Bill Clinton. From the back of the room, Hillary Clinton yelled "get off it Tom."[50] This surprise attack generated tremendous media coverage of the encounter. Reactions were mixed to Mrs. Clinton's confrontation. Most political spouses campaign for their partner, but few of these political spouses directly confront the opponent. Hillary Rodham Clinton made it clear that when you go after her husband, she will come after you publicly. With superior name recognition and funding, Bill Clinton won the primary and general election for governor of Arkansas in 1990.

A year later, he would travel throughout the state asking people if he could break his promise to run for the presidency. The Clintons decided that they had enough support from the people of Arkansas to break a campaign promise and consider a presidential run in 1991 and 1992.

Unlike the rushed decision-making process in 1987, a Clinton presidential bid in 1991 and 1992 seem to be well planned. Bill Clinton had established himself as the leader of the Democratic Leadership Council, a group that advocated moving the Democratic Party more to the center of the political spectrum. He traveled around the nation supporting popular issues such as welfare and education reform. Moreover, while incumbent George H. W. Bush remained popular after a successful 1991 Gulf War, the U.S. economy had started to weaken. As governor of Arkansas, economic development was always the most important issue in the state. Bill Clinton knew how to talk about economics and relate it to everyday citizens. With this background and the timing of the 1991 recession, Clinton had a ready-made platform to challenge George H. W. Bush.

During this time when he was pondering a presidential run, Bill Clinton gave a speech at a Little Rock hotel in May 1991. According to a state trooper who accompanied him, Clinton spotted a young state employee named Paula Jones and asked the trooper to invite her to his hotel suite. This encounter between the Arkansas governor and a low-level Arkansas state employee in 1991 would become the basis of a major Supreme Court case and an impeachment of the president of the United States. As president, Bill Clinton would vehemently deny that anything improper occurred between him and Paula Jones. In fact, Clinton said her could not recall meeting her.[51] Paula Jones would allege the Clinton made an obscene sexual advance toward her and told her to keep quiet about. Whatever the real facts, Bill Clinton would again put himself in a position to be attacked by the media and his political opponents. He would never seem to understand how his relationships with other women or even the appearance of these relationships could destroy his life-long political ambitions.

Rumors about Bill Clinton's relationships with other women were a constant in Arkansas political life in the 1980s. They were kept alive by political opponents and observers of the political scene in Arkansas. A former Miss America from Arkansas admitted to a brief relationship with Clinton. A lifelong friend Dolly Kyle Browning also asserted a long-term relationship with Bill Clinton that continued after his marriage to Hillary Rodham. Various other rumors emerged concerning women who were involved in the Arkansas political and social scene in Little Rock.[52] As in most instances like these, only the people involved know the real truth. During the Paula Jones case and the Whitewater investigation in 1998 conducted by special prosecutor Kenneth Starr, Clinton, for the first time would testify under oath about specific instances of adultery.

Yet as the Clintons entered the 1992 presidential campaign, the adultery issue was a major roadblock for their success. In 1987, Clinton had ended his presidential ambitions for that year because of the rumors about his personal life. The issue had to be addressed in 1992 or the campaign could never really move forward. Hillary Clinton would soon come to rescue her husband's campaign in New Hampshire in February 1992. Their relationship again would be a central part of the focus of his presidency during his initial two years in office in 1993 and 1994. Of course, the Clinton marriage would again dominate his presidency with the Whitewater investigation and Monica Lewinsky scandal. Again these examples highlight a major problem with the concept of members of an immediate family holding the office of the presidency at different times. Personal family issues impact presidential campaigns and the presidency itself to such a degree that these issues seemingly would overwhelm a family trying to attain *two* presidencies.

In a move to rebut rumors about Bill Clinton's infidelities, both Bill and Hillary Clinton appeared at a Washington breakfast in September

1991. Clinton addressed the concern that his marriage had serious problems. He told a group of reporters "what you need to know about Hillary and me is that we've been together nearly 20 years. It has not been perfect or free from problems; we're committed to our marriage and its obligations to our child and to each other."[53] It was a brilliant preemptive strike against reporters who would later ask about the issue.

However in the new age of tabloids and twenty-four-hour news coverage in the early 1990s, the issue would not die. In January 1992 just before the New Hampshire primary, the Clinton's presidential campaign almost imploded. Encouraged by Republicans in Arkansas, Gennifer Flowers, a former news reporter and lounge singer, sold her story about Bill Clinton to the *Star,* a tabloid newspaper. In the newspaper, Flowers detailed a twelve-year relationship with the governor of Arkansas. She also had taped some of their mutual phone conversations about the affair.[54] Even though Bill Clinton denied the story, Gennifer Flowers' accusations dominated media coverage in New Hampshire and around the nation. The Clinton campaign would be forced to respond in a more detailed way than offering simple denials.

In order to preserve his drive for the most powerful political office on earth, Bill Clinton's campaign would have to turn to the one person who could offer him credibility on the issue: Hillary Clinton. In a *60 Minutes* interview broadcast after the Super Bowl, much of the United States was introduced to the Clintons. With his wife by his side, Bill Clinton disputed the allegations of Gennifer Flowers, but he did not dispute the overall charges of adultery. He acknowledged causing "pain in his marriage" but he said he was committed to Hillary and their marriage. Hillary Clinton strongly said that she was not just "standing by her man" but that she was also committed to her marriage. Steve Croft, the *60 Minutes* interviewer later said that Hillary Clinton gave the more effective performance; "she's tougher and more disciplined."[55] From most quarters, Mrs. Clinton's performance drew good reviews. She had provided a strong defense against her husband's largest political weakness.

Bill Clinton's campaign would recover in New Hampshire even after another controversy surfaced about his avoidance of the Vietnam draft. Hillary Clinton again offered critical support and guidance. She encouraged Bill Clinton to face these issues directly with the people. Speaking about charges of womanizing and avoiding the draft, Bill Clinton told a New Hampshire audience "they say I'm on the ropes because other people have questioned my life after years of public service...I'm going to give you this election back, and if you give it to me, I won't be like George Bush. I'll never forget who gave me a second chance and I'll be there for you till the last dog dies."[56] The speech showcases the Clintons ability to persevere in a highly charged political atmosphere. Many observers were sounding the death knell for Clinton's campaign after the draft allegations surfaced again in New Hampshire. Against conventional wisdom, Bill Clinton continued and wound up finishing a surprising second in the New Hampshire primary. His wife's public support and his political determination kept his campaign alive.

After they survived in New Hampshire, Bill Clinton soon became the clear front-runner for the nomination. The campaign won an impressive victory in the state of Georgia and then moved on to sweep the Southern states on Super Tuesday. The Clinton campaign beat back two relatively weak challengers, Paul Tsongas of Massachusetts and former California Governor Jerry Brown. Even with this momentum, the Clinton's marriage and relationship was still a central topic of the campaign.

Bill Clinton himself put his wife's role in his future administration at the center of his campaign. During his announcement speech in Arkansas in 1991, he said, "when you think of Hillary think of our real slogan, buy one get one free."[57] Bill Clinton also made it clear that his wife would have an unprecedented role in his administration. He said that she would have more power than Eleanor Roosevelt who is usually cited by historians as the most influential first lady. Clinton told an audience in 1992, "if I get elected president, it will be an unprecedented partnership far more than Franklin Roosevelt and Eleanor. They were two great people but on different tracks. If I get elected we will do things differently."[58] During a victory speech after the Illinois primary, Hillary Rodham Clinton gave the longer speech and said "*we* believe passionately in this country."[59] Tom Brokaw, an NBC anchor, commented on the air about the dominant role Hillary Clinton was assuming in the victory speech.

Early in the campaign of 1992, both Clintons were making the point that there would be an important qualitative difference between the Clintons' relationship and the presidency from previous first couples. In a democracy, the legitimacy of executive leadership rests with the electoral process. Most elected presidents have been advised by their spouses regarding both policy and politics. However the Clintons were suggesting something substantially different. They were suggesting a shared presidency. Other observers have labeled this proposed relationship as a "co-candidacy" or a "co-presidency." They were suggesting a transfer of power from the elected official (the president) to an unelected and nonappointed person (the first lady). More confidently, they also did not deny the idea of two consecutive Clinton presidencies. Candidate Bill Clinton told writer Gail Sheehy in 1992 that after his two terms there could be "eight years of Hillary Clinton, why not?"[60] No such relationship had ever been proposed by a presidential candidate.

This close political partnership did provoke a backlash during the late stages of the 1992 primary campaign. When Democratic presidential candidate Jerry Brown questioned Hillary Clinton's integrity by stating that she may have guided government business to her private law firm, Mrs. Clinton shot back. "I suppose I could have stayed home and baked cookies and had tea parties, but what I decided was to fulfill my profession."[61] Hillary Clinton wanted to make clear that she could have her career, but in making the point she offended some stay-at-home mothers. During the end of the Democratic primary season, conservative opponents and observers questioned her role in a Bill Clinton presidency. Moreover, the couple's business dealings in Arkansas were also coming under scrutiny. One particular investment, the Whitewater land development, with their close friend Jim McDougal, would provide their political opponents with ammunition to accuse the Clintons of illegal behavior during their time as Governor and First Lady of Arkansas. Unlike the charges of adultery, the Whitewater investigation would center on Hillary Clinton not Bill Clinton. The Clintons promised an unprecedented relationship in the White House, but they also provided their political opponents with two targets not just one.

Mrs. Clinton may have seen these criticisms as sexist, but she was well aware of their impact. As detailed previously, she fundamentally changed her image in 1982 when her husband was seeking political redemption in Arkansas. Again in the spring and summer of 1992, she downplayed her role as Bill Clinton's most important adviser, but she would remain a forceful presence in the campaign and assert herself during the postelection transition.

The Clinton campaign of 1992 has been reviewed favorably in the film documentary *The War Room*. The film focuses on James Carville and George Stephanopoulus as brilliant strategists who helped Bill Clinton win the presidency. This recognition ignores the serious trouble the Clinton campaign was in during the spring of 1992. Even though Bill Clinton established himself as the clear front-runner for the Democratic nomination, he trailed George H. W. Bush and independent candidate Ross Perot in most polls. Perot had entered the race in the spring of 1992 because he claimed that people were begging him to take on the two traditional parties.

Undoubtedly the Clinton team ran a great campaign to unseat an incumbent president. Yet a combination of unique circumstances occurred in the summer of 1992 to help the Clintons attain their lifelong dream. In the early summer of 1992, the Clinton campaign made the unusual decision to nominate another Southerner as their vice presidential candidate. The team of Al Gore and Bill Clinton brought forth a message of youth and vitality. The selection received widespread favorable media coverage. Unlike previous efforts, the Democratic Convention of 1992 was well organized and media friendly. During convention week in New York City, Ross Perot shocked his own supporters by dropping out of the race. Those voters who were seeking change had only one place to go and that was Bill Clinton. Perot would reenter the race in fall, but he had lost his momentum. His reentry also provided another candidate who constantly attacked Bush and thereby helped Clinton.

Another important development was the negative tone of the Republican Convention in Houston. On the first night of the convention, defeated presidential candidate Pat Buchanan was given time to speak before the convention. Buchanan was a former Nixon speechwriter and a conservative populist. He announced that there is a religious war going on in the country and he went directly after Hillary Clinton, "The agenda that Clinton and Clinton would impose on America—abortion on demand, a litmus test for the Supreme Court, homosexual rights, discrimination against religious schools, women and combat units that's change all right...that's not the kind of change America needs...it's not the kind of change we can abide in a nation that we still call God's country."[62] Never in modern American politics has a potential first lady been attacked at the opposing party's convention before an election. Clearly Hillary Clinton would be a force in the Clinton administration, but Buchanan's attack on her backfired. The convention received overwhelming negative publicity and George H. W. Bush and Dan Quayle left the convention trailing the Clinton campaign by double digits.

Through political toughness, good planning, and good luck the Clintons triumphed in 1992. This improbable political victory would allow Bill Clinton to assume the presidency as its youngest occupant since his idol John F. Kennedy. Bill Clinton had promised a new type of politics and administration. What President Clinton could not predict would be the strangest two years for the American presidency in recent memory. The years 1993 and 1994 highlight the problems and the tensions involved with Bill and Hillary Clinton assuming power.

The Clintons Begin

The last hours before the Clinton presidency began were tumultuous for Bill and Hillary Clinton. According to some reports, they swore at each other as they were leaving from Blair House (across from the White House) to pick up President George H. W. Bush and his wife Barbara on inauguration day.[63] This innocuous incident between a couple meant nothing at the time but it foreshadowed the first two years of the Clinton presidency. The presidency would have tremendous passion and ambition but it also would have many difficulties because of the Clintons' unusual marriage.

Although her role had been downplayed in the latter stages of the 1992 campaign, Hillary Clinton would assert herself strongly in the planning stages of the Clinton transition. Her chief of staff, Maggie Williams, declared before the inauguration that Hillary Rodham Clinton would be "a different type of first lady."[64] Unusual for a first lady, Hillary Clinton would have her own office in the West Wing of the White House. She would have an expanded staff with higher salaries than the staff of Barbara Bush. Hillary Clinton was also given sole authority of picking a female attorney general.[65] After Cabinet nominees interviewed with the president; they would then have to be approved by the first lady who held her own interviews.[66] As journalist Bob Woodward described it, there were three power centers in the White House; one belonging to the first lady, one belonging to the vice president, and one belonging to the president.[67] The first lady's office area and staff were known as "Hillaryland."[68] This unprecedented power given to the first lady would cause tremendous strain on the Clinton presidency and their own relationship.

To portray the first two years of the Clinton presidency as a widespread failure is incorrect. During the two-year span, the Clinton administration had many notable successes. The *Family Medical Leave Act* was passed early in the Clinton administration that promised unpaid leave to employees with family health issues. The Clinton economic package barely made it through Congress, but it did pass. Focusing on deficit reduction, this package raised taxes and cut spending. By the end of the 1990s, the federal deficit would be eliminated. Against long odds and the NRA (National Rifle Association) lobby, the Congress passed the *Brady Bill*, a bill that required a five-day waiting period for the purchase of handguns. While the bill fell short of many of the desires of gun-control advocates, it remains the most significant gun-control legislation passed on the federal level since the 1960s. Clinton also went against his allies in the labor movement and strongly supported the North American Free Trade Agreement (NAFTA). This important free trade agreement passed with the help of many of the Republicans in Congress.

Yet, the combination of personal and policy struggles during the first two years of the Clinton presidency was perplexing and significant. Ultimately, the voters would reject the first two years with a stunning electoral debacle for Democrats in the Congressional midterm elections of 1994. For the first time since the 1950s, Republicans controlled both houses of Congress.

On the personal front, the Clintons would have to endure death of the president's mother and the first lady's father. A report surfaced in June 1993 that Bill Clinton's father was a bigamist and Clinton had a half-brother who he did not know. Vince Foster, close family friend and White House lawyer, committed suicide because he could not handle the pressures of Washington. In December 1993, reports surfaced of affairs that President Clinton had while he was governor of Arkansas. One of these alleged affairs was with a woman named "Paula." These reports would eventually lead to Paula Jones filing a sexual harassment suit against the president of the United States. In the same month, two major newspapers would call for an investigation into the Clintons' involvement with the failed Whitewater land investment in Arkansas.

These monumental personal distractions intersected with the difficulties of the beginnings of the Clinton presidency. From the start, the Clinton administration was not focused or well organized. The administration had to go through three appointments before an attorney general nominee was able to pass through Congress. Between the election and the inauguration, Clinton had publicly reaffirmed his support for gays serving in the military. This show of support led to a firestorm in Congress and in the military. The issue took up vast amounts of the administration's time in the early months. In October 1993, Somalia insurgents killed nineteen American servicemen and dragged their bodies through the streets. American forces had been placed there by the administration of George H. W. Bush for humanitarian assistance, but their role and mission were unclear during the first year of the Clinton administration. A comprehensive crime bill was defeated late in 1994 because of lack of congressional support. Most importantly, health-care reform legislation was so badly handled that it never came up for a vote in Congress. Presidential advisor David Gergen described the failure of health care: "Not since the Vietnam War had there been such a public policy debacle."[69]

The relationship between Bill and Hillary Clinton would be central in these political and policy failures. During a chaotic transition, the Clinton team organized policy clusters to examine upcoming issues the administration would face. With all this attention on particular issues, the organization and administration of the White House itself was never clearly articulated. At the beginning of the administration, Cabinet level appointments and other executive appointments were way behind schedule. In the middle of the administration's first year, Clinton's first chief of staff, Mack McLarty, told incoming presidential adviser David Gergen that the White House was organized in an unusual way, "in this White House, as you will find, we usually have three people in that top box; the President, the Vice President, and the First Lady. All three of them sign off on big decisions."[70] Gergen eventually concluded that the vice president found particular issues in which he could complement President Clinton. Yet the first lady could never really define her own role. Elizabeth Drew, a respected Washington writer, wrote a book about Clinton administration's first two years in office entitled *On the Edge*. The White House ordered presidential advisers to cooperate with Drew on the book. Drew concluded that due to legal concerns, the first lady was never given a specific title in the administration, yet "she was basically put in charge of domestic policy for the administration—economic policy excluded."[71] The Clintons were attempting a copresidency.

This arrangement made it inevitable that the Clinton White House would be unorganized and inefficient. Many decisions could not be made without the approval of both the president and the first lady. More importantly this arrangement also presented difficult constitutional issues. The founders had worked long and hard during the summer of 1787 to provide the nation with an energetic single executive who would be checked by the other branches of government. The Clintons were attempting a plural executive that the founders explicitly rejected. For all her talents and recognition, First Lady Hillary Clinton had not been elected or appointed to any office in the executive branch of government. Yet, in the early years of the Clinton administration, she was put in charge of domestic policy. When not serving the president's interests, high-level presidential appointees including vice presidents can resign. The first lady as a domestic copresident put the presidency in uncharted territory. She was accountable to no one—not the Congress or the president. Simply put, you cannot fire your own wife. Also, if Hillary Clinton ever assumes the presidency, she could not fire her own husband.

The idea that Hillary Rodham Clinton simply grabbed for power is an imprecise caricature. In truth, President Clinton believed in this power-sharing arrangement. He had stated as much in his campaign kickoff speech in 1991. He also put his wife in a terribly difficult position early in the administration. On his first week in office, President Clinton appointed his wife as the head of a health-care reform task force. The goal for this task force would be nothing less than to overhaul the entire U.S. healthcare system. Healthcare represented more than one-seventh of the entire U.S. economy. The enormity of the project almost ensured its defeat. Democratic president Harry Truman once attempted legislation that would mandate health coverage for all Americans; the American Medical Association and other power players in Washington had rebuffed his efforts. The Clinton proposal eventually ran into similar opposition. The health-care reform process showed stark policy consequences of having the president and the first lady share power on a major policy issue.

To limit the influence of interest groups, the health-care reform task force met in secret. Both associations of doctors and insurance groups complained that they were being left out of the process. The key for the health-care reform effort was mandatory insurance coverage for all Americans. To reach this lofty goal, the Clinton task force produced a report that ran over 1,300 pages and included a massive reorganization of the health-care sector. Many advisors in the White House thought the plan was too broad and too expensive. Congressional leaders also wanted another more centrist plan that could attract bipartisan support.[72] Yet, the first lady demanded that any plan presented to Congress include mandatory coverage. She convinced the president to dare the Congress to pass a health-care reform bill that did not include mandatory coverage. In his 1994 State of the Union speech, Clinton held up a pen and said he would veto any version of health-care reform that fell short of mandatory coverage. The stunt made for good pictures on television but it enraged congressional leaders especially Republicans. Presidential adviser David Gergen knew that the pen incident would ruin the chance for compromise in Congress. Democratic Speaker of the House Tom Foley had told Mrs. Clinton to drop the visual from the president's speech. Gergen went directly to the first lady and asked her to drop it as well. She responded, "No, we're going ahead."[73] Because of the demand of mandatory coverage, the bill never even came up for a vote on the floor of the House or the Senate.

This depiction of the political relationship in the White House between the first lady and the president is troubling. It appears the first lady made all the important policy and political decisions on the president's most important legislative item. The president had abdicated his leadership to the first lady on this important issue. It brings into context an important question, if President Clinton really believed something else about the health-care debate could he have ordered the first lady to change course?

The Clinton administration and the first lady herself would pay a high political price for the health-care reform defeat. Republicans in Congress would use the health-care debate as a vehicle to attack both the president and first lady. Opponents took to the airwaves to label the health-care reform effort as a bureaucratic nightmare. The mainstream press and political talk radio went after the first lady. Both the *New York Times* and the *Washington Post* began to thoroughly investigate the couples' Whitewater land dealings. Their partner in the Whitewater deal, Jim McDougal, had illegally used money from a failed Arkansas Savings and Loan to pay off debts and make campaign contributions. Because of the pressure by the press and their political opponents, the Clinton administration ultimately asked the attorney general to appoint a special prosecutor to review the Whitewater matter in early 1994. Unbelievably, this request in early 1994 would eventually lead to the impeachment of Bill Clinton in 1998. White House counsel Bernard Nussbaum strongly objected to this recommendation. He believed that the investigation would not stop at Whitewater. He said the special counsel would use a "roving searchlight" to investigate everything about the president and the first lady.[74] Nussbaum would turn out to be a prophet as the Paula Jones' lawsuit and the Whitewater investigation would eventually merge. Ken Starr eventually would take over as independent counsel with the approval of a judicial panel. In 1994, the Whitewater investigation would follow the first lady and mute her message on health-care reform.

First Lady as a Political Target

In November 1994, Democrats across the country were hammered in the midterm elections. The Republicans took the House with a clear margin under the leadership of the Newt Gingrich, a conservative Republican from Georgia. The Republicans also managed a three-vote majority in the U.S. Senate. For the first time since the 1950s, the

Republicans controlled both houses of Congress. It was an obvious and serious repudiation of the Clinton administration.

As a result of the failure of her health-care initiative and the first lady's response to the Whitewater investigation, the loss in the 1994 midterm elections was blamed on Hillary Clinton in many quarters. Some polls showed disapproval of her heavy involvement in her husband's administration.[75] This criticism was too simplistic. The president let the administration begin in organizational chaos. The president's staff also did not offer the first couple the type of guidance and support that could have made the transition to power much smoother. Instead of continually working with the president to put forth a centrist agenda, a Democratic majority in Congress viewed a Democratic presidency as an opportunity for pork-barrel opportunities not substantive legislative accomplishments.

Yet the unusual political relationship that Bill and Hillary Clinton shared was a major reason for the problems of the Clinton administration. With this idea of shared responsibility, no clear lines of authority existed in the White House. Presidential adviser David Gergen writes that Mrs. Clinton became so defensive about the media and the Republican opponents that her mood helped to drag down her husband's presidency.[76] Even Mrs. Clinton realized that the White House would have to change after the 1994 elections. She called in their infamous political enforcer Dick Morris.[77] Morris told the president and the first lady that they had moved too far to the Left. Reportedly, he also told the president privately that his wife's policy-making role had to be publicly downgraded.[78] After the disastrous 1994 midterms, Bill Clinton was seen as vulnerable for his 1996 reelection campaign.

Yet again, the Clintons would find a way back from political oblivion. In the period from 1995 to his reelection in 1996, Bill Clinton slowly worked his way back in back onto solid political round. Clinton deftly handled the tragedy in Oklahoma City when antigovernment terrorists destroyed the federal building. The Republicans in Congress led by Newt Gingrich attempted serious budget reductions to the popular Medicare and Medicaid programs. Clinton refused to sign the Republican budget into law and a government shutdown ensued in late 1995. The White House framed the budget story to the president's advantage. Eventually the Republicans backed down and Clinton scored an important political victory. After his success with the budget, no dynamic challenger emerged for the presidential race in 1996. Senator Bob Dole was the eventual Republican nominee and he was no match for Clinton's political skills. President Clinton would win an easy reelection race with large electoral vote count. After the political humiliation of 1994, Clinton became the first Democratic president to win reelection since Franklin Delano Roosevelt.

Yet the situation was not nearly as positive for the first lady. In January 1996, she was called before a federal grand jury by Kenneth Starr with the Office of Independent Counsel. To this point, Starr's investigation into the Whitewater land dealings had basically come up short. The investigation had led to the indictment of Hillary Clinton's former law partner Webb Hubbell. Hubbell had been an assistant attorney general in the Clinton administration, but he was charged with defrauding his clients as a private attorney in Arkansas. Starr's investigation also ensnared the governor of Arkansas Jim Guy Tucker and Jim McDougal, the Clintons' former business partner.[79] Tucker and McDougal were charged with helping a friend obtain a fraudulent small business loan. None of these rather minor issues had much to do with the president or the first lady.

In a dramatic display, the first lady had to report to the Federal Courthouse in Washington and give testimony before a federal grand jury. The first lady was brought before the federal grand jury when missing financial records strangely appeared in the White House. Even after Mrs. Clinton's testimony, the Starr investigation had little evidence of wrongdoing by the president or the first lady.[80] The focus on the first lady herself was historical and legally questionable. Again, the first lady was not an elected official so how could she be accused of public corruption? The tight political relationship between the president and the first lady made her not just a political target but a legal one as well.

Impeachment and the Frozen Presidency

By the second Clinton term, Starr's investigation was yielding few results. This dynamic changed dramatically when the Whitewater investigation and the Paula Jones' case collided in January 1998. After delaying the Paula Jones' case after his reelection, President Bill Clinton would have to answer questions in a deposition involving the case. The Jones' attorneys alleged that after the encounter with Clinton at the hotel in Arkansas in 1991, Jones was denied promotion and benefits. To bolster their case, the Jones' attorneys attempted to show a pattern of this behavior by questioning women who were allegedly romantically involved with Bill Clinton either in Arkansas or in Washington. In essence, this allowed the Jones' attorneys to have a free pass to investigate Bill Clinton's private life. One of these women questioned was former White House intern Monica Lewinsky.

Before the president's deposition in the Paula Jones case on January 17, 1998, the Office of Independent Counsel had received information that the president was trying to influence Monica Lewinsky's testimony. They asked and received permission from Attorney General Janet Reno to include the Lewinsky matter as part of their Whitewater investigation. In 1994, White House counsel Bernard Nussbaum had been right. What started as an investigation into a land deal in Arkansas was now an investigation of perjury and obstruction of justice concerning an affair between the president of the United States and a White House intern. The Whitewater case and the Office of Independent Counsel were no longer centered on Hillary Clinton; they were headed directly toward the president. Ironically the only person who could save him was his political partner and wife, Hillary Rodham Clinton.

During his testimony before a federal judge, Bill Clinton denied ever being alone with Monica Lewinsky, and he denied having a sexual relationship with Monica Lewinsky. He also denied trying to influence her testimony. After the story was leaked to the papers four days later, Clinton assured his wife and his aides that "nothing improper had occurred."[81] He specifically told his deputy chief of staff John Podesta that he did not have oral sex with Monica Lewinsky.[82]

Clinton's presidency was in trouble. If it could be proven that he lied in a federal court proceeding, Republicans in Congress surely would call for his impeachment. He needed to fight back strongly and confidently. In three interviews given on the day the story broke, the president was neither calm nor convincing.

The only way to change the political momentum was for both the president and the first lady to adamantly deny the charges. His famous White House denial to the American people "I did not have sex with that woman, Miss Lewinsky" helped to slow the calls for his resignation. Yet the person who would be the most effective character witness for the president was the first lady. She appeared on the *Today* show and strongly defended her husband. She claimed "a vast right-wing conspiracy" was trying to bring down her husband. She told the nation that she believed her husband and that the charges were false.

After her first two difficult years in the White House and the ongoing Whitewater investigation, Hillary Clinton was a political negative for her husband's administration. Yet with her strong performance on the *Today* show, she helped to stabilize his political standing once again.[83] She also infuriated conservative Republicans with her claims about a right-wing conspiracy.

The Clintons spent the spring and summer of 1998 traveling throughout the world. Stymied by a Republican Congress on his domestic initiatives, the president sought release in foreign policy. Yet the critical month of August 1998 came quickly. The Office of Independent Counsel struck a deal with Monica Lewinsky and granted her immunity. Lewinsky testified that she had a sexual relationship with the president, and she had a stained blue dress as evidence. The Office of Independent Counsel would charge that the president committed perjury in his deposition in January 1998. Without any legal recourse, the president and his lawyers agreed to testify in a deposition with Ken Starr and his deputies. On August 17, 1998, the president gave a long and tortured explanation of his relationship with Monica Lewinsky. His whole defense rested upon the definition of sexual relations.

Clearly the President had lied. Although he never said it directly in his testimony, his deposition made the point. That night in an address to the nation, President Bill Clinton admitted that he had misled the country, his wife, and his friends. The president's personal behavior again threatened his presidency. His actions would eventually lead to his impeachment by the House of Representatives. His spurned wife would have to rescue him again.

A Presidency on the Brink

With his August 1998 admission of an affair with Monica Lewinsky, Bill Clinton's political life was once again in jeopardy. At this time, his Republican opponents were the least of his concerns. Because he had lied to his wife, his Cabinet, and his political supporters, Clinton had a few political friends that he could rely upon. His wife was not speaking to him and he literally was sleeping on a couch.[84] Some senior Democratic congressional leaders were close to asking for his resignation.[85] Donna Shalala, his secretary of health and human services, lectured the president about his moral behavior in front of other Cabinet officers. Bill Clinton had dedicated his entire life to gaining the presidency and he was in real danger of being forced from office.

This circumstance shows the profound impact that a family relationship can have upon the presidency. Clearly, Clinton's political opponents from Arkansas and elsewhere had aided the Paula Jones case. Yet his political dilemma went far beyond the efforts of his opponents. If President Clinton simply told his wife about the Monica Lewinsky affair at the beginning of 1998 when he was confronted, the year-long legal drama with the impeachment proceedings would have never occurred. Surely, President Clinton would have endured personal and political damage. Yet this damage most likely would have been short-term. By lying under oath and lying to the American people, it placed his office in peril. In his biography, President Clinton gives the reasons for his deception. "I didn't want to hurt her (Hillary) or Chelsea, that I was ashamed of what I've done and I had kept everything to myself in an effort to avoid hurting my family and undermining the presidency."[86] Clinton wanted to save his marriage and his job.

This turmoil in 1998 would have major policy consequences. Because of the exhaustive efforts to defend himself, much of his presidency lost energy and direction. Visitors to the Oval Office were concerned about the president's focus. Health and Human Services Secretary Donna Shalala said about Clinton, "it's almost as if the government adjusted to his limping."[87] Because he could not reveal the truth to his wife, Bill Clinton had frozen his presidency.

Foreign policy was an even larger concern. Saddam Hussein and Osama bin Laden were presenting President Bill Clinton in the late 1990s with difficult challenges. Just before President Clinton went to testify to the Office of Independent Counsel in August of 1998, two U.S. embassies in African countries were bombed. The bombings killed hundreds including twelve Americans. Although his terrorist network was not well known to the American people at the time, the bombings were linked to Osama bin Laden. In many respects, the African bombings signaled the beginning of a sustained conflict by Islamic terrorist groups. The bombing of the World Trade Center in 1993 and the Khobar Towers in Saudi Arabia in 1996 showed that terrorists could directly impact the interests of the United States.

The bombings in 1998 coincided with a declaration of war against the United States from Osama bin Laden. This type of activity was a new threat against the United States. This would not be a conflict against a nation-state; it would be an ongoing conflict against a shadowy organization. This new type of security challenge would require the full attention and focus of the U.S. government. The Monica Lewinsky affair and resulting impeachment made sure that the focus and attention were not there. In response to the embassy bombings, President Clinton ordered missile strikes in Afghanistan and the Sudan. The missile strikes did not kill bin Laden, but more importantly they raised critical political questions back home. Republican senator Arlen Specter speculated that foreign governments would see the strikes as a response to Monica Lewinsky not Osama bin Laden.[88] Because the Monica Lewinsky scandal had become so all encompassing, the president's foreign-policy options may have been limited. In a pre-9/11 world, if President Clinton had tried to pursue these terrorist cells even more aggressively, he would have been accused of diverting the American people's attention away from his sex scandal.

Saddam's Hussein's Iraq would also challenge President Clinton during the impeachment scandal. Iraq was under a UN mandate to open its nuclear facilities for inspection by international inspectors. In December 1998, the UN issued a report stating that Iraq was denying access to UN inspectors. Just as the House of Representatives was considering impeachment proceedings against the president of the United States, Bill Clinton ordered missile strikes against Iraq.[89] Even though his defense secretary and the government of Great Britain believed these strikes were necessary, President Clinton again was accused of using military action to divert attention away from his political problems. Again further action may have been limited because of these political concerns. In effect, a vigorous presidency was not possible because of the Lewinsky scandal.

Collision of Family Problems and Presidential Problems

President Clinton's marital problems severely impacted his second term. When his wife did learn the truth about the Lewinsky affair, Bill Clinton effectively handed the keys of his presidency to Hillary Clinton. Many Republican legislators, and some Democrats like Senator Kent Conrad from South Dakota thought the president should consider resigning. If his wife had abandoned him publicly at this time after the August 1998 admission, it would have been difficult for President Clinton to survive politically. If his wife could not forgive him, how could the rest of the country? In her biography, Hillary

Clinton stated that her marriage was in trouble after President Clinton's August 1998 testimony.[90] If she had decided to seek a divorce in September 1998, other Democrats surely would have followed in seeking his divorce from the presidency.

In effect, the leadership of the greatest democratic constitutional republic in world history would be decided by the outcome of a marital dispute as a result of a midlife crisis. This absurd situation definitively shows how family relationships can shake the foundations of the presidency itself. The situation also highlights the central role Clinton's marriage played in his presidency.

Clearly the Clinton presidency had notable successes with the passage of welfare reform and NAFTA on the domestic agenda, and the positive outcomes in Bosnia and Ireland in the foreign-policy arena. Most importantly, the economic success of the Clinton years was unparalleled in recent American history. Yet when the Clinton marriage and political relationship took center stage in the presidency, serious problems emerged. Their unusual relationship resulted in a chaotic first two years in office, continuing investigations by their political opponents, and the eventual impeachment of the president for the only second time in the history of the Republic. Again the attempted removal of a democratically elected president did not center upon treason or crimes against the state, President Clinton's impeachment came about because he could not tell his wife the truth about an affair. The toxic combination of the Clintons and the office of the presidency present important questions and concerns about another Clinton presidency.

The impeachment scandal had two other monumental political effects. It ensured that the drive for political power between the two most important families in American politics in the 1990s would continue and intensify. On the very date that President Clinton was not convicted by the Senate for impeachable offenses, Hillary Clinton began planning to run for the Senate from the state of New York. The impeachment scandal had made her a more sympathetic and likable public figure. Her poll ratings increased dramatically during this period.[91] Among all the major figures in the scandal that included Bill Clinton, Ken Starr, Monica Lewinsky, Linda Tripp, Hillary Clinton was the only one who survived with her reputation intact.

The scandal also had another important impact It allowed the inexperienced oldest son of the man Bill Clinton defeated for the presidency to make his own run for the White House. George W. Bush said he would "restore honor and dignity" to the White House.[92] The simple message was that George W. Bush may not be an experienced man but he was a good man. This message would connect with the public who were weary of political scandal. In many respects, George W. Bush has Bill Clinton to thank for his election victory in the year 2000. Incredibly, the Clinton impeachment scandal helped to make George W. Bush and Hillary Clinton formidable political figures and possible presidents.

Chapter Six

The Bush Redemption

> "Would you like me to run as Sam Smith? The problem is I can't abandon my background."[1]
> —George W. Bush in 1978 during his first political campaign.

To introduce himself to the nation and the world as a presidential candidate in 2000, George W. Bush appeared in an introductory film at the Republican National Convention in a pickup truck with his dog. Bush's consultants and handlers had made a conscious choice to make the governor of Texas appear as genuine and down-home as possible. Bush, the son of a defeated presidential incumbent George H. W. Bush and grandson of a Connecticut senator, had learned in the modern politics of the late twentieth century that image and values trump complicated policy issues in presidential campaigns. Throughout his father's political career his opponents had painted George H. W. Bush as not being a real conservative who understood the problems of the average man. In 1964 and 1970, George H. W. Bush was viewed to be an Ivy League carpetbagger competing in Texas politics. In his run for the presidency in 1980, George H. W. Bush was criticized for not being conservative enough for Republican primary voters. Even after winning the Gulf War in an impressive fashion during his presidency, Bush was viewed as an out-of-touch elitist who could not relate to the working class.

George W. Bush had seen all these campaigns and worked in most of them. He understood the lessons well. He would deftly use his experience and connections to put together an unlikely campaign to beat the incumbent vice president. He would continually contrast his character and values with those of Bill Clinton and Al Gore in 2000. In an election during a period of economic prosperity and few obvious foreign-policy crises, impressions and images of the candidates were the most important dynamic. George W. Bush would not lose this battle over image. In his acceptance speech at the Republican Convention in 2000, Bush went right after the Clinton administration. "Our current president embodied the potential of a generation. So many talents. So much charm. Such great skill. But in the end, so much promise, to no great purpose." Bush promised to "swear to uphold the honor and dignity of the office."[2] He had learned from his father's experiences; define your opponent before you get defined.

Deciphering his own role in his father's legacy would be the main factor in George Bush's business and political life. George W. Bush "clearly idolized his father," but at the same time, he did not want to be seen as his father's direct political heir.[3] Navigating his place in his "father's shadow" would be tremendously difficult for George W. Bush.[4] As many sons attempt to do, George W. Bush would try to "live up to his father's expectations without repeating his father's mistakes."[5] Unlike Joseph Kennedy, George H. W. Bush never demanded that his sons seek political office. Yet, his father's legacy was one that George W. Bush could not escape. When to follow his father's example and when to go his own way would be the tension that would dominate George W. Bush's life course and political career. Most men have to figure out how to deal with their own father's past on their own terms. Because of his life choices, George W. Bush would have to navigate this tension in the public eye and eventually in the White House itself. Ironically, George W. Bush's determination to not repeat the mistakes of his father has led him to make serious public policy errors of his own. The modern American presidency is challenging enough without the added burden of following your own father in the office.

His father's legacy has been a mixed blessing for George W. Bush. He had no foreign-policy experience, and yet he became the first presidential son since John Quincy Adams to win the presidency. His situation presented a difficult paradox and highlights the thesis of the book. The Bush name had given him access to a large national political network, and without the brand name, it is exceedingly difficult to imagine George W. Bush ever becoming president. However, his name and connections would not ensure success as a president.

In the modern birthplace of constitutional representative democracy, George W. Bush used his family background to beat the political system. The Bush fund-raising apparatus excluded most of the other potential Republican rivals for the presidency by the time the primaries had begun in early 2000. His family's political advantages also allowed George W. Bush to downplay his relative lack of national political experience. However, the name also carried substantial personal and political baggage that would act as a negative force in George W. Bush's presidency. Following his father's example, he asked many of the same senior advisors including Dick Cheney, Colin

Powell, and Condoleezza Rice to guide his foreign-policy team. Yet, clearly rejecting his father's policy, these same senior advisers would lead George W. Bush to invade Iraq and place the United States in the most serious political and military quagmire since the Vietnam War. The name would help give him the most powerful political office in the world, but it would not allow him to succeed in that office.

Early Years

The idea that George W. Bush would be president of the United States would have been unlikely in the late 1970s. He had difficult time finding his way in life. As a son of a military, business, and political star, George W. Bush had a crushing burden of expectations. His drive to meet these self-inflicted expectations shaped his early adult life and led him to successive business and political failures. When he was eighteen, his father ran for the U.S. Senate from Texas as a Republican. As noted in chapter 4, George H. W. Bush's campaign in 1964 would be a challenge because Texas still had many conservative Democrats who voted that way. In the summer of 1964, George W. Bush traveled throughout Texas on behalf of his father. Seeking to establish themselves as true Texans, the Bush campaign employed a traveling musical caravan known as the Bush Bluebonnet Belles; the campaign song was "the sun is gonna shine in the Senate someday. George Bush is going to chase them liberals away."[6] This early campaign experience would be invaluable. George H. W. Bush lost the race in the 1964 but George W. Bush would learn politics as a Southern Republican who ran on values not a Connecticut Republican who ran on issues.

His early adult years would resemble a consistent attempt to follow in his father's accomplishments. Even though George W. Bush was raised in Texas, he followed his father's example and attended Andover, a prestigious New England college preparatory school. Bush was a popular student but average academically. Even at his high school, his father's reputation preceded him. George H. W. Bush was a legend at Andover Academy; George H.W. Bush had been named "Best All-Around Fellow." He was known as a baseball star and a military hero complete with his portrait hanging in a student hall on campus.[7]

Andover would just be the beginning of George W. Bush's attempts to fulfill his father's legacy. Even though he considered the University of Texas his first college choice, he ended up at Yale, his father's alma mater. Yale was not a good fit for George W. Bush. In a much-publicized incident, George W. Bush later revealed that the Yale University chaplain told the younger Bush after the 1964 election regarding his father's loss, "I know your father. Frankly, he was beaten by a better man."[8] This rude remark made an impression on the younger Bush. It helped to solidify his thinking about Ivy League academics and elites. Bush believed that Northeasterners and intellectuals looked down on average Americans. He would contrast his behavior and appearance with those of his more liberal classmates.

He liked to be viewed as confident, macho, and fun. He did not want or strive to be intellectually superior. This distrust of academic and cultural elites would be a trademark of George W. Bush's political career. He believed these intellectual elites "thought they could create a government that could solve all our problems for us."[9] Even though he was born to a Connecticut establishment family, he would live his life as an unabashed, conservative Texan who believed in the limits of government not its possibilities.

George W. Bush graduated in 1968 from Yale University. Unlike his father he was not a star athlete or student; he graduated in four years and was ready to pursue his father's legacy again. He emerged as a confident and arrogant young man who was searching for his place in life. In 1968, the Vietnam War was at its height. Like other men his age, George W. Bush would have to confront the possibility of being drafted. After graduation he made a prompt decision to apply for the Texas Air National Guard, and he joined the 147th fighter wing. The commander of the fighter group asked George W. Bush why he wanted to join the Texas Air National Guard, Bush replied "I want to be a fighter pilot because my father was."[10] George W. Bush's service in the National Guard became controversial in his later political campaigns. It is unclear whether he was given preferential treatment in accessing a slot in the Guard, but other well-connected Texans were also in the Guard. Moreover, by joining the Guard, Bush greatly diminished the chances that he would be sent to Vietnam. Unlike the Iraq War of present day, only a small percentage of national guardsmen were sent overseas in the late 1960s. Yet, George W. Bush's Guard experience was not without danger. He engaged in a year of continuous pilot training in a fighter jet and was given generally good marks as a pilot. When his father was running for the U.S. Senate from Texas for a second time in 1970, George W. Bush's pilot training was featured in a newspaper article in Houston.[11]

After his training, George W. Bush returned to Texas and attempted to find a career. He worked on his father's unsuccessful 1970 U.S. Senate campaign.

Again he had the opportunity to observe how campaigns function. After the campaign, he took his first private-sector job with a family friend as an assistant trainee for a corporation that purchased overseas horticultural interests.[12] The corporate life did not suit George W. Bush, and he left after less than a year. Clearly George W. Bush was "drifting." Robert Gow, the head of the company, believed that Bush was trying to find a way to find his father's success. He saw "a son following his father every step of the way."[13]

George W. Bush's difficulty in following his father's footsteps was evident in 1972. After a night of heavy drinking, George W. Bush arrived at the new Bush home in Washington DC with his younger brother Marvin in tow. A disappointed George H. W. Bush asked to see his oldest son. When George W. Bush saw his father in their family study, he said "I hear you're looking for me, you want to go mano a mano right here."[14] For a twenty-six-year-old man to challenge his own father to a fight after a night of drinking shows how far George W. Bush had to go in his maturation. He was still searching for his place in the Bush family and his life.

George W. Bush received some of that direction when he was accepted into Harvard Business School in 1974. His mother thought that Harvard was "an important place" for George W.[15] Unlike his undergraduate experience at Yale, his graduate studies at Harvard were more practical and applied. Bush understood the case-study approach much better than the theoretical writings he had to read as an undergraduate. He also was able to renew his distrust of that Northeasterners and academic elites. Harvard also gave him an opportunity to make a serious change in the direction of his life. A degree from the Harvard Business School could have been a ticket to a well-paying position with a Wall Street firm. But George W. Bush did not seek to follow his grandfather; he wanted to follow his father. Thus with two Ivy League degrees, he returned to Midland, Texas where people generally did not trust Ivy Leaguers. He returned to Texas to begin in the oil business. He wanted to start a successful oil drilling business just like his father.

The Apprentice Bush

Returning to Texas would be an extremely active time for George W. Bush. With financial help from one of his uncles, George W. Bush started a fledgling oil-drilling business prophetically named Arbusto. In its first few attempts to drill for oil, Bush's company came up empty. Also during this time, he met and soon married Laura Welch. She was a quiet librarian and she complemented his brash and outgoing style. They were married in the middle of his first political campaign. The long-time incumbent Democratic congressman from Midland, Texas, unexpectedly decided not to run for reelection in the 1978 congressional elections. Even though he was just starting his business and his marriage, the open seat presented a great opportunity for the younger Bush.

The campaign would also be a clear example of how George W. Bush struggled with his father's legacy. The Bush name offered him tremendous advantages, but it also could be politically damaging. George H. W. Bush was heavily involved in the 1978 campaign but he had to keep his involvement low key. In the Republican primary for the congressional seat, George W. Bush faced a former mayor of Odessa, Texas, Jim Reese. The primary became a preview of the Ronald Reagan and George H. W. Bush battle for the Republican nomination in 1980. Reagan endorsed Jim Reese and the Bush family was incensed.[16] George H. W. Bush had spent nearly two decades trying to build up the Republican Party in Texas and to have his rival for the Republican presidential nomination endorse someone else was difficult to take.

The heated primary became an attack on George W. Bush's connection to his father. Reese's campaign claimed that "Rockefeller Republicans" represented by Bush's father were coming in to Texas to take over the Republican Party.[17] To rebut the charges that his father was running his campaign, George W. Bush pulled out his birth certificate at campaign appearances to show his middle name was different than his father's.[18] George W. Bush also encouraged his father not to make public campaign appearances.[19] He would win the primary, but these concessions to the political attacks of his opponent must have been difficult for George W. Bush. The father whom he idolized could not be a public part of his campaign. The situation highlights a dilemma that George W. Bush would face throughout his political career. He desperately needed his father's political connections and organization, but he also tried not to repeat the mistakes his father had made. When to use his father's expertise and advice and when to follow his own instincts would be a constant source of tension for George W. Bush. It is tension that would follow him into the White House.

His Democratic opponent in the 1978 congressional race sensed that George W. Bush was having a difficult time using his father's legacy. Kent Hance, a state senator with a long history in West Texas portrayed George W. Bush as a spoiled carpetbagger who did not understand Texas. George H. W. Bush's efforts to raise money on behalf of his son aided this portrayal. George W. Bush received contributions from all over the United States including baseball commissioner Bowie Kuhn and Mrs. Douglas MacArthur. Bush's opponent told Texas audiences that his parents and grandparents were farmers unlike Bush whose father was a lifelong politician who was responsible for "the mess we are in right now."[20] Referring to George W. Bush, his opponent added, "George Bush hasn't earned the living he enjoys."[21]

To complete the portrait of Bush as an out-of-touch Easterner, Kent Hance's campaign highlighted two of Bush's campaign miscues. One of George W. Bush's campaign commercials showed him jogging across the plains of Texas. Hance publicly ridiculed the ad by saying that "the only time folks around here go running, is when someone is chasing them."[22] To attract young college students at Texas Tech, the Bush campaign promised to throw a "Bush Bash" with free beer for college students. The Hance campaign jumped on the issue and sent out letters to conservative Christians in the district claiming that Bush was attempting "to persuade young college students to vote for and support him by offering free alcohol."[23] In conservative West Texas with a number of dry counties, the idea of offering free beer to college students was offensive.

The final attempt to frame Bush as an outsider came in the form of a whispering campaign about secret eastern societies that were attempting to establish a world government. A talk-show host from Odessa, Texas, "wanted to know if the young Bush was a tool of some shadow government."[24] Bush replied "that I won't be persuaded by anyone, including my father."[25] The talk-show host ended up supporting Bush's opponent because "Bush never worked a day in his life.... Everything was handed to him."[26] Hance summed up his argument against Bush at the Lubbock Press Club, "There's somewhat of a tendency to ride the coattails, I think, of his father." Bush could only reply, "Would you like me to run as Sam Smith? The problem is I can't abandon my background."[27]

Even though he had outspent Hance, Bush lost a close race by 6 percentage points. This first failed campaign is critical in understanding Bush's political future. Even though the younger Bush had attended elite schools and had lived in Washington, DC, for part of his life, he would present himself in the future as a down-home Texan. During the most serious foreign-policy crisis the United States had faced since Vietnam in 2001, President George W. Bush promised to find Osama bin Laden "dead or alive." This casual talk concerning an important foreign-policy issue is an example of how the 1978 race shaped his political outlook. Reflecting on the campaign in later years, Bush's opponent Kent Hance remarked that Bush would never be "out good-old-boyed again. He's going to be the good old-boy next-door."[28] In his campaigns against Texas governor Ann Richards and Vice President Al Gore, he was the "good old-boy" and he won those elections.

The 1978 campaign also revealed the challenges and opportunities that his father's name presented. Without his father's assistance, George W. Bush could have never been a competitive candidate in 1978. Since college, he had moved from job to job and did not have a record of distinction. Yet, his father's contacts allow him to win a tough Republican primary and run a close race in the general election. However, the connection with his father doomed his chances to win the general election. Clearly George W. Bush was a stubborn and confident man. He would embrace part of his father's legacy, but he also wanted to stand out on his own. He did not like to be called Junior and he believed in his own abilities. Even with this confidence, balancing his father's past with his own future would continue to dominate George W. Bush's life.

After his bitter election loss of 1978, George W. Bush returned to his oil business in Texas. He would soon have two young children to provide for. His business went through several iterations, and he was able to raise capital through his family connections. Yet, the oil business in Texas was in a difficult time. By the mid-1980s, several oil companies in Texas would go bankrupt. The declining price of oil had dried up most of the investment. George W. Bush had to cut back on salaries and hope for the big oil strike. His big strike never came. In order to salvage his company's assets, he sold his company to Harken Energy. Bush received a yearly salary and a spot on the company's board of directors, but he had to lay off his employees.[29]

The failure of George W. Bush's oil venture would start a pivotal period in his life. With his father as the sitting vice president of the United States, the pressure on George W. Bush was immense. "His father was raising the bar of achievement yet again."[30] A Bush cousin remarked "I think all the boys felt the pressure...The fact that he also carried his father's name added enormous built-in pressure."[31] At one point his oil company was ranked 993rd in the state of Texas. During this period, friends and observers saw that George W. Bush was drinking more heavily. He summed up this situation by saying, "I'm all name and no money."[32] For a proud man, the business failure would be difficult especially when it was compared to the success of his father.

His Father's Advisor

After his failed business venture, George W. Bush was at an important crossroads. Given the tremendous opportunities, he had come up short in both business and in politics. In the mid 1980s, his father was the leading contender for the Republican presidential nomination. His younger brother Jeb was immersed in the business and politics of Florida. Jeb would soon be leading the Commerce Department in Florida and was seen as a rising political star. At this point, George's younger brother "outshone him."[33] To further highlight George W. Bush's problems, a drunk George W. Bush confronted a newspaper reporter who was sitting with his family at a restaurant in Washington, DC in 1986. In front of the reporter's four-year-old son, Bush swore at the reporter and told them that he would not "forget what you wrote."[34] The reporter had simply predicted that Bush's father would not win the 1988 presidential nomination. A Bush relative put it bluntly, "George had a lot of bravado...A lot of that had to do with the drinking and Laura simply wanted it to stop."[35]

After his fortieth birthday, George W. Bush did stop drinking. The decision to stop drinking came about not only to assure his own family but also not to embarrass his father. During this time, George W. Bush was also undergoing a major change with his religious faith. With the help of the Reverend Billy Graham, George W. Bush became an evangelical Christian. Unlike his father who had difficulty talking about his religious beliefs, the "born again" George W. Bush expressed his religion and religious beliefs openly to his family and others.

He began going to Bible study with his friend Don Evans who would become the future commerce secretary of the United States.[36]

The intensity of George Bush's religious beliefs would become a major part of his life and his future politics. As he was looking for a new career opportunity, he agreed to join his father's presidential campaign as an adviser. A major part of his duties was to provide outreach to Christian conservatives. He traveled the country meeting with ministers on his father's behalf. These contacts would be invaluable over a decade later when he began his own presidential quest. White evangelical Christians have become a major force in American politics since Ronald Reagan's first presidential campaign in 1980; the Bush campaign was determined to solidify this alliance with the

Republican Party. George W. Bush's newfound religious passion aided this alliance tremendously.

George W. Bush's experience with his father's 1988 campaign helped to lay the groundwork for his own political ambitions. He got to work with one of the leading political strategists in the country, Lee Atwater. Atwater was a top political operator who believed in confrontational politics. George W. Bush believed in the same political style. In the 1988 presidential campaign, he was known as "the enforcer" because he aggressively defended his father at every turn. Campaign officials found that George W. Bush's style was markedly different than his father's. "He wasn't just decisive, he was the most decisive person I'd ever met in my life," noted Doug Wead who traveled often with Mr. Bush during the campaign.[37] This decisiveness would be both hailed and severely criticized during George W. Bush's own presidency.

The campaign also marked a new chapter in his relationship with his father. George W. Bush became a confidant and troubleshooter for his father. During a campaign in which Democratic presidential contender Gary Hart withdrew because of a sexual affair, George W. Bush made sure that reporters knew that his father did not have similar problems. In a conversation leaked to reporters, George W. Bush is quoted as saying "and the answer to the big A question is NO."[38] The younger Bush traveled extensively on behalf of his father and solidified friendships in his parents' large political network.

George W. Bush also observed the importance of a consistent campaign message. Both he and his father had been defined in previous Texas campaigns as elite outsiders. Lee Atwater would not allow George H. W. Bush to be defined in this way again. In a campaign that had very little substantive policy disputes, the Bush forces devastated Democratic opponent Michael Dukakis by showing him to be a Northeastern liberal. George H. W. Bush called Dukakis a card-carrying member of the American Civil Liberties Union (ACLU) and said Dukakis believed in "Harvard boutique liberalism."[39] Even with a highly controversial vice presidential selection of Dan Quayle, the Bush campaign took the lead after the political conventions in the summer of 1988 and never looked back.

The 1988 campaign had important impact on George W. Bush. In his autobiography, George W. Bush writes "I learned a great deal from my Dad's presidency and campaigns...I learned the value of personal diplomacy as I watch my dad build friendships...I learned that is difficult to protect incumbency."[40] The 1988 campaign served as the greatest political apprenticeship that George W. Bush could have ever received. He met his father's political supporters across the country; he learned the value of attack politics, and it also gave him the confidence to seek political office on his own.

Baseball and Politics

George H. W. Bush's clear victory in the 1988 presidential race was also a win for his son George W. Bush, but his son did not want to remain in Washington so he moved back to Texas. Just about at that time the business opportunity of a lifetime found its way to George W. Bush. A group of investors sought to buy the Texas Rangers, a major league baseball team that played in Arlington, Texas. Some of investors did not want the public scrutiny that went along with owning a baseball team. Peter Ueberroth, the commissioner of baseball, suggested that they talk to George W. Bush. Bush had been a lifelong baseball fan and was interested in being involved with a major league team. For an investment of $850,000, the investors made Bush a managing partner and became the public face for the team.

The job was a dream combination for Bush of both politics and business. He would soon have an office that overlooked the stadium and had a box seat where the public could see him at every game. He even had a baseball card made up of himself that he could autograph at games.[41] The team experienced some success and even acquired Texas legend Nolan Ryan. In order to make the finances work however, a new stadium was needed. The old Arlington Stadium was not attracting enough fans for the team to break even. The team ownership wanted to build a new stadium to make the team more profitable. The city of Arlington agreed to increase its sales taxes to help pay for part of the new stadium. Later, this taxpayer-financed stadium would help Bush make a real profit when he sold his interest in the team. This taxpayer-funded deal stands in stark contrast to most of George W. Bush's ideas about the limited role of government.

Bush understood the possible political implications of his involvement with the team. In 1989, a reporter asked George W. Bush about his future political plans. Referring to his new job with the Texas Rangers, Bush candidly stated, "this job has a very high visibility which solves the political problem I'd have" "what has the boy done?"[42] The political rumors regarding George W. Bush started to emerge even when his father was still president. George W. Bush considered running to be Texas governor only four months after his father had won the presidency. Immediately, his public statements showed the challenges of dealing with his father's legacy. George W. Bush told reporters in 1989 that "his chances are good partly because 'people will know who I am.'" He then quickly added, "my mother and father are important to me but their opinions are their opinions."[43] In other words, his father's name would give him an advantage but he did not want to be seen as his father's puppet. Karl Rove, the Texas political consultant and long-time Bush family friend, wanted Bush to run in 1990. Yet, his mother and President Bush's advisers thought his gubernatorial plans would be a great distraction. George W. Bush himself thought it might be too early. He told a reporter "I could run for governor... but I am basically a media creation. I've never really done anything. I have worked for my dad.... that's not the kind of profile you have to get elected to public office."[44] The Bush name and a tough political strategist would soon make George W. Bush a political star. A man who said in 1990 "I have never really done anything" would be president of the United States ten years later.

The Campaign for Governor in 1994

Ironically, George W. Bush's political career would be jumpstarted following his father's crushing defeat in the 1992 presidential race. Although he was not as fully involved as in the 1988 race, George W. Bush was again an adviser to his father in the 1992 campaign. He saw the infighting and disloyalty that emerged from his father's campaign. He told his father's staff that his father had started his reelection campaign too late.[45] The emergence of another Texan, Ross Perot also bothered the younger Bush. Even with his heroic status from the victory in the Gulf War, his father had been portrayed by the Clinton campaign as being an out-of-touch and being unconcerned about the problems of average Americans.

George W. Bush took several lasting impressions from his father's defeat. He understood that modern presidential campaigns were never-ending. Money needed to be continually raised and an organization needed to be strengthened at all times. He also believed that his father's White House advisers had been disloyal and politically weak. After the Gulf War victory, President George H. W. Bush had no agenda to offer the American people. His father's critics pounced on this vacuum of leadership. When George W. Bush would get elected, he made sure that legislators, media, and political foes would know that he is in charge.

George W. Bush also had specific personal scores to settle after the 1992 election. Texas state treasurer Ann Richards during the 1988 Democratic National Convention famously commented on Bush's father, "Poor George, he can't help it, he was born with a silver foot in his mouth."[46] For Ann Richards to publicly attack their father during a nationally televised event burned the Bush family. It brought back the most serious political attack against the Bush family—the idea that George H. W. Bush was a societal elite who had not earned his way in life. Richards had become Texas governor in 1990 and she was soon becoming a national political star with her trademark white hair and her tough sarcasm. She was also tremendously popular in Texas and her popularity was threatening the status of the fledgling Republican Party in Texas.

A second personal vendetta George W. Bush took upon himself was directed toward Bill Clinton. His father was shocked that the nation would choose the controversial Bill Clinton over him. George W. Bush was equally outraged. Joe O'Neill, a family friend from the Midland, Texas, described how George W. Bush felt about Bill Clinton. "He has no respect for Clinton morally. And morals count in the Bush family."[47] "Bush harbored his father's loss like a wound."[48] George W. Bush would spend the next eight years defeating the political legacies of Ann Richards and Bill Clinton.

First Son Becomes Governor

The Bushes do not like the talk of dynasty, but when President Bush lost his reelection, two of his sons immediately took up the political battle. Jeb Bush would try to take on a popular incumbent for the governor's office in Florida and George W. Bush would do the same in Texas. George W. Bush had already shown interest in the job in 1990. He now had the added incentive of payback for his father's presidential loss in 1992.

George W. Bush had taken his father's loss badly. He immediately poured himself into training for a running a marathon in Houston.[49] He also was planning for a political marathon. Soon after his father's loss, he had decided to run for governor of Texas. Many observers and friends encouraged him not to run in 1994 against Richards. Richards was popular and a national figure in her own right. In his autobiography, George W. Bush writes that his own mother did not believe he could beat Richards.[50]

Bush had three political advantages in the 1994 race that most political observers missed, and these advantages were tied back to his father.

First, as a result of the bizarre start of the Clinton administration in 1993, some voters had buyer's remorse. As detailed in chapter 5, the Clinton administration that had started with so much promise was struggling in its first year. After the embarrassing defeat of 1992, Republicans started to mobilize against the young Clinton administration. The Clinton administration with its shared powers between Bill and Hillary Clinton seemed to represent everything about the "baby boom" generation that conservatives did not like. George H. W. Bush had retired from politics and would not seek office again. For some Republicans there was no better way to seek revenge for the 1992 election than by electing another Bush and defeating a strong Clinton ally Ann Richards.

Another major advantage George W. Bush would have in the 1994 governor's race were the services of Karl Rove. Rove had been a long-time political operative and had an impressive record of getting Republicans elected in the state of Texas. George W. Bush had met Karl Rove when Rove worked for the Republican National Committee in the early 1970s. As chairman of the Republican National Committee, Bush's father had defended Rove from charges that he taught dirty tricks to other Republicans during the Watergate period. In a controversial election to be chairman of the College Republicans, George H. W. Bush declared Rove to be the winner. Bush believed that Rove's opponent had been disloyal to the Party by going to the press about Rove's tough tactics. Instead of investigating Rove for possible campaign violations, George H. W. Bush made Rove his assistant at the Republican National Committee.[51] George H. W. Bush had protected Karl Rove; twenty-seven years later Karl Rove would help make his son the president of the United States.

Rove first met George W. Bush when Bush arrived in Washington to see his father. Rove's first impression of George W. Bush was simple and direct. "He was cool" Rove remarked.[52] Rove maintained his relationship with the younger Bush through the years. As Rove was growing his political consulting business in Texas, he was in the perfect place to manage George W. Bush's political career. By 1993, Rove had run many campaigns across the country and was helping to fortify the Republican Party in Texas. He also had numerous business contacts throughout Texas. Since they first met in the 1970s, Rove had maintained a positive impression of George W. Bush and thought he could be a political star. He was ready to take him to the governor's office and beyond.

The third advantage Bush had was his father's political fund-raising network. Since his father began in Texas politics in the early 1960s, he had maintained a list of fund-raisers and supporters throughout the state. As his father rose to the presidency, his list of supporters expanded dramatically. Texas was a business-friendly state with no restrictions on individual campaign contributions. Contributors who had fond memories of his father made sure that George W. Bush had the money to run his campaign. The George W. Bush campaign knew they could not feature the older Bush too prominently in public, but the candidate himself proposed an important role for his father. He told reporters "I don't think he'll be holding my hand campaigning everywhere for me. I can handle my own self. But I hope he raises me a whole bunch of money."[53]

Highlighting the importance of Bush's connection to his father in the 1994 gubernatorial race was the lack of a Republican opponent. Two other prominent Texans had considered running for governor on the Republican ticket in 1994. Bush and Rove had watched George H. W. Bush being wounded by a challenge within his own party from Pat Buchanan in 1992. The Bushes were determined not to let it happen again in Texas. Rob Mosbacher whose father had been a cabinet secretary under Bush's father was also considering a race for governor. The young Mosbacher had the money and connections to make a serious bid. George W. Bush visited Mosbacher personally and asked him not to run. Mosbacher soon made the announcement that he would not run for governor. Even though his family had millions in oil money, Mosbacher decided not to run because "he wasn't interested in spending up to 15 million (dollars) going to war with the entire Bush family and then Richards."[54] The other potential Republican candidates also dropped out. Even with his relative inexperience, Bush was not challenged for the Republican nomination. Politicians in Texas marveled on how Bush cleared the field of potential Republican rivals. They called it "the only one day gubernatorial primary in Texas history."[55] Six years later, Bush would use the same strategy of heavy fund-raising and family connections to clear the path to the Republican nomination for president in 2000.

For the general election in 1994, the Bush campaign put together a disciplined campaign that focused on four issues: education reform, crime, welfare reform, and tort reform. As mentioned in chapter 3, George W. Bush rarely discussed policy issues with his father as he was growing up. At Yale and Harvard where many students engaged in political discussions, Bush was notably not interested in these political issues.[56] He had vast experience with political campaigns but he was not conversant on many policy issues. For example, he did not understand the difference between Medicaid, the medical program for the poor and Medicare, the medical program for seniors.[57] Accordingly the campaign instituted strict message discipline. The issues were a brilliant selection of topics that concerned Texans. Although the crime rate had recently been reduced, incidents of violent crime led most new newscasts in Texas in 1994.[58] Conservative Texans took to the law and order theme. Bush's other issues were difficult to oppose. Everyone believed in the need for better schools and welfare was one of the least popular government programs in Texas. Tort reform was not a high-profile issue but it brought in huge dividends from businesses that donated large sums of money to Bush's campaign. For example, Ken Lay and other Enron managers gave nearly $150,000 to Bush's gubernatorial campaign in 1994.[59]

While George W. Bush was being disciplined, Ann Richards was not. At various times in the campaign she called the younger Bush "Shrub" and a "Jerk." She was personally popular, but it was a difficult year for Democrats. Her loud support of Bill Clinton in 1992 came back to haunt her two years later. Governor Richards also had to suffer personally from a whispering campaign about her sexual identity. As governor, she had appointed a woman commissioner to the Utilities Board in Texas. The commissioner let it be known that she was a lesbian. Some of Richards' political opponents in the state took this to mean that she was "filling state government with lesbians."[60] A state senator from East Texas who was also one of Bush's campaign chairmen told the *Houston Post* that East Texans did not approve of gays serving in government "It is part of their culture and frankly part of mine that (homosexuality) is not something we encourage, reward or acknowledge as an acceptable situation."[61] The quote sparked widespread media coverage throughout the state. The Bush campaign denied approving the quote of the state senator, but the damage had been done to Richards.

Bush's disciplined campaign led to a widespread victory across Texas. In Florida, his brother Jeb had come close but ultimately failed to unseat an incumbent governor. Against the predictions of many political pundits, George W. Bush had won an amazing victory. On the most important night of his professional life, George W. Bush still could not escape the issues of his family's political legacy. When he talked to his father on a night of his victory, George H. W. Bush apparently was heartbroken at Jeb Bush having lost in Florida.

George W. Bush told a relative "it sounds like dad's only heard that Jeb lost. Not that I have won."[62] Many in the Bush family were surprised that George had won and Jeb had lost. George W. Bush was now the political star in the family.

The Texas Rehearsal

Only two years after his father's disastrous campaign, George W. Bush quickly became one of the most prominent Republicans in the nation. He was governor of the second-largest state in the nation. His administration moved to capitalize on his political standing. Working with conservative Democrats in the Texas legislature, Bush was able to pass most of his campaign agenda in his first legislative session. He passed popular pieces of legislation involving local control of education, welfare reform, and harsher treatment of juvenile criminal defendants. He won praise for his early legislative victories and for his ability to work across party divisions. Bush made it obvious that he wanted an agenda that everyone could understand. He was attempting to avoid the mistakes of his father who had conceded the domestic agenda to the Democrats in Washington. He described his legislative approach as "Focus is good, an agenda that everyone understands and is clear."[63] Six years later he would attempt the same type of governance in Washington, DC. The simple and direct approach was meant to be a stark contrast with his father's governance style. As George W. Bush encountered a wider variety of issues with more complexities, this style would not serve him as well.

His early success in Texas immediately brought him the notice and the attention of important supporters of the Republican Party nationally. Robert Dole, the Republican front-runner for the presidential nomination in 1996 sought his endorsement for the presidential race. At the 1996 Republican Nominating Convention in San Diego, Bush was treated as a celebrity. He remarked that the political "baton had been passed" in his own family to him.[64] He was given a speaking slot in prime time at the convention. In his speech, he argued that Americans are in a "cultural crisis" and advocated for more personal responsibility.[65]

Bush became even more popular after the 1996 election. Republican national leaders were not providing a real alternative to the political skills of Bill Clinton. Republican speaker of the House Newt Gingrich was outflanked by Bill Clinton in the 1995 budget negotiations. Senate majority leader Robert Dole could not generate much excitement about his presidential campaign. The result was that Bill Clinton, the most disliked president in recent history among Republicans, had won an easy reelection. Republicans were looking for a star candidate, and Bush had more advantages going for him than other Republicans around the nation.

During 1997 and 1998 the momentum increased for George W. Bush to make his own run at the presidency in 2000. Some of his Texas supporters encouraged him to run. Bush told a reporter in late 1997 that "he was not afraid to lead. I've got a clear view of the future. I believe I know what the world ought to look like."[66] One Republican pollster said of Bush in 1997 "(What) I think our Party will be looking for in 2000, it's someone younger, a baby boomer, and not elitist. He meets all those tests."[67] His father George H. W. Bush also said in 1997 that he wanted his son to be in the White House.[68]

The rush to push George W. Bush to the presidency brings about an important issue that most of his supporters failed to examine. Was he ready? By late 1997, George W. Bush had only been a governor for three years. This self-described late bloomer ran his oil company into financial problems during the 1980s. He found his first professional success in helping to run a professional baseball team. Yet, even this financial success came about with a large taxpayer contribution in the form of a publicly financed stadium. His wife Laura talked about how her husband in his adult life was "ready to be rescued" through their marriage and his faith.[69] Bush should be given credit for maturing and correcting his life's course, but should he have been given the presidency of the United States?

Supporters of Bush in 1997 and 1998 highlighted his first term as governor as a critical reason why he should become president. However with a closer analysis, it is easy to conclude that five years as governor of Texas was not sufficient experience for a future president. Bush was lauded for working with Democrats in Texas. He hoped to change the tone in Washington with bipartisanship. However translating the Texas example to Washington would be extremely difficult. Many Texas Democrats in the state legislature came from a Southern Democratic Party that was conservative. Conservative Democrats in past elections had beaten both Bush's father and Bush himself. Many of the state legislators had little in common with national congressional Democrats who were practicing the partisanship of the Clinton years in Washington. Bush's down-home charm would not work in Washington among Democrats.

Moreover, Texas government was based upon the idea of a weak governor. After the turbulence of the Civil War, military rule, and

Reconstruction in the South, many Southern state constitutions were written with weak central authority. Most Texans also believe in minimalist government. In addition the Texas legislature meets only once every two years for 180 days. A sitting governor only has to interact with the legislature for only three out of every twenty-four months. The characteristics of Texas government do not translate well to the large and complex federal government.

Thus why was a person who had matured late in life and was governor of a state that had a weak governor system such an enticing potential candidate in 1997 and 1998? The Bush name gave potential supporters both comfort and excitement. Without this family legacy, a candidate with George W. Bush's credentials would not have been considered for the presidency. After six years of the Clinton administration, Republican supporters wanted an attractive candidate with a known background. George W. Bush provided this. With this Bush mystique driving the early presidential nominee process, other Republican candidates would be overlooked. American democracy does provide almost anyone the opportunity to run for office, but the campaign of 2000 did not offer most candidates the chance to be seriously considered.

Accordingly, the 1998 campaign for governor of Texas was a dress rehearsal for the Bush campaign in 2000. Bush faced a little-known Democratic opponent who was not well financed. At the beginning of the campaign, one survey had Bush winning by 50 percentage points.[70] At the end of the 1997 Texas legislative session, the legislature had passed a $1 billion tax cut. The cut was much lower than Bush originally proposed but his political team deftly took credit for the reduction. Even though he faced little opposition, Bush raised a huge amount of money. Karl Rove and his political team concentrated on getting Bush the highest percentage possible of the vote. They engaged in an effective outreach to Hispanic voters in Texas. He won nearly half of the Hispanic vote and almost 70 percent of the entire vote. His brother Jeb also won an impressive victory in Florida on the same night in November of 1998. The Bushes now were the most successful political family since the Kennedys.

George W. Bush's victory had made a strong statement. He was a popular governor from a large state with a strong political name who had just passed a tax cut. He also was a politician who had been talking about the cultural crisis in the nation that called for more personal responsibility. Since the Republican Convention in 1996, George Bush was clear and direct about his thoughts about the morality of the country. He thought the country was in a moral crisis. Just as his message was reaching a national audience, his baby boomer counterpart Bill Clinton was caught in the middle of a sex scandal. The scandal would lead to the impeachment of Bill Clinton and would give the country a two-year media soap opera complete with sex, lies, and a videotaped deposition. In the view of Republicans, Bush's message of cultural problems and personal responsibility was the perfect antidote to the scandals of the Clinton years.

Clearing the Field

The 2000 presidential campaign is best known for what actually occurred after the election with the controversial recount in Florida. Scholars and commentators have questioned the legitimacy of the American electoral process because of the multitude of problems with the 2000 election. This issue is undoubtedly important, but the more important issue that needs examination is the Republican nomination process in 1999 and 2000. A former president's family took over and dominated the nomination process in 1999 and 2000.

In a methodical and overwhelming fashion, the Bush family inherently limited the choices of the Republican electorate. Even though the nomination should have been wide-open because of a lack of an incumbent, George W. Bush's political team led by Karl Rove dominated the process. With the exception of John McCain, the Bush political team muscled and deterred all other Republican candidates. After the reforms of the early 1970s, both political parties democratized their nominating process. Candidates would be chosen after a series of primaries and caucuses. By allowing the Party faithful to choose their nominees for elections, the nomination process was taken away from party bosses at the political conventions. The political domination exhibited by the Bush family in 1999 in 2000 would have made the old party bosses proud.

By early 1999, numerous candidates were showing their interest in running for the Republican nomination including former vice president Dan Quayle, magazine publisher Steve Forbes, former transportation secretary Elizabeth Dole, and former Tennessee governor Lamar Alexander. Karl Rove instituted a bold strategy in early 1999. Instead of having his candidate travel throughout the nation meeting fund-raisers, he had Republican elected officials and fund-raisers come to Austin, Texas, to meet George W. Bush. It was a clever strategy because the younger Bush was very charming and persuasive in personal settings. He was less convincing as a stump speaker especially when he had to speak without notes.

His father George H. W. Bush played a critical role in the early days of his son's campaign. He used his contacts throughout the national Republican Party to encourage important political contributors to support his son over other Republican candidates. His own former vice president Dan Quayle called Bush and asked him to remain neutral in the Republican nominating process. George H. W. Bush made it abundantly clear that he would be supporting his son strongly and rebuffed Quayle's efforts. The older Bush remarked "We all have to do what we have to do."[71]

The Bush family asked for commitments to the campaign from friends and supporters throughout the nation. Bush biographers Peter and Rochelle Schweizer described the network: "the Bush family had a nationwide network that included literally tens of thousands of family members, friends and supporters. Their commitment was in a way to the Bush family itself not simply one particular candidate."[72] George W. Bush had developed a strong core of fund-raisers in Texas. His brother Jeb had done the same thing in Florida. Thus, the Bush family put together a fund-raising apparatus that included George H. W.'s supporters from his long career in public service that included being Republican National Committee chairman, vice president of the United States, and president of the United States. This network was then combined with supporters of the governors in two of the largest states in the country.

A Republican fund-raiser in 1999 put it simply, "the Bush family has done everything they could to shut off the oxygen supply of everyone else and it's worked."[73] Incredibly by the summer of 1999, a year and a half away from the general election in 2000, George W. Bush had received endorsements from over 120 Republican members of Congress and numerous governors. Karl Rove was attempting to make George W. Bush the inevitable nominee and his strategy was working.

The Bush strategy to overwhelm their Republican opponents was evidenced in a straw poll in Iowa in August 1999. The Iowa straw poll was a weird event in the campaign process. The straw poll was conducted at a huge barbecue sponsored by the Republican Party of Iowa. The poll was only opened for those who bought tickets to the barbecue and stayed around to cast their preference for a candidate. Thus, campaigns could literally buy votes. For this barbecue, the Bush campaign put on an organizational juggernaut. The campaign brought in huge tents and country music singers. The campaign won the straw vote because they bought the most tickets.[74]

Bush's fundraising success and the Iowa straw poll sent a direct message to the rest of the Republican field. Months before voters would actually make their preferences known in the caucuses and primaries, several potent candidates dropped out because they could not compete against the Bush organization.

Because of the fund-raising success, Karl Rove could implement a fifty-state strategy. He would not only focus on the first caucus state, Iowa, but also the first primary state of New Hampshire. He had the resources to compete in almost every state during the nomination process. This strategy produced one real challenge for the Bush campaign. Unlike other candidates, Bush had not spent much time in New Hampshire before the primary in February 2000. During the last week before the primary, Bush brought in his family members to campaign on his behalf. George H. W. Bush casually put his arm around his son and called him a "boy." This public appearance was mocked by the press.[75]

John McCain and his traveling bus had caught fire with the media and the New Hampshire public. With the help of independents who could vote in the New Hampshire primary, McCain won a resounding victory.

The inevitability of the Bush nomination was now in doubt, but the McCain campaign may not have realized what they were up against. As Bush biographers Peter and Rochelle Schweizer have written, when McCain accepted his congratulatory call from George W. Bush after the New Hampshire primary in the presidential suite at a New Hampshire hotel, a picture of George H. W. Bush looked down upon McCain celebration.[76] The Bush campaign would use all organization and resources, and direct them toward the South Carolina primary.

The primary turned out to be brutal. George H. W. Bush still had many supporters from his important 1988 win in the South Carolina primary. George W. Bush's campaign targeted religious Conservatives who made up an important part of the Republican Party in South Carolina. Bush made a controversial appearance at a fundamentalist Christian school, Bob Jones University. The Bush campaign filled the TV and radio airwaves with campaign commercials. They used direct mail for more personal attacks including questioning McCain's commitment to the pro-life position of the Republican Party.[77] Other Bush supporters even made harsher attacks. A Vietnam veteran had claimed that John McCain had "abandoned" his fellow veterans by not supporting veterans' causes and programs. E-mails were sent out charging that McCain had an illegitimate child. McCain's wife and children were the subject of rumors and innuendos.[78] The Bush campaign denied that it had a role in the attacks on McCain's family, but again the damage was done. Bush went on to a solid eleven-point victory in the South Carolina primary. With Karl Rove using the fifty-state strategy, the Bush campaign had a clear advantage in most of the remaining states. After South Carolina, George W. Bush would be the overwhelming favorite to be the Republican nominee for president.

As the inevitability of the George W. Bush nomination became clear, the Bush campaign set its sights on Vice President Al Gore, the eventual Democratic nominee. George W. Bush had learned from his own campaign and his father's campaigns to define your opponent early. In March 2000, Bush claimed that the vice president would say or do anything to get elected.[79] The Bush campaign would continually make the character of Al Gore a major issue in the campaign. With the Clinton impeachment scandal still fresh in minds of many voters, the Bush campaign would promote their candidate as the anti-politician. Somehow, the grandson of a U.S. senator and the son of the U.S. President would run as a political outsider.

As Republican supporters gathered for their convention in Philadelphia in August 2000, they had tremendous hope that Bush could beat the incumbent vice president Al Gore. George W. Bush had unified the party and had emerged as a likable alternative to the sitting vice president. Yet the campaign had one glaring vulnerability: George W. Bush's experience and readiness for the office. Bush had been governor for only five years and had limited experience in national affairs and foreign policy. Contrasted with Vice President Al Gore who had been a U.S. senator and in the White House for eight years, Bush's experience looked shallow.

At this moment in the campaign his father George H. W. Bush offered invaluable assistance. Bush's father had tried to stay out of public view during the campaign since his son's loss in New Hampshire. Yet behind the scenes, his father was still intimately involved. When George W. Bush chose a vice presidential nominee that would be the most important decision in the campaign, his father recommended that Dick Cheney oversee the selection process. Cheney was a conservative Republican from Wyoming and was Bush's defense secretary during the first Gulf War. After George W. Bush worked with Cheney during the selection process, his father made a critical suggestion.

He advised George W. Bush to choose Cheney as his vice president.[80] The younger Bush listened to his father's counsel and selected Cheney. Cheney would emerge in the next Bush administration as the president's most important adviser and a leading advocate for the going to war with Iraq. His father's suggestion helped to define his son's presidency. For the purposes of the campaign, Cheney's selection helped to answer the argument about George W. Bush's experience. The selection offered the public the assurance that the younger Bush would have a calm and steady Washington veteran by his side.

Vice President Gore's campaign said the selection of Cheney showed that Bush was simply taking orders from his father. President Bill Clinton had criticized the campaign of George W. Bush by charging that the only reason the younger Bush was running was because "My daddy was president."[81] Clinton's criticism infuriated the Bushes. George W. Bush was always wary of being seen as being part of a political dynasty. Yet, the motivation to redeem his father's loss in 1992 was strong among Republican supporters. The GOP chairman from the Nebraska delegation at the convention said: "it's going to be sweet revenge... but after eight years of Clinton and what he's done to the moral standards of the country it's going to be sweet revenge that a Bush is kicking Clinton out of the White House. I don't care if it's George P. Bush, Jeb Bush or George W. Bush, I'm just glad that a Bush is kicking them out of White House."[82] Another delegate expressed the opinion of other Bush supporters regarding George H. W. Bush. "Some people feel sorry we took a good man and he lost, and people allow themselves to be swayed by a 'new Democrat.'"[83]

Unlike the 1978 campaign where George W. Bush tried to diminish the influence of his father, he talked about how much respect he had for the man.

Still he rejected that he was part of a political dynasty. "Dynasty is the wrong word... Dynasty has got the sense of royalty... democracy is a field where you have to earn people's respect it's not something you'd been given."[84] George W. Bush would fail to recognize just how much he had been given. He and his campaign had been relentless for over a year in their pursuit of the presidency. Yet without his lineage, George W. Bush would not have been the nominee in 2000.

While the controversial end to the 2000 presidential election provided drama and excitement, many observers ignored the fact that the general election campaign was nondescript. The candidates had emerged from their conventions in a close race with Vice President Gore having a small lead. Candidate George W. Bush made several speaking mistakes in September and thus remained behind the vice president. Then, Vice President Gore handled the three televised debates badly and soon slipped in the polls. The election in the final week was going to be close with George W. Bush holding a slight lead.

Among other battleground states, the state of Florida was emerging as a must win for both campaigns.

By fate, luck, and good planning, Jeb Bush was the governor of Florida. During the last week of the campaign, the Bush family came to Florida on behalf of George W. In an appearance at the First Baptist Church in Orlando, Governor Jeb Bush summed up the argument for his brother. "My brother learned right and wrong at the knees of George and Barbara Bush."[85] In a campaign that had been devoid of many substantive issues, the Bushes were making a direct appeal. Because of the scandals of the Clinton era, it was time to put a good man from a good family back into the White House. The argument was that his policies for the country mattered less than his overall character. Governor Jeb Bush introduced his mother as "one of the great character builders I've ever met."[86] When former president Bush took the stage, he talked about his respect for the White House, and he felt that "'we served with honor.' I can guarantee you that George W. Bush will restore honor and respect and dignity to the White House...let's return honor and respect to the political process."[87] The Bushes were reassuring the public with a simple message, since the Bush family is good, George W. Bush will be good.

Ironically, character issues almost derailed George W. Bush late in the campaign. Four days before the election, a news report emerged that George W. Bush had been arrested for drunken driving in 1976. While Bush had openly talked about his battle with alcohol, he had never mentioned the arrest. The Bush campaign that attacked Al Gore over lies and exaggerations was seen as hypocritical by some observers. The incident also highlights how George W. Bush could never fully escape his father's legacy. The incident occurred in 1976 when George W. Bush was drifting. This minor arrest almost cost him the presidency.

The 2000 election voting controversy has been well documented. The importance of the Florida recount for the purposes of this book is how the Bush family supported George W. Bush and ensured his assumption of the presidency. Although George W. Bush's advisors wanted the younger Bush to establish his own credentials, at the first sign of a controversy in Florida they reached back to his father's political team. James Baker was asked to lead the recount effort in Florida. Baker had a long history with George H. W. Bush going back to his presidential campaign in 1980. He was chief of staff to Ronald Reagan and secretary of state to George H. W. Bush. Although the Bushes had a falling out with Baker after the unsuccessful 1992 campaign, he was still regarded as a tough political professional. Baker was described as "the leading political operative of his generation."[88]

There was evidence that Al Gore received more votes than George W. Bush in Florida, but Baker skillfully led a team of lawyers and public relations consultants to rebuff the legal and political arguments of Gore's recount team.

The best chance for a Gore's team to win the recount battle was when the Florida Supreme Court ordered all uncounted votes in the state to be tabulated. The Bush team appealed to the U.S. Supreme Court; the Supreme Court granted a stay for Bush and ordered the recount stopped. The reason for the stay was that George W. Bush would be a victim of "irreparable harm" because different Florida counties would count votes in a variety of ways. In essence George W. Bush was arguing that he was not receiving fair treatment from the Florida Supreme Court.

For George W. Bush, son of the U.S. president and brother and of the Florida governor, to argue that he was being treated unfairly in the election process again highlights all of the advantages of being part of the Bush family.

Just fourteen years earlier, George W. Bush was a business failure and drifting. Because of his family connections and his own competitive nature, he became president of United States. He had used his father's good name to rise quickly in Texas politics. He used his father's connections to assemble a national political machine with money and endorsements. Finally, when the election was in doubt, he used his father's best political operative who worked in concert with his own brother to secure the election for him. The founders would not recognize this type of American democracy.

The Bush Restoration

"I don't have any idea about foreign affairs, this isn't what I do."[89] According to author Bob Woodward, this is the statement that Governor George W. Bush made to Condoleezza Rice in 1998. His father George H. W. Bush had arranged a meeting between Rice and his son to discuss foreign policy. Rice had been his father's National Security Council aide during the first Bush administration. Examining the challenges in George W. Bush's foreign policy is important for this analysis because it shows the heavy impact of his relationship with his father regarding policymaking.

George W. Bush's honesty is revealing. For a son of a former president, former vice president, former ambassador to the UN, former head of the CIA, and former envoy to China to admit that he had no idea about foreign affairs is startling. Yet the statement may reveal the true nature of the relationship between father and son involving politics. George H. W. Bush would be intensely involved behind the scenes in his son's presidential campaign. He saw it as his role to introduce political and policy experts to his son, but not to directly advise his son on policy unless asked. George H. W. Bush would have a substantial impact on his son's personnel decisions, and these personnel decisions played a crucial role in developing Bush administration policy. As the younger Bush made it clear to Condoleezza Rice, foreign policy was not his focus. Much like his first term as governor in Texas, he had some idea of a domestic agenda, but he desperately needed help forming his foreign-policy agenda. It would be an irony of history that a candidate that professed little knowledge of foreign affairs would go on to serve in a presidency that would be dominated by foreign policy.

Even before the disputed presidential vote was resolved in late 2000, the second Bush administration was taking form. Bush had determined that Dick Cheney, the vice president-elect, would lead the transition. As stated previously, Bush's father had strongly recommended Cheney for the slot of vice president.[90] Andy Card, another of his father's presidential aides, was named chief of staff. Even though his father's former staff would be leaders in his own administration, George W. Bush was adamant that he would not repeat the mistakes of his father's administration. Although he campaigned as a compassionate conservative, he would continue to show his conservative credentials to connect with the base of his own Republican Party. He demanded loyalty from his aides and was wary of the Washington media. He would be decisive and offer a clear agenda for his first few months in office.

When the Bush administration assumed office in January 2001, they got off to a quick start and set the policymaking agenda. Bush offered the "big six:" tax cuts, education reform, Medicare reform, faith-based social policy, military reform, and partial privatization of Social Security.[91] The early agenda was heavily based on domestic policies and was extremely aggressive for a president who lost the popular vote and won a disputed election. The younger Bush had learned from his father's mistakes that the president is expected to lead.

Bush's early months as president went relatively smoothly. His administration benefited from the clumsy exit of the Clinton administration.

During the last week of the Clinton administration, Bill Clinton gave out questionable pardons including one to a husband of a campaign contributor who was a fugitive. Hillary Clinton came under great scrutiny for the amount of gifts and White House furniture that she ordered to be packed up and sent to the Clintons new address in New York. This public attention and criticism of the ongoing Clinton scandals gave the Bush administration some breathing room with the media and the public.[92] Bush's signature tax-cut plan would become law by June 2001. The administration was more than holding its own in Washington; Bush was setting the agenda.

Foreign Policy

George H. W. Bush continued to assist his son in 1997 and 1998 to prepare for his run for the presidency. He asked his friend Prince Bandar Bin Sultan, the Saudi Arabian ambassador to the United States, to meet with his son to talk about his presidential ambitions. As stated above, the younger Bush was candid about his lack of foreign-policy credentials. He told the ambassador "I don't have the foggiest idea what I think about...foreign policy."[93] The Saudi ambassador's discussions with Bush revealed a presidential candidate who needed some tutoring. Later during the presidential campaign, the younger Bush would again ask the Saudi ambassador for advice. According to writer Bob Woodward, the younger Bush asked the ambassador "why should I care about North Korea?" The ambassador reminded candidate Bush that nearly 40,000 troops were in South Korea, and in the event of an attack by North Korea, the United States would be at war.[94] Referring to some of the policy experts whom his father had assembled, Bush replied, "I wish those assholes would put things just point-blank to me. I get half a book telling me about the history of North Korea."[95]

This incident reveals George W. Bush to be impatient about the complexities of foreign policy. From his own admission, he had a tremendous amount to learn about foreign relations. Yet, he was not interested in all the different factors that might impact the relationship between the United States and another country. He once told a congressman that he doesn't do nuance. He was a leader of instinct and gut.[96] This decisiveness benefited George W. Bush when he used it on such issues as tax cuts. It would not serve him as well in the field of international relations. He wanted to be decisive but he did not understand and know the complexities of foreign policy. With his lack of background, options concerning foreign affairs would have to come from others. Many of the major players of his father's foreign-policy team must have seen the younger Bush's inexperience as an invitation to fill the vacuum with their own options.

Into this vacuum, Dick Cheney emerged as the most powerful vice president in the history of the United States. With his father's advice, George W. Bush selected Dick Cheney. When George W. Bush made the selection he told an aide that "there will be a crisis in my administration and Dick Cheney is exactly the man you want on your side in a crisis."[97] With the emphasis of his presidency on defense and foreign affairs, Cheney quickly became the president's "most trusted confidential adviser."[98] The situation offered a rare opportunity to Cheney. He would be delegated some of the powers of the presidency without being elected president. He had briefly thought about running on his own in 1996, but soon realized he did not have the personality to raise money and glad-hand his way across the country. George W. Bush's confidence in Cheney gave him tremendous power without the obligation of holding media press conferences and trying to stay popular with the public. Cheney's reach would touch every major issue in the administration. He would also be a strict guardian of the power of the executive branch. The selection of Dick Cheney would be the personnel appointment that had the most influence on George W. Bush's presidency, and Cheney had come from his father.

By the year 2000 Colin Powell was one of the best-known and popular Americans. He had been chairman of the Joint Chiefs of Staff under Bush's father. He had executed a successful war plan in the First Gulf War with the idea of using overwhelming force. This military doctrine became known as the Powell doctrine. Powell had a good relationship with George H. W. Bush. The elder Bush asked Powell to meet with his son when he was a candidate. Unlike Cheney, Powell was uncertain about whether George W. Bush was ready to be president. Powell's friend and chief assistant Richard Armitage had been attending meetings of George W. Bush's foreign-policy advisers during the campaign. According to Bob Woodward, Armitage felt that Bush had a "dreadful lack of experience...and he was not sure that the younger Bush understood the implications of the United States as a world power."[99] Powell would eventually agree to be the Bush's secretary of state but his initial reluctance would ensure that he would never develop a close relationship with the younger

Bush. In comparison to Cheney's relationship with Bush, Powell would be often on the outside looking in.

Condoleezza Rice was another former adviser to former president Bush. She served as a deputy on the National Security Council in the first Bush administration. When she first met with the younger Bush concerning his campaign, she was told by Bush he wanted her to "run my foreign policy for me."[100] She would be put in charge of the National Security Council and attempted to coordinate policy between the departments of State and Defense. This job would be extremely difficult in the second Bush administration.

Paul Wolfowitz was a senior defense official in his father's administration but played a critical role in George W. Bush's administration as well. Wolfowitz had served in the first Bush administration as a senior aide to Dick Cheney at the Pentagon. Wolfowitz had been one of the few senior officials in the first Bush administration who argued that the First Gulf War was ended too soon. In 1991, Wolfowitz believed the United States should have aided the Shiite majority by overthrowing Saddam Hussein.[101] He came to lead the disjointed relief operation to feed the Iraqi refugees during the chaos after the First Gulf War. This relief effort ultimately led to a ten-year commitment to provide aid and military cover for thousands of Iraqis. When Wolfowitz was out of power and a dean at a prominent university, he led an effort to call for regime change in Iraq.[102] He would take these passionate beliefs with him when he signed up for another stint as undersecretary of defense in the administration of George W. Bush.

Don Rumsfeld would be an exception. He was the one major figure on George W. Bush's foreign-policy team who was not highly recommended by his father. Rumsfeld and the senior Bush did not get along. According to Bob Woodward, the senior Bush thought Rumsfeld was "arrogant, self important, too sure of himself and Machiavellian."[103] Yet Cheney had a different view. Cheney wanted strong leadership at the Pentagon and Rumsfeld would offer this leadership. Without Dick Cheney, Donald Rumsfeld would not have been defense secretary.

These appointments would also ensure that eventually George W. Bush's foreign-policy team would be dysfunctional. These capable individuals had different allegiances; some to the father, some to the son, and some to themselves. The vacuum that George W. Bush's foreign-policy leadership provided would invite a continuous power struggle that severely deterred the effectiveness of the administration. George H. W. Bush's recommendations should have provided steady foreign-policy leadership; instead these personnel decisions created a foreign-policy disaster. These experienced advisors seemed to be serving themselves instead of serving George W. Bush. A family legacy was no substitute for foreign-policy experience.

The first instance where this power struggle would be evident was in an early showdown with China. On April 1, 2001, the Chinese military intercepted an American military plane by claiming that it had crossed over into Chinese airspace. The Chinese forced the plane to land and took twenty-four American crew members prisoner. In its first foreign-policy test, the administration did not choose military confrontation but diplomacy. Colin Powell dispatched Saudi Arabian ambassador Prince Sultan to approach the Chinese and gain the release of the American prisoners. The Saudi ambassador did this successfully.[104]

Less than a month later, President George W. Bush was being interviewed by ABC's Charlie Gibson; Bush told Gibson that the United States would use "the full force" of the U.S. Military to defend Taiwan from Chinese aggression. The president's words sounded like a fundamental shift in American policy.[105] The United States was always committed to helping Taiwan in the event of a surprise attack by China. Bush's statement made it sound like the United States would assist Taiwan in an offensive mission against China. The Chinese were furious because they thought that the new president was taking an aggressive posture toward them.

The second Bush administration needed help. They called upon Brent Scowcroft to talk with the Chinese. Scowcroft was Bush's father's closest national security adviser.[106] After his presidency, George H. W. Bush and Scowcroft had written a book called *A World Transformed* examining foreign policy in the post–cold war world. George W. Bush had not selected Scowcroft to be part of his administration. Scowcroft was too close to his father and the new Bush administration did not want to be seen as a carbon copy of the first Bush administration. Yet when George W. Bush made his first serious foreign-policy mistake, they did call upon his father's closest adviser. Scowcroft quietly and professionally assured the Chinese that the United States had not changed its policy. A crisis was diverted but it took the expertise of his father's closest adviser to do it.

During the summer of 2001, the Bush administration faced another potent danger. Since the terrorist attacks on American embassies in Africa in 1998 and failed attempts during the millennium celebrations in the year 2000, the CIA and other U.S. intelligence agencies had been warning about a terrorist attack on U.S. soil. CIA director George Tenet had warned National Security Council adviser Condoleezza Rice numerous times about a possible attack. Tenet thought that Rice was not taking the threat seriously enough.[107] Like other previous administrations including the Clinton administration, no clear course of action to deter terrorism was apparent. In most cases, the intelligence did not describe detailed threats. In an open and free society like United States it was difficult to know what to defend.

On September 11, 2001, the United States entered a new national security era. The terrorist attacks in New York and Washington killed nearly 3,000 Americans and shocked the national economy. The attack had not come from a nation-state but a terrorist group. For forty-five years after World War II, the national security policy for the United States was determined by its rivalry with another superpower, the Soviet Union. After the fall of the Soviet Union in the early 1990s, George H. W. Bush hoped for a New World Order. The hopes for a New World Order were sabotaged by the brazenness of Islamic terrorist groups such as Al Qaeda.

The true leadership of the Bush foreign policy was on display on September 11th. Vice President Dick Cheney was in effect, the chief operating officer for the day. President Bush had gone to Florida to give a speech in front of schoolchildren. When he received word of the attacks, the vice president suggested that President Bush get on a secure plane and not come back to Washington. Meanwhile as Washington itself was being attacked, Cheney was put in an underground secure bunker at the White House. From the secure bunker, he directed the American government during this major crisis.[108] This would not be the first instance where Cheney would assume a dominant role in foreign policy.

The first three months after the September 11th attacks would mark the high point of George W. Bush's foreign policy. George W. Bush gave an inspiring address before Congress about his response to September 11. The brutal nature of the attacks and the threat of Al Qaeda to other nations brought the United States much sympathy and support from around the world. The Bush administration was able to put together a broad coalition to support its efforts in Afghanistan. Surprisingly, the Pentagon did not have a plan to confront Al Qaeda in Afghanistan.[109] The CIA put together a covert plan to aid a group inside Afghanistan and have the U.S. military provide air support to this group. By providing massive military and intelligence assistance to the Northern Alliance, Al Qaeda and the Taliban soon fled most of Afghanistan. The United States suffered few casualties but it also experienced one obvious setback; Osama bin Laden was not captured.

The United States had extensive international cooperation for its efforts in Afghanistan. The UN aided the effort with peacekeeping forces after the fall of the Afghan capital. The North Atlantic Treaty Organization (NATO) assisted with combat troops and infrastructure systems during the attack on Afghanistan. The United States initiated a new relationship with Pakistan including giving Pakistan a billion dollars in economic assistance. Although its leader General Musharraf came to power in a military coup, Pakistan would become the second largest recipient of American foreign aid.[110] Much of the international community was willing to assist the United States in its war against Al Qaeda.

Even with the success of operations in Afghanistan, the problems in the Bush foreign-policy team were apparent. During the first few weeks after the attacks the Pentagon and the CIA clashed over who exactly was in charge of the Afghanistan operation.[111] Conflicts between the Pentagon and the State Department were also apparent. The success of the attacks also gave some in the Bush administration tremendous confidence in its judgment and policy ideas.

This administration infighting and overconfidence that many in the Bush administration displayed after Afghanistan would lead to the United States to engage in a high-risk military operation in Iraq.

Finishing His Father's War

President Bush argued that after the September 11th attacks, a new, more serious threat had emerged. This more serious threat was the possibility that a nation in collaboration with a terrorist group would attack the United States with weapons of mass destruction (WMD). As a result of this possible threat, the Bush administration set its sights on the nation of Iraq. In truth, the second Bush administration's focus on Iraq occurred much earlier. In 1999, Richard Perle and Paul Wolfowitz were foreign-policy advisors to George W. Bush's presidential campaign. During the campaign they suggested that George W. Bush take a different approach with Iraq.

This policy was in direct contradiction of his father's administration. As late as 1998, George H. W. Bush defended his decision not to pursue Saddam Hussein to Baghdad. The senior Bush argued that to go to Baghdad would leave the United States without an "exit strategy."[112] Incredibly, the son was going to try to improve upon the father's most important foreign-policy accomplishment. He was also going to do it in a way that suggested that his father had been wrong.

Only a day after the 9/11 attacks, Secretary of Defense Donald Rumsfeld suggested to Bush that the United States go after Iraq as well as Afghanistan. Rumsfeld believed that the senior Bush had made a fundamental mistake in letting Saddam Hussein survive in power.[113] He wanted to correct the mistake. By November 2001, the administration began planning for the war in Iraq.

During his campaign for reelection in 2004, in a show of unity, President Bush appeared at several campaign events with his one-time rival Senator John McCain. Reportedly, President George W. Bush told McCain "I don't want to be like my father. I want to be like Ronald Reagan."[114] The younger Bush had seen his father get torn apart in the 1992 campaign because he went back on his promise not to raise taxes. The younger Bush at all times wanted to appear confident and decisive. The idea for the United States to attack another sovereign country and remove the country's leadership was unquestionably bold and decisive.

However, this idea was an enormously complex and dangerous one as well. Clearly, the administration vastly underestimated these complexities. The president claimed that the 9/11 attacks had made the situation in Iraq intolerable for the United States. The United States would be replacing a secular (although brutal) regime with a Shiite-dominated democracy. Deposing Saddam would give the country of Iran enormous power and influence in the Middle East; Iran's fellow Shiites would now rule Iraq. Since the hostage crisis of 1979, Iran had been a constant foe of the United States.

The connection between Iraq and terrorist groups was presented as one of the most important reasons to invade the country. Yet the secular dictatorship of Saddam Hussein had little to do with the Islamic fundamentalism of Al Qaeda. The two entities were not natural allies and evidence of their collaboration was weak. Syria and Iran had a much-longer record and clearly identifiable links to terrorist groups who had attacked United States interests.

After the initial invasion in Iraq, the United States would have to occupy a nation with 25 million people with three distinct religious sects. In the eyes of most Iraqis, the United States was an enemy that had been bombing the country ever since the beginning of the First Gulf War in 1991. For a Western superpower to engage in a long-term occupation of a traditional Middle Eastern country with a complicated ethnic mix would be enormously difficult. Finally, locating and disarming any possible nuclear or biological weapons presented serious risk. If Iraq did have WMD, the United States might be engaging in the first nuclear battle since Hiroshima and Nagasaki.

Even with all of those potential risks, the Bush administration embarked on a year-and-a-half march to war. In the first State of the Union address after 9/11, President Bush made it clear that Afghanistan would not be the only military target. Bush referred to an "axis of evil" that included Iraq, Iran, and North Korea. To place these three countries in any type of axis was strange. Iran and Iraq were sworn enemies who had fought a long war in the 1980s. The brutal North Korea regime seemingly had no connection to the two countries as well. Bush's argument focused on WMD. In his address he said, "I will not wait on events while dangers gather. I will not stand by as peril draws closer and closer. The United States of America will not permit the world's most dangerous regimes to threaten us with the world's most destructive weapons." In June 2002, Bush offered the rationale for war. In a speech to the cadets at West Point he said, "if we wait for threats to fully materialize we will have waited too long."[115] This doctrine became known as preemption. It was a fundamental shift in U.S. military strategy. This strategy would depend upon excellent intelligence and brilliant postwar planning. The Bush administration would offer neither.

Other foreign-policy experts were wary of the new preemption policy. George W. Bush's father's most trusted adviser, Brent Scowcroft, made a strong argument against the possibility of war in a *Wall Street Journal* editorial in August 2002. Scowcroft argued that Iraq was not an imminent threat to the United States. Moreover, attacking Iraq would undermine the war on terrorism with the allies of the United States. The editorial was a damaging blow for the second Bush administration.[116] Here was his father's closest adviser saying that the son was making a terrible mistake. Former secretary of state James Baker also expressed concerns to President George W. Bush. Secretary of State Colin Powell also tried to an inform George W. Bush about the perils that a war with Iraq might bring.

Yet the son's most trusted adviser had a totally different view. Ever since the September 11th attacks, Vice President Dick Cheney had become fixated on possible mass-casualty attacks against the United States. Even though he argued against going after Saddam in 1991, he firmly believed the United States should dispose the Iraqi dictator twelve years later. Cheney would also lead the younger Bush to seek more executive power than any president since Richard Nixon using national security as the basis for expanded presidential powers.[117]

Cheney would make it clear that the administration saw a threat in Iraq. In a speech in late-August 2002, Cheney definitively stated that Iraq had WMD. This statement was way ahead of most intelligence accounts of Iraq's WMD. The vice president said, "simply stated, there is no doubt that Saddam Hussein now has weapons of mass destruction. There is no doubt he is amassing them to use against our friends against our allies and against us."[118] The vice president was not only claiming that Iraq had WMD, but also that they were planning to use them against the United States. This ominous prediction would help to end most of the debate in Washington. Saddam Hussein was a real threat who was planning to attack United States. The United States could not wait.

Unlike the vigorous debate over the First Gulf War in the early 1990s, the U.S. Congress offered minimal resistance to President Bush's authority to go to war against Iraq. In the fall of 2002, Bush was still popular because of his response to the September 11th attacks. Some Democrats thought voters punished them when they voted against going to war against Iraq during the First Gulf War in 1991. Even though the Democrats held a very slim margin of control in the U.S. Senate, no credible opposition emerged to Bush's war plans. Some Democrats wanted to get the Iraq War vote over with before the November 2002 elections. President Bush was given the authority without much of a debate in Congress. This early war vote did not help the Democrats because the party lost seats in the House and the Senate in 2002.

The United States was about to enter the first preemptive war in its history. Vice President Cheney and Secretary of Defense Donald Rumsfeld were prepared to initiate action at any time. The State Department desperately wanted to get UN approval for the upcoming attack on Iraq. President Bush asked Powell to make a presentation before the UN. With the assistance of the CIA director, Powell put forth a persuasive argument before the UN. Powell declared "we have first-hand description of biological weapons factories on wheels and on rails. Our conservative estimate is Iraq today has a stockpile of between 100 and 500 tons of chemical weapons agents."[119] Powell received favorable reviews from across the country.[120] The nation had been assured by one of its most trusted leaders that the threat was real. George W. Bush entered the presidency with less governmental experience than any president since 1920. His administration was proposing a bold and dangerous military engagement in the Middle East. Yet with his father's respected aides Dick Cheney and Colin Powell describing the threat as real and imminent, no wide-ranging political opposition to the war in Iraq developed. Ironically, his father's advisers had sold a policy to the nation that his father had explicitly rejected eleven years earlier.

As of this writing, the problems and challenges brought forth by the U.S. involvement in Iraq are well documented. Initial military action quickly deposed Saddam Hussein, but the battle plan for the Iraq War has now come under heavy criticism for ignoring the long-term situation in Iraq. No WMD were discovered. Moreover, the U.S. government was not ready for the second phase of the war after the initial military victories. The first postwar planning meeting took place only three weeks before the war began.[121] The United States is now responsible for a country of 25 million people. The occupation produced one problem after the other. President Bush and his advisors did not understand the nature of the internal conflict going on in Iraq in regards to the insurgency.

After the fall of Baghdad in April of 2003, the American organization and management of the war effort was in chaos. Donald Rumsfeld would refer to the problems in Iraq as overstated. The State Department and the Department of Defense were in the midst of constant interagency battles. Condoleezza Rice had the difficult task of trying to coordinate policy between the Pentagon and the State Department.[122] The Coalition Provisional Authority under Paul Bremer acted as separate entity from other parts of the U.S. government. In effect for a year, Paul Bremer was the viceroy of Iraq—a strange way to introduce democracy to the nation.[123]

Results of the War

The mismanagement of the war in Iraq has had severe consequences. As of the fourth anniversary of the war in March 2007, more than 3,200 U.S. Troops have died and more than 25,000 troops wounded with 10,000 of the troops wounded seriously.[124] Fiscal costs of the war effort are over $350 billion not including future veterans healthcare needs.[125] One of the impacts of the Iraq conflict has been severe for the U.S. military especially the U.S. Army and the National Guard. In a report to Congress, the Pentagon stated that not one Army unit has the personnel and equipment it needs to complete their present mission.[126] For the Iraqis themselves, the war has extracted an even greater cost. More than 2 million Iraqi refugees have fled the country since 2003.[127] By one estimate, nearly 60,000 Iraqi civilians have been killed in sectarian conflicts or by terrorism.[128]

The United States can point to the successful removal of Saddam Hussein and the areas of Iraq that are experiencing stability and prosperity such as the Kurdish area in the north; yet overall, the Iraqi policy has been a disaster for the Bush administration. Although never uniformly popular across the world, the standing of the United States is at a new low.[129] Most likely, the human and fiscal costs of continuing the Iraqi operation are too much for the United States in the long term. If a stable government cannot be produced, Iraq may continue to fall into anarchy with most of its population facing daily security concerns. This bold policy of attacking Iraq to find weapons and spread democracy throughout the Middle East now is being labeled as the largest foreign-policy mistake in recent American history.[130]

The Iraq Study Group was a bipartisan team formed by Congress to examine the administration's policy in Iraq and made this sobering assessment in late 2006; "the situation in Iraq is grave and deteriorating; there is no path that can guarantee success."[131] The group was led by James Baker who had been secretary of state under George H. W. Bush and had also secured the Florida vote for the younger Bush in the 2000 election. It represented another chapter in the complicated relationship between father and son. The Iraq situation had gotten so bad that his father's secretary of state would have to help to get him out of the situation. This group recommended a mixture of diplomatic and military changes. The group recommended that the president and the administration engage in diplomatic overtures with Iraq's neighbors such as Iran and Syria about the future of Iraq. It also advocated a redeployment of U.S. Troops in Iraq.

This new mission would focus on combating terrorism and securing the borders of Iraq. Initially, the president and his advisers rejected most of these recommendations. Even after four difficult years of war, the president and some of his advisers were wary of following James Baker's advice. The president did not want to be seen as running to his fathers' friends when the going got tough.[132] A month after the report was issued President Bush offered a radically different strategy. Instead of a redeployment of American troops, there would be a surge of American troops. President Bush would not admit to his policy being wrong and he did not want to be seen as advocating policies of his father's administration that he had rejected early in his own presidency. The foreign policy of the United States was caught in the middle of an intergenerational struggle between two men from the same family.

The Shadow Remains

The complicated relationship between George H. W. Bush and George W. Bush dominated the younger Bush's life and presidency. This relationship also highlights the two major themes of the book. (1) In a democratic system that is supposed to be open to all, family political machines run against the American democratic ideal. (2) Family legacies and the office of the presidency do not mix. The personal relationships between family members can dominate policymaking. As the lone superpower left in a complicated and unstable world, the leadership of the United States should not be subject to family passions and vulnerabilities.

The simple truth is that George W. Bush would have never been considered for the presidency without his father. George W. Bush had to grow up and develop in the long, wide shadow cast by his father. Being a relative of a vice president or president is strangely difficult. George W. Bush compounded these difficulties by seeking the office of presidency itself. George W. Bush had no clear professional direction in his life until after the age of forty. He spent much of his young adulthood moving in between unsuccessful business and political ventures. He drank too much in several instances of public drunkenness. He had good political instincts and helped his father during his numerous political campaigns. As a result of the Bush name and voters' regrets about the Clinton administration, George W. Bush was elected governor of Texas two years after his father was defeated in the 1992 presidential election. He won this race even though he had held only one successful professional job in his life. Upon entering office he immediately became a national name and celebrity. Only three years into his term as governor, he decided to run for the presidency of the United States.

With his father's contacts and fund-raising apparatus, he forced out most of his Republican opponents early in the process for the 2000 presidential race. When Senator John McCain threatened his nomination, the Bush campaign and other supporters buried Senator McCain's campaign under a deluge of TV commercials, direct mail, and anonymous negative e-mails. Because of the economic success in the 1990s, George W. Bush's presidential campaign in 2000 ran against the character of Bill Clinton and Al Gore. The Bush campaign presented itself as being able to restore the dignity that his father had shown in the White House. In the wake of the Clinton impeachment scandal, it was a successful message.

After a lackluster campaign, the 2000 presidential campaign was decided in the state of Florida, the state where candidate Bush's brother Jeb was governor. The Bush campaign turned to his father's most experienced political operative James Baker to win the disputed Florida election. Thus, in order for George W. Bush to win the White

House; he had to call upon his father's secretary of state and his own brother who was the governor of Florida.

Obviously the most critical policy decision that George W. Bush made in his presidency was his decision to invade Iraq. The direction of Iraqi war was dominated by the relationship between father and son. Bush adored his father but he also wanted to be seen as his own person. Even though his father had decided not to take the fight to Baghdad in 1991, his son was more decisive and reckless. The younger Bush bragged that he did not examine the nuances of all the decisions he would make. He used his gut and he used his instincts.

This type of decision making draws upon emotional reserves. One of these emotions was revenge for his father. In late September 2002, six months before the war, President George W. Bush was at a campaign event in Texas. He told his audience that Saddam Hussein needed to be removed because "this is a guy that tried to kill my dad."[133] George W. Bush was referring to an assassination plan in Kuwait when Bush's father was visiting the country in 1993. Kuwaiti authorities have blamed the plot on the Iraqi government. President Clinton ordered a missile strike against Iraq in retaliation for the assassination plot. Apparently, President Clinton's actions were not enough for George W. Bush. President George W. Bush again in 2003 mentioned the assassination plot as a reason to go after Saddam Hussein. Naturally any son would want to defend the safety of their father. However, for the president of the United States to use as a partial justification personal revenge to take the nation to war is unacceptable. This scenario highlights why multiple family presidencies do not serve the nation or the presidency well. With the tremendous power of the U.S. Military, Americans expect their leaders to use caution in judgment when committing military troops to action. For George W. Bush, the war in Iraq seemed all too personal. According to a member of George W. Bush's White House communications staff, Bush told his press secretary one of the reasons the United States was going after Hussein was that "I don't like motherf****** who gas their own people...I am going to kick his sorry motherf****** ass all over the Mideast."[134]

Because George W. Bush entered the presidency with less governmental experience than any president in eighty years, he leaned heavily on some of his father's advisers for guidance on foreign policy. Dick Cheney would become his most prominent adviser, and the strongest advocate of war with Iraq. Ironically, President George W. Bush did not solicit nor take the advice of the one person who might have prevented the tragedy in Iraq: George H. W. Bush.

His father's good name and wide political network helped to give him the presidency. He took his father's advice on his vice presidential selection and other foreign policy appointments, but there were limits to the relationship. No record exists of former president Bush advising his son on policy. When asked by a former U.S. senator why the former president does not advise the younger Bush on his Iraq policy, Barbara Bush reportedly replied, "he doesn't think he should unless he's asked."[135] Apparently the senior Bush had tremendous reservations about his son's Iraq policy but did not relate them to his son.[136] George H. W. Bush's closest adviser Brent Scowcroft said that the former president was in "agony" because of the war and its aftermath.[137] The father had given his son to the nation and put some of his advisers close to him to offer assurance to the public, but he could not make him succeed. The failures of the second Bush Presidency offered a warning to the American people that family presidencies are dangerous anomalies.

Chapter Seven

From First Lady to President?

"It's her turn now."[1]
—Democratic Convention delegate in 2000 commenting on Hillary Clinton.

On February 12, 1999, the president of the United States was delivered an acquittal in his impeachment trial before the U.S. Senate. For only the second time in the history of the Republic, a president had been impeached with the possibility of being forcibly removed from office. For the preceding thirteen months, Bill Clinton had performed masterful political gymnastics to remain in office. He had survived lying to a federal judge and to the American public. He survived the indignity of appearing before the nation on TV and admitting that he had an affair in the White House with a young intern. He had survived an impeachment from the House of Representatives and a trial in the U.S. Senate. To celebrate his victory in the U.S. Senate, his closest political partner, his wife Hillary, did not hold a reception. Instead, on the very day their personal and political nightmare was over, she began planning her own political future. Even before the Senate had officially voted, she was meeting with her political adviser Harold Ickes about running for the U.S. Senate from New York in the 2000 election.[2] This odd juxtaposition was the culmination of a long road for Hillary Rodham Clinton. After more than twenty-five years together, she would no longer put her political desires second to his.

A major premise of this book is that multiple family presidencies do not serve the nation or the institution of the presidency well. These family connections help to give candidates huge advantages, but they can interfere with effective governance. And communication having to follow in her husband's footsteps would be enormously challenging because the Clintons' personal relationship dominated their political relationship as well. As she would attempt to move out on her own politically, this essential dynamic would not change. Because of the personal and political difficulties Bill Clinton had put her through, she believed it was her time. However, no matter how hard she would try, her future would look a great deal like her past; her relationship with Bill Clinton would be a dominant factor in anything she attempted to do.

Why would she begin planning for her own campaign on the very day her husband was acquitted by the U.S. Senate? In some ways, she had been waiting for more than twenty-five years to concentrate on her own career. At her time at Yale Law School, she had put together an impressive resume. As noted in chapter 5 she could have stayed in Washington, DC. and began her legal career in social activism. Instead, she moved to Arkansas to be with her future husband Bill Clinton. She put her career ambitions on hold while her husband began his political career. Because the governor's salary in Arkansas was relatively small, she had to become the breadwinner for the family. Because of numerous mistakes, Bill Clinton lost his gubernatorial reelection in 1980. As a result of this devastating loss, his political career was in jeopardy. Hillary Clinton helped to run the 1982 campaign that put Bill Clinton back in office. She had changed her name and even her hairstyle to be more accommodating to voters. After the victory in 1982, Bill Clinton put his wife in charge of his most important policy objective, school reform in Arkansas. She testified before the Arkansas legislature and helped to pass reform legislation in the mid-1980s.

Moreover, during his time as governor, she had to endure rumors about her husband's infidelity. Bill Clinton canceled his plans to run for president in 1988 partly because of accusations concerning affairs he had with other women.[3] By 1990, Hillary Clinton was so frustrated with her husband that she considered running for governor herself.[4] According to several biographies about Hillary Clinton, both Clintons considered a divorce in the late 1980s.[5]

Their relationship recovered, and they began a long-shot bid to win the presidency in 1992. During the very first primary of the 1992 election in New Hampshire, she had to endure the media spectacle of a former TV reporter, Gennifer Flowers, publicly stating that she had a twelve-year affair with her husband.

She then had to go on national television and attempt to convince the nation that her husband was a good man.

After they had won the election in 1992, she sought an important role in her husband's presidency. She was given the difficult assignment of reforming the nation's health-care system. During the first two difficult years of the Clinton presidency, her health-care efforts were a disaster. Also, her husband had agreed to the appointment of a special prosecutor that began examining their past land deals in Arkansas. The Whitewater investigation would begin a long torturous road that led to the impeachment of Bill Clinton. Yet before the Monica Lewinsky scandal emerged, the Whitewater investigation was centered on Hillary Clinton. She had to testify before a grand jury and by some accounts was close to being indicted.[6]

After all of these difficult moments, her husband had been reelected by a wide margin. Yet his second term would be dominated by a scandal involving a sexual relationship with a White House intern. Again she had to publicly defend her husband on national TV. She then found out that he had lied to her and the nation. Simply put, Bill Clinton owed his wife.

The Decision

The decision to run for the U.S. Senate from New York was a definitive turning point for Hillary Clinton. The impeachment of her husband had presented her with an unusual opportunity. Because she was one of the few public figures in the impeachment scandal that could provoke some sympathy, her standing with the public increased. As she contemplated what she would do with her life after her husband's presidency, many options were available. The fact that she chose to engage again in the brutal political process displayed her strong ambition when she had other worthwhile and attractive alternatives.

Hillary Clinton has on numerous occasions cited Eleanor Roosevelt as a role model. Yet, when her two terms as first lady were over, she did not follow the example of Eleanor Roosevelt. In an interesting twist of history, Harold A. Ickes Sr., father of Hillary Clinton's advisor, had approached Eleanor Roosevelt in the mid-1940s about running for the U.S. Senate after the death of her husband.[7] Eleanor Roosevelt said she did not want to run for elected office. Instead she used her energies and public stature for two main objectives. President Truman had appointed her as a U.S. representative to the international working group that was forming the UN. Eleanor Roosevelt passionately worked on forming the UN making sure that it would become a functioning world body. For her efforts, she became known as "First Lady of the world."[8] She traveled extensively and brought attention to issues such as war refugees and world poverty. She also became a major political figure within the Democratic Party. She wanted the party to stay with its progressive roots that came from the New Deal era. She became known as an important social voice in the Democratic Party in late 1940s and 1950s.

Hillary Clinton could have adopted a similar role. Some of her best reviewed work as first lady was her advocacy of women's issues around the world. Her speech as first lady to the UN Conference on Women held in Beijing, China, challenged the Chinese government to allow women the same civil rights as men.[9] Her speech was lauded by Democrats and Republicans because she had taken a tough position with the Chinese.

The role of women in society and the world at large has become even more controversial in recent years. The rise of Islamic fundamentalism has continually put women in Islamic nations in difficult circumstances. Women in some of these countries are not allowed to show their faces in public, and some of these countries also forbid women from attempting professional careers. As a former first lady, Hillary Clinton could engage the world on this important topic using her celebrity status. When she made the decision to run for the U.S. Senate from New York, she rejected this type of Eleanor Roosevelt model of a post–first lady's life. Just because she is a woman, she would not be confined to women's issues.

Another important question to examine is: why New York? As first lady she traveled to New York often but she had no residency there. She was raised in Illinois; she went to college in New England, and lived in Arkansas for twenty years. Moreover, as first lady of Arkansas she continually pressed issues concerning the plight of that state. She led education reform efforts there and also ran a legal aid clinic for the poor. Arkansas remains one of the poorest states in the nation. It ranks close to Mississippi and Louisiana in the number of residents in poverty. Accordingly her type of social activism is still desperately needed in Arkansas; the state could use a former first lady who could vigorously make its case in the U.S. Senate.

Yet, Hillary Clinton left Arkansas behind. New York with all of its political and economic power was more attractive. Mrs. Clinton's stated that one of the reasons she engaged in the Senate campaign was because it "would enable me to be involved in a lot of the issues and causes that I care about." The state of Arkansas was awash in these important issues, but New York presented a more enticing opportunity.

Mrs. Clinton's attempt to represent New York also showed a fundamental shift in American politics. The Bushes who started out as New England patricians are now Southern conservatives. "Bubba" Bill Clinton and his wife Hillary have moved to New York to chart their own political future. These personal moves reflect the political transformation of the nation. The Northeast is now seen as a base of the blue Democratic Party. The South is now the base of the red

Republican Party. Mrs. Clinton's attempt to try to represent New York adds to the political division in the nation. Instead of pursuing the Democratic agenda where conservative politics have done well recently, the Clintons decided to take their progressive politics to a more welcoming environment. By moving to New York, a polarized political system became even more polarized. If her presidential ambitions are to be successful, the former first lady of a Southern state for twelve years will have to struggle to try to win at least one Southern state.

New York presented a different type of opportunity for Hillary Clinton. To represent one of the largest states in the nation and the economic center of Western capitalism was a much bigger prize than leading a nonprofit foundation or representing Arkansas. If she was going to take the political stage in her own right, she was going to do it in a very large way. Again the reasons for this move to New York directly relate back to her relationship with Bill Clinton. She had subjugated her ambitions and her career for him for more than twenty-five years. This was her turn. If she could win New York, she would immediately be an elected national political power. New York could obviously be a launching pad for presidential ambitions. Author Gail Sheehy believed that she was seeking redemption with her run for the U.S. Senate. Redemption from the health care-reform defeat; redemption for the Whitewater investigation; redemption for her husband's impeachment.[10]

Following George W. Bush's example in Texas, Hillary Clinton attempted to clear her own party's primary of any real opposition. The New York Senate seat was an attractive opportunity because New York rarely has an open Senate seat. Several well-known Democrats were supposedly considering the race. John F. Kennedy Jr. before his tragic airplane crash had even been mentioned as a possible candidate.[11] Yet, no one stepped forward because the rumblings of a Hillary Clinton candidacy had begun in late 1998.

New York Representative Nita Lowey had shown interest in the Senate seat. Lowey had represented New York for ten years and especially understood the issues of the struggling upstate economy. Lowey was a dedicated Democrat who could have run a credible race. Yet, she made it clear that she would not challenge Hillary Clinton if she got in the race. Lowey did not want to challenge "the most famous woman in America."[12] By June 1999, it was apparent that Hillary Clinton was going to run for the U.S. Senate. Lowey quickly withdrew consideration for her candidacy and endorsed Clinton. George W. Bush had put together a one-day primary for the governorship of

Texas; Hillary Clinton had done the same thing for the U.S. Senate race in New York—a state where she had never resided. The primary became a coronation.

Running from the White House gave Hillary Clinton huge advantages in the race. Most of her travel would be paid for by U.S. taxpayers. In her role as first lady she had access to military aircraft and Secret Service protection. This allowed her to travel quickly and without inconvenience. Even before her official announcement, Hillary Clinton made numerous trips to New York. In 1999, the Republican National Committee objected to her use of military aircraft to travel to New York. The White House suggested that the trips were not for her campaign but were part of her duties as first lady.[13] By March 2000, Mrs. Clinton's trips to New York cost nearly $200,000 by one congressional estimate. The campaign paid back a small fraction of the cost of the trips but approximately 80 percent of the costs were not reimbursed.[14]

The White House residence was also used as a meeting place for Mrs. Clinton's early strategy in the New York race. Carl McCall, the highest-ranking African-American elected official in the state, was granted a night in the Lincoln bedroom with his wife. A large group of New Yorkers came to visit the first lady in March 1999 at the White House including the head of the New York City's teachers union.[15]

The most obvious advantage that Hillary Clinton would enjoy would be accessing the Clintons' fund-raising network. In July 1999, a group of Hillary Clinton supporters put together a plan to raise $25 million for the New York Senate seat. She started off with $1000-a-head breakfast in New York City. In August 1999, an exclusive party in the Hamptons was planned with many A-list contributors. The famous dress designer Vera Wang also offered to have a brunch at her house.[16] A business executive supporting Hillary Clinton's senatorial bid put it like this, "the cult around her is Kennedy-like,... people can't do enough for her."[17] The state of New York provided a mix of the economic and the celebrity elite. The Clinton campaign would take advantage of both sectors.

At a party near the Democratic National Convention in Los Angeles, a star-packed gathering raised $1 million in one night for the First Lady's senatorial bid. The event included Cher singing to President Bill Clinton *If I Could Turn Back Time*. Brad Pitt, Jennifer Aniston, John Travolta, and Gregory Peck were also in attendance. Bill Clinton sang *Ain't No Mountain High Enough* with Diana Ross.[18] Nita Lowey was a dedicated representative from upstate New York who may have represented her state very well, but she would never get Brad Pitt and Jennifer Aniston to one of her fund-raisers. Moreover, helping to lead her fund-raising efforts was Terry McAullife, the experienced fund-raiser who helped Bill Clinton raise his campaign warchests. Al Gore called McAullife, "the greatest fundraiser in the history of the universe."[19]

The first lady could also call upon some of the best political strategists in the country. As noted above, Harold Ickes was a long-time political operative who was more dedicated to Mrs. Clinton than the president. Mandy Grunwald who handled press and public relations in the successful 1992 Clinton campaign also made her services available to the first lady. Her husband's strategic pollster Mark Penn signed on to help the first lady. James Carville, the hard-edged strategist also was available to Mrs. Clinton as an adviser.[20]

Most importantly she had the advice and full support of her husband, the president of the United States. In the 2000 election cycle, President Clinton offered advice numerous times to his wife and other candidates. He was known as "strategist in chief."[21] A Democratic senator put it simply, "the guy can't live without a campaign in his life."[22] Besides being a top fund-raiser, the president made personal calls on behalf of his wife seeking endorsements. He also advised the campaign about ads and helped with her speaking engagements. When she was about to announce her candidacy, President Clinton advised his wife on how to relate to voters. In an interview, Mrs. Clinton described one of these training sessions with her husband, "he's listened to me and he said, 'no, now don't do that. Do it like this.' For me, it was revelatory about how hard it was to step over the line to become the candidate. It's like I had watched my husband do surgery every day for years and then all of a sudden they hand you the scalpel...I really had my eyes opened as to how tough this is."[23]

Even though, he was the president of the United States at the time, Bill Clinton devoted time and energy to his wife's campaign.

When speaking of assisting both Vice President Al Gore and his wife Hillary Clinton with their campaigns in 2000, President Clinton remarked, "I owe them a great deal."[24] In regards to his wife, she probably could not have agreed more. During their volatile relationship, she had saved him politically numerous times; it was now time to make up for those past transgressions and advance his wife's career. Their mutual affection and his sense of obligation to her would make it a reality that President Clinton would be a dominating presence in his wife's political career. This presents potentially troubling consequences if Hillary Clinton ever wins the presidency.

Clinton versus Giuliani

The advantages that Hillary Clinton had in the U.S. Senate race did not mean that she was a sure winner. Although family legacies aid tremendously in American politics, they can also attract fierce resistance. For much of 1999 and at the beginning of 2000, Hillary Clinton's most likely opponent was going to be New York mayor Rudolph Giuliani. Giuliani was a moderate Republican and had become a popular but polarizing mayor of New York. He was a tough former federal prosecutor who led an effort to make the city of New York more livable. Even in a Democratic state such as New York, he would be a formidable opponent. In December 1999, Giuliani lashed out at the Clintons and other Democratic families such as the Kennedys and the Cuomos. Giuliani was upset that a local district attorney was investigating one of his top political advisors. Giuliani was also upset that Bill Clinton's federal housing secretary Andrew Cuomo, son of former governor Mario Cuomo, was blocking one of the city's efforts to deal with homelessness in New York City. Giuliani charged that his political aide was being investigated because "Mrs. Cuomo, Kennedy Cuomo was doing her thing last night, you have Bobby Kennedy now getting very active on the watershed. You have Andrew Cuomo trying to take funds away from the city...and they're all thinking about how they can help Al Gore or Hillary Clinton...it actually is silly."[25]

Also, a relative of the Bush family attacked the first lady's bid for the U.S. Senate. Jonathan Bush, the brother of George H. W. Bush and the uncle of George W. Bush predicted major problems for the Clinton campaign. Bush said that Clinton "will get very intense scrutiny when she's a candidate...and she will not pass the test...but she makes Geraldine Ferraro [former vice presidential candidate] look like the Virgin Mary."[26] He told the press, "you people will have a field day with Hillary Clinton. She's dead, I think."[27]

The chairman of the New York Republican Party was so incensed at the prospect of Hillary Clinton running for U.S. Senate from New York that he let off a brutal verbal attack. In an interview with reporter John Harris in July 2000, he called the first lady, "opportunistic, hypocritical and egotistical...cold blooded and hotheaded...brash, calculating and scheming...power hungry."[28] The chairman continued with his ire, and said "in a ruthless quest for power, she claims to be a 'New Democrat' but she's a fraud, a phony and a pretender...she's a hard-core, hard line, hard ultraliberal who uses people and hates

Republicans."²⁹ With emotions like these, her campaign experience would inevitably be difficult and controversial.

The Campaign

Hillary Clinton's campaign started with an important endorsement. The sitting senior Democratic senator from New York, Daniel Patrick Moynihan, stood next to Hillary Rodham Clinton and endorsed her candidacy for his seat. The Moynihans and the Clintons were not close. Hillary Clinton had attempted to bypass Moynihan's important Senate Finance Committee during her health-care reform efforts. Yet, six years later he would endorse her as a candidate for the U.S. Senate. At that point she had become the only viable Democratic candidate and he also wanted to see his seat in the hands of a prominent person. Moynihan was seen as one of the few Senate intellectuals, and his support of Clinton was critical in the early part of her campaign.³⁰

Clinton also did not want to be seen as a carpetbagger. Accordingly during the second half of 1999, she engaged in what she called a "listening tour" around New York state to learn about the issues in the state. This tour allowed her to campaign without really having to answer difficult questions about New York politics. The tour was a brilliant concept because it allowed the candidate to learn about the state without taking firm policy positions. She also traveled all over the state of New York to many parts that do not receive much political or media attention. Her travels to upstate New York contrasted nicely with the lack of attention Rudolph Giuliani was showing to other parts of New York outside the city.

With the successful launch of her campaign, two major incidents occurred in the fall of 1999 that almost derailed her whole campaign effort. Both of these incidents pitted the politics of a New York senatorial candidate versus the policies of her husband's administration. In August of 1999, President Clinton offered clemency to sixteen members of a Puerto Rican nationalist group. This group instigated a series of terrorist acts in the 1970s in New York to highlight the issue of Puerto Rican independence. The law enforcement community in New York thought the clemency was a terrible idea as some of the violent acts in the 1970s had killed citizens and injured police officers. The sixteen Puerto Ricans were not accused of taking part in the bombings but were part of the support network of the terrorist group. The Republicans charged that President Clinton was trying to gain favor for his wife with New York Puerto Rican voters. Hillary Clinton first supported the clemency, but three weeks later changed her mind and asked for the clemency to be removed.[31] With her change of mind, she simultaneously offended both law-enforcement officers in New York and New York's Latino community. The White House rejected any notion that the clemency offer was politically motivated, but the circumstances did not look good. This situation highlights a serious problem with having a sitting first lady running for a U.S. Senate seat. Does she carry political water for her husband or will she represent voters in New York?

In November 1999, in her role as first lady, Hillary Clinton took a trip to the Middle East. She visited both Israel and Palestine. At a day-care center in Ramallah, Palestine, Yasser Arafat's wife appeared with Mrs. Clinton. In Arabic, Arafat's wife charged that Israel was using poison gas on Palestinian children. When Mrs. Arafat was done with her speech, Mrs. Clinton kissed her on both cheeks. The kiss was seen as a sellout to Jewish voters in New York. Mrs. Clinton claimed that she did not understand the translation of Mrs. Arafat was saying. The visual was terrible for the Clinton campaign; the kiss indicated that Clinton supported the Palestinian position.[32] The Jewish vote was crucial in New York City. Again the situation shows the conflict between her duties as Bill Clinton's wife and her duties as a potential New York senator. First ladies have to be diplomatic in all situations; senators do not. This question of how Mrs. Clinton was going to balance her strong political partnership with her husband against her own judgment and against the needs of her constituents is an important one. It will be a question that will also follow her during her presidential campaign.

Fortunately for Mrs. Clinton, her Republican opponent Rudy Giuliani was struggling with his own issues during the 2000 campaign. He was not as active a campaigner as Hillary Clinton. Even though upstate New York had been traditionally Republican, Mrs. Clinton put forth an aggressive effort to get some of these voters. Giuliani did not match this effort. The mayor was concerned with both personal and mayoral issues in New York City. In March 2000, an African-American man was shot and killed by an undercover New York City Police Department (NYPD) officer. The man apparently had no drugs or weapons in his possession. The black community in New York was outraged and called for an investigation. Giuliani who had been an outspoken advocate of the NYPD during his time as mayor ordered that the juvenile arrest records of the dead man be released. Giuliani said the victim had a "pattern of behavior" that led to the shooting.[33] The mayor seemed to be convicting the dead man because of his past behavior. Hillary Clinton criticized Giuliani by charging that he was "dividing the city."[34] The case was a turning point in the campaign and gave Hillary Clinton her first lead in the polls.

Later that spring, Giuliani also revealed to the public his many personal challenges. In April 2000, he told a New York press conference that he had prostate cancer and that he was unsure whether he would continue the campaign.[35] He talked openly about the disease and his treatment options.

Giuliani was praised for his openness and courage facing the disease. Yet just when most of the public was rallying to his side because of his cancer, Giuliani exposed another personal bombshell. A New York newspaper reporter happened to view a late-night dinner in a public restaurant between Rudolph Giuliani and a woman who was not his wife. When asked about the woman, Rudolph Giuliani responded that she is "a friend, a very good friend."[36] A couple days later, Giuliani told a shocked roomful of reporters that he and his wife Donna Hanover lead "separate lives." He also said he hoped to put together an arrangement that would be good for his estranged wife and their children.[37] The problem for Mayor Giuliani was that while he was telling the nation about his separation from his wife, he had failed to inform his own wife that they were separated. Mrs. Giuliani (Donna Hanover) appeared hours later in front of the mayor's mansion in New York and charged that her husband had a relationship with one of his staff members.[38] Giuliani's marriage was literally breaking apart in front of reporters and TV viewers. Giuliani moved out of the mayor's mansion soon after and his wife stayed in the mansion.

For Mrs. Clinton who had suffered the humiliation of the Monica Lewinsky scandal, the irony of having a political opponent with marital problems was obvious. Giuliani could not take the moral high road with Mrs. Clinton as his marriage was falling apart. Later in the month, Giuliani citing health concerns withdrew from the Senate race. Because of a weird set of circumstances, Hillary Clinton was now the favorite to become the U.S. senator from New York. Giuliani would recover and become a national hero during the aftermath of 9/11. The 2008 presidential election almost became a rematch between these two political titans. In the 2000 campaign, Hillary Clinton's campaign was more disciplined than the mayor's campaign, but Giuliani clearly had more passion and charisma.

The Giuliani departure did not mean that Hillary Clinton would not be challenged in the general election. A young congressman from Long Island, Rick Lazio, would put together a credible campaign.

Yet, the Clinton campaign would deftly use the advantages of running as a well-known first lady.

Her husband appeared with her several times during the campaign and watched her get nominated at the New York Democratic Convention. Her campaign worked with Vice President Al Gore's presidential campaign to put together a coordinated effort in New York. New York's Democratic leanings on the presidential level would help Hillary Clinton in her Senate bid.

The most important event in the general election campaign came in September 2000 during a debate between Clinton and Lazio. NBC's Tim Russert served as moderator. Russert asked Mrs. Clinton whether she would apologize for "misleading the American people" when she denied on the *Today* show in 1998 that her husband was having an affair with Monica Lewinsky. Clinton calmly answered "I didn't mislead anyone. I didn't know the truth..., my husband made it clear that he did mislead the country as well as his family."[39] Even in her Senate race, Hillary Clinton had to deal with the political implications of her marriage. She was able to keep her composure in the debate. Shortly after the first debate, the Whitewater Independent Counsel announced that there was not enough evidence to charge either Bill or Hillary Clinton with any crimes connected to their Arkansas business dealings. In the space of a week during the New York campaign, she had put behind her, for a short time, both personal and political baggage.

Senator Clinton

With the help of the presidential race at the top of the ticket, Hillary Clinton would go on to a landslide win in the New York Senate race. She beat her opponent by 12 percentage points. By any measure it was an impressive victory. Her friend and minister, Don Jones, summed up the meaning of her victory. It was "vindication."[40] Vindication for all that she had been through and vindication for the Clinton family. Because of her victory and the loss of the Gore-Lieberman presidential ticket, the Clintons would remain the most important Democratic family in the nation. Even with all the personal strife, the Clinton marriage had endured, and she acknowledged Bill Clinton's importance in her political life, "I would not have been standing there without the support and work of my husband."[41]

Hillary Clinton would attempt to establish her own dignified and understated Senate career. She knew that she could not appear as a celebrity Senator and gain the trust of her Senate colleagues. She would attempt to be as low key as possible in an attempt to be just an ordinary Senator. Yet a series of events would occur that would inexorably tie her Senate career to her husband's past actions as president. She agreed to a book contract with a major publisher for over $8 million. She signed the book contract before she was sworn in as Senator because Senate rules would not allow such lucrative deals. As her family was leaving the White House, they took a long list of furniture and gifts with them. The Clintons argued that this was the normal procedure but the impression it left some voters with was that they were raiding the White House before leaving.[42]

After she was sworn in as a Senator, two major pardon scandals erupted. An explicit power granted the president by the Constitution is the power to pardon those with criminal offenses. A couple of weeks after she was sworn in, Hillary Clinton had to answer press questions about pardons her husband had granted four Hasidic Jews from New York before he left office. These Orthodox Jews were from an area called New Square in New York. New Square is a tight Jewish community that usually votes in a bloc, and Hillary Clinton won the votes of nearly everyone in that particular Jewish community. The Hasidic Jews who were pardoned had been convicted of stealing millions of dollars from the government.[43] These suspicious pardons also became public at the same time the news broke that Hillary Clinton's brother Hugh Rodham was paid $400,000 to lobby for presidential pardons. The New York Attorney's Office was investigating these issues along with another controversial pardon granted by President Clinton to fugitive Marc Rich. When asked about her involvement in the pardon of the Hasidic Jews, she said that she had sat in on a meeting at the White House concerning the pardons but she did not offer an opinion.[44]

All these incidents drew widespread publicity and hurt Senator Clinton's reputation. She eventually was cleared of criminal wrongdoing, but just as she was attempting to establish her own career as an elected official, the actions of her husband and her brother reminded voters of the scandal-plagued Clinton years in the White House. She was accused of making a "sloppy exit" from the White House.[45] She had moved to another state and won a seat in another branch of government, but she still could not escape her husband. The promise of the Clintons always seems to be accompanied by questionable judgment and political scandal.

Because of these early problems, Hillary Clinton drew low poll ratings in New York. Yet she worked to become a decent colleague in the Senate in the spring of 2001. She said she wanted to be a "workhorse" not a "showhorse."[46] Fellow senators complemented the way in which she did not seek special treatment as well as her ability to be prepared. She concentrated mostly on local noncontroversial issues such as an economic package for upstate New York. She worked to slowly rebuild her political profile to New York citizens.

Hillary Clinton also had to consistently tamp down speculation that she would run for president in 2004. In April 2001, she denied a report that she was thinking about running for president. She remarked that she was going to be "the best senator I can be."[47] She worked with other senior senators to understand the institution and attempt to get funds for New York. In particular, she had a close working relationship with Senator Robert Byrd of West Virginia who was the senior Democrat on the Senate Appropriations Committee.[48]

September 11th

The terrorist attacks of September 11, 2001 challenged both the economic and political system in the United States. Yet these attacks would be especially difficult for a senator from New York. Her own daughter was in the city during the day of the attacks and she now had to help secure funding to help New Yorkers begin to recover. A week and a half after the attacks, President Bush hosted both Senator Hillary Clinton and her New York colleague Senator Chuck Schumer. When the senators brought up the request for aid, George W. Bush replied, "I'm with ya."[49] Bush also assured the New York senators that he would seek retribution for the attacks. "When I take action, I'm not going to fire a $2 million missile at a $10 empty tent and hit a camel in the butt. It's going to be decisive."[50]

Hillary Clinton worked with George W. Bush during the days after the terror attacks. By December 2001, she and Senator Schumer had secured billions of dollars in recovery relief for New York. Yet even in this time of political cooperation and reconciliation, she still had to defend the past policies of the Clinton administration. Four days after September 11, Senator Clinton commented on a plot to kill Osama bin Laden during the last hours of her husband's presidency. She said the plot had failed because the intelligence was not solid.[51] Facing criticism for doing little to combat terrorism, both Clintons wanted to make it very clear that they had taken the terrorist threat seriously. Yet critics of the Clinton were not mollified by these assertions.

From First Lady to President? 167

Her Most Important Vote

Her judgment on foreign policy would be severely tested in the fall of 2002. As examined in chapter 6, President George W. Bush had used his political strength coming from the September 11th attacks to advocate a more aggressive foreign policy. This new foreign policy included the doctrine of preemption—the idea that United States would act against potential threats before they could materialize. This was a significant departure in national security policymaking in the United States. Hillary Clinton's decision making involving her vote on the Iraq War is important to examine for several reasons.

First, her war vote was her most important vote as a Senator. The decision to give the president authority to use military action is obviously one of the most solemn responsibilities that a member of the legislature can have. Second, the decision to go to war in Iraq was a radical shift in how the United States had previously engaged the rest of the world. A war in Iraq could have major policy consequences for the next thirty years.

Third, the influence of Bill Clinton in Hillary Clinton's vote for authorization of the war is important as well. Before the second Bush administration, Bill Clinton had worked continuously to moderate the image of Democrats. Since the Vietnam War the Democratic Party was viewed by too many voters as being weak on national defense. As part of being a "new Democrat," Bill Clinton wanted to appear as tough on foreign policy as his Republican counterparts. Some Democrats who had voted against the First Gulf War in 1991 felt their vote against the war had cost them politically. In 2002, only a year after the 9/11 attacks, it would be difficult for Democratic senators to vote against the second Iraq War. Even though Iraq had no connection to the September 11th attacks, ambitious Democrats did not want to appear to be soft on national defense. Most of the Democratic senators who were potential presidential candidates in 2004 including future vice presidential candidate John Edwards would vote for the authorization. The political pressure to vote with the president was so intense in 2002 that Democratic senator Max Cleland of Georgia later admitted he voted for the authorization for war with Iraq even though he had serious misgivings about the war. Cleland was involved in a close reelection race. In the race, he was being accused of being soft on terrorism.[52] Cleland voted for the war but would lose his reelection anyway.

Senator Clinton's decision making in this crucial hour may provide some guidance in how she would act as president. She heavily relied on her husband during this critical juncture. He was seen as her "main counsel on the Iraq War vote."[53] Her husband was generally aligned with his "party's hawks, endorsing the move to disarm Iraq while promoting the need for more skillful diplomacy along the way."[54] Bill Clinton attempted to appease both sides of the war debate. Thus Hillary Clinton also attempted to find some middle ground between the Left of the Democratic Party and George W. Bush. If Bill Clinton exercised this type of influence in a Hillary Clinton presidency, the Clintons would return to a copresidency status.

Bill Clinton's impact on Hillary's Clinton thinking was evident in her public statements about the war. When asked in September 2002 (one month before the vote) her view on a potential war with Iraq, Mrs. Clinton made it clear that she would support President Bush, "if I was convinced it's the right thing, we're going to do it and I would have no problem with that at all...I think the world knows that we all know, which is that the Congress is going to give this President this authority."[55]

Only a month after her voting to give the president authority to go to war, Senator Clinton then criticized the president. In an interview in front of a group of college students in November 2002, Senator Clinton said President Bush seemed to be anxious to go to war. "To talk all the time like you're inviting war, anxious to go to war, does a great disservice to the country."[56] She also suggested that some in the Bush administration were trying to finish the work of George W. Bush's father, "a lot of people have old scores to settle" she told Chris Matthews of the TV show *Hardball*.[57]

Yet, her attempts to both support and criticize the war at the same time shifted again in early 2003. Her criticism of the president was generally muted in the two months before the war began. She did not berate President Bush for failing to get a second UN resolution that would support U.S. action in Iraq. Three days before the start of the war, Senator Clinton told reporters that she hoped President Bush would get more international support, but she said "I don't think it's useful now to go back and Monday morning quarterback."[58] She did not want to jeopardize her political position at the time. In late 2002, Gallup Poll released its annual list of the most admired men and women come on Americans. Strangely, George W. Bush was listed as the most admired man in the nation and Hillary Clinton was the most admired woman.[59] To launch her own presidential bid four years later, Hillary Clinton would make criticism of the Iraq War a central part of her campaign. The middle ground had evaporated.

The Clintons Next Turn

After the initial success of the Iraqi invasion in March and April 2003, the political circumstances began to shift against President George W. Bush. He was still an incumbent president who had seen the nation through a terrible tragedy, but as the Iraq occupation dragged on, his approval ratings began to fall. Democrats began looking for a credible candidate to take on Mr. Bush in his reelection in 2004. As the most famous Democratic senator, attention turned to Hillary Clinton. A reporter discovered that Hillary Clinton's pollster had actually been researching the viability of her running in 2004.[60] As the year 2003 went on, Hillary Clinton increased her criticism of President Bush. She called President Bush's administration "radical" because the administration was trying to destroy the "central pillars of progress in our country during the twentieth century."[61] Yet, she decided against running in 2004. She knew better than anyone the difficulties of running against an incumbent president.

John Kerry's failed presidential bid in 2004 would have important effects on Hillary Clinton's political future. Kerry had voted for the Iraq War authorization, but in 2004 he also voted against funding the Iraq War. The Bush campaign skillfully painted Kerry as indecisive and weak. Kerry's infamous comment that he had voted for the funding for the war before he voted against it essentially ceded the Iraqi issue to the Republicans in the campaign of 2004.[62] The public had not completely turned against the Iraq War at this point, and the Bush campaign was able to cast the incumbent president as a protector of the American people. Democrats had been beaten on national security issues once again. The close election of 2004 was little consolation to the Democratic critics of the Bush administration; they were ready for change.

After the 2004 election, Hillary Clinton in effect became the leader of the Democratic opposition. The 2004 election had not brought many Democratic leaders to the forefront. She was the most obvious person to lead the Democrats into the next presidential election four years later. She had helped establish a Democratic think-tank in Washington to combat conservative critics and Internet bloggers. Her home in Washington also became one of the best places to raise money for Democratic candidates.[63] During the 2004 and 2006 elections, she traveled extensively campaigning for Democratic candidates and gaining their loyalty.

Most importantly, she was the wife of the first Democratic president to win two terms since Franklin Delano Roosevelt. After their messy exit from the White House in 2001, Bill Clinton's popularity and status had increased again dramatically by 2004. The Clintons' pollster Mark Penn commented on Bill Clinton that "he almost always rises back up to the surface even if events seem to beat him down for awhile.... and he's become less of a polarizing figure, more of a uniting figure."[64] Moreover, as the troubles of the second Bush administration continued to mount, Bill Clinton's presidency looked better and better to some voters. Bill Clinton would be vital to Hillary Clinton's presidential hopes. He would be her chief fund-raiser, strategist, and policy adviser.

Unlike her Senate bid in the year 2000, there was no real question about whether she would run for president in 2008. She first had to win her own Senate reelection in 2006; the Senate campaign would act as a dry run for her presidential race. Just as George W. Bush had accomplished in his own gubernatorial reelection in 1998, Hillary Clinton essentially cleared the field of any real opponents in her 2006 Senate race. One of her early Republican opponents, Jeanne Pirro, a district attorney for Westchester County in New York withdrew from the race after a series of campaign problems. One of her problems was the publicity her husband Albert Pirro received from the tabloid press in New York. Albert Pirro had served prison time and also fathered an illegitimate child.[65] The Clintons marriage looked good in comparison.

The mayor of Yonkers, New York ended up being the Republican nominee for U.S. Senate. He had difficulties raising money, and he could not contend with the name recognition of Hillary Clinton in the Democratic-leaning state. Hillary Clinton would win a landslide victory in Senate race in 2006 and have $14 million left over to contribute to her own presidential bid.

Her position was so strong in the Democratic Party by the fall of 2006 that a potentially dangerous rival for the Democratic nomination in 2008 had dropped out. Mark Warner, former governor of Virginia, decided not to challenge for the nomination. He had a successful term as governor of Virginia and was well liked by moderates in the Democratic Party. Yet, he did not want to endure the grind of a presidential campaign.[66]

The circumstances seemed to be favoring Senator Clinton's bid for the nomination. The Democratic nomination was open because John Kerry had failed to beat an incumbent president with low approval ratings in 2004. She and her husband had recovered from numerous scandals and a difficult exit from the White House in 2001. The Clintons once the ultimate outsiders in the Democratic Party were now the party establishment. Endorsements, fund-raising, and organization would all be strengths of a Hillary Clinton candidacy. It seemed to be her time.

Even with all of these advantages, a major challenge would emerge to threaten Hillary Clinton's candidacy for the Democratic nomination: fellow Democratic senator Barack Obama. As of the writing, the outcome of the 2008 campaign is unknown, but examining the impact the Barack Obama candidacy had on Hillary Clinton's campaign reveals how important Bill Clinton would be in Hillary Clinton's campaign and potential administration.

Barack Obama signaled his intention to run for president in late 2006. His entry into the race completely juggled the Democratic field. Several senators and governors were putting together campaigns to challenge Hillary Clinton for the nomination. Yet, by late 2006, no other candidate received the attention and excitement that Barack Obama brought to the Democratic race. Obama, a forty-five-year-old African-American senator from Illinois, had wowed the 2004 Democratic Convention with a speech about national unity. After his win in Illinois in the 2004 Senate race, he served two years in the U.S. Senate. He decided that the Democratic field needed him in the race because people were tired of "slash and burn, highly ideological politics that bogged us down over the last several decades."[67] His message was obvious; the Democratic Party and the country needed to move beyond the Clintons. The success of his campaign in the Iowa caucuses showed the power of his anti-Clinton argument.

He also had two other important advantages in comparison with Hillary Clinton. Although he was not in the U.S. Senate at the time, he was publicly on record as opposing the Iraq War from the beginning. In the early stages of the 2008 campaign, the Iraq War was the most important issue to Democratic primary voters. Obama stood out from other major Democratic contenders because he had opposed the war from the beginning. Among Democratic activists, this would be a real advantage.[68]

He also was seen as a "warm campaigner" who attracted large crowds and much enthusiasm.[69] He was attracting a tremendous amount of media coverage and interest from political observers around the country. President George W. Bush's media adviser, Mark McKinnon, called Obama, "the most interesting person to appear on the political radar screen in decades. He's a walking, talking hope machine and he may reshape American politics."[70]

The emergence of Obama forced Hillary Clinton to begin her campaign in early 2007. The Clinton campaign knew Senator Obama was a serious threat to win the nomination. After Obama held a

Hollywood fund-raiser in mid-February, a former Clinton supporter David Geffen told Maureen Dowd of the *New York Times* that he was supporting Obama because he was "inspirational and he was not from the Bush royal family or the Clinton royal family."[71] Geffen went on to say that the Clintons were liars. The Hollywood producer had hit a nerve. A former supporter of her husband's was claiming that the only reason Hillary Clinton was a leading candidate was because of her family legacy and her dishonesty.

Soon after the interview was published, the Clinton campaign released a statement that attacked both Geffen and Obama. During the two weeks after the statement was released, Hillary Clinton's ratings among African-Americans plummeted.[72] The attack on the Obama campaign backfired badly.

Initially, Bill Clinton's role in his wife's campaign had been mostly behind-the-scenes. This changed dramatically after the threat from Barack Obama appeared. Bill Clinton made numerous calls to Democratic allies in important primary states to get support for his wife. South Carolina State senator Darrell Jackson said he was supporting Hillary Clinton because he got a personal phone call from Bill Clinton. The African-American senator stated, "they made somebody like me feel real honored."[73] Jackson decided that Hillary Clinton's time in the White House as first lady was an important reason for his support, "the vast difference between Hillary Clinton and Obama is that she has the Rolodex and she doesn't need a tour of the White House."[74] The Clinton campaign was not going to run from Bill Clinton, they were going to embrace him. Hillary Clinton would run on her credentials and her experience; and the core of that experience was being Bill Clinton's wife as first lady.

Hillary Clinton also emphasized how important her husband is to her and her future administration. A week after the Barack Obama controversy had occurred, she told an audience in San Francisco that Bill Clinton would be used as a diplomat around the world. She called her husband "the most popular person in the world right now."[75] Her campaign also distributed talking points to supporters so they could answer criticisms about the Clintons attempt to win a second presidency within the family. The memo was written in a question and answer format. One of the questions was: how do you combat "Clinton fatigue for those who say they don't want the drama of the Clintons again?" The answer on the memo stated "a lot of Americans will gladly take eight great years of economic prosperity and peace that the Clinton administration delivered…we can do this again with experienced leaders like Hillary at the helm."[76]

To shield his wife from criticism, Bill Clinton publicly stated in March 2007 that Senator Obama and Hillary Clinton had similar voting records concerning the Iraq War. In a conference call, Bill Clinton stated, "the dichotomy that has been set up to allow him to become the raging hero of the antiwar crowd is factually inaccurate."[77]

When challenged by Senator Obama, Hillary Clinton's campaign fought back with the message that she was the more experienced candidate and she was the candidate closest to Bill Clinton. Most of that experience would come through being the wife of Bill Clinton. "Two for the price of one" from Bill Clinton's campaign in 1992 was back as a campaign strategy.[78] With her husband helping to lead the counterattack, Hillary Clinton regained her status as the front-runner as of June 2007. After her stunning defeat in the Iowa Democratic caucuses, the campaign again turned to her husband to help her in the state of New Hampshire. If she ultimately loses the nomination, Democratic voters would have rejected the idea of multiple Clinton presidencies and the continuation of the Clinton saga.

Why Not Two Clinton Presidencies?

As of this writing, the consequences of a possible Hillary Clinton presidency are unknown. Yet the potential problems that another Clinton presidency may present can be discussed. With a son of a former president in the White House having numerous difficulties in his second term, and the wife of a former president seeking the office, these issues are relevant and important. This book has two central tenets. Multiple family presidencies are not democratic and run against the ideals of the founders. Second, the pressures of following a close relative into the White House combined with the inherent expectations of the office do not serve the nation or the presidency well because personal relationships end up impacting public policy. A potential Hillary Clinton presidency would again highlight these two basic themes.

Hillary Clinton's Presidency Would Be Undemocratic

As a former first lady, Hillary Clinton has enormous advantages in running for president. Senator Barack Obama may overtake her, but they will be taking on an experienced and tested political organization known as the Clintons. Moreover, if Hillary Clinton does not win the presidency in 2008, she likely still would be considered for future Democratic presidential nominations. The impact of her presidential campaign on American democracy is troubling. Just like George W. Bush, she has used her family connections to put together a tremendous campaign infrastructure. By some estimates her campaign raised $125 million dollars *before* the primaries and caucuses began in January 2008.[79] Besides Senator Obama, these totals should dwarf all the other candidates. All presidential candidates have to raise money, but it is so much easier for candidates with family connections.

What she cannot secure through money, she will get through endorsements. Just as George H.W. Bush did for his son, Bill Clinton has made hundreds of calls around the country asking directly for Democrats to support his wife. It is difficult for a governor, mayor, or a city council member to say no to a former president of the United States.

On the day she announced her run for president in January 2007, her campaign organization already had approximately 200 political professionals working for her; this number includes her Senate staff. From these professionals, she has demanded and received both discipline and loyalty. They are ready to respond to attacks, stroke potential donors, and organize her appearances all on a moment's notice.[80]

As mentioned in chapter 2, if she succeeds in winning the nomination and general election in 2008, a new era of American presidential dynasties would be born. A typical American college graduate in the year 2012 would have never seen a sitting president who was not named Bush or Clinton. For the birthplace of modern constitutional democracy, this presidential handoff between families is troubling. Moreover, it would hypocritical for President Hillary Clinton to preach to other nations about the sanctity of democracy when it takes a family political machine to win presidential elections in the United States.

Her successful candidacy would bring a woman into the presidency for first time in the nation's history. This circumstance is not inconsequential. Women were the last Americans to gain their full right to vote, and a woman becoming president should be a hallmark moment in American democracy. Yet having a former first lady as the first woman president diminishes that achievement. The first women president should not be elected because she was a wife of a former president. She should be elected because the nation views her as a leader in her own right. Both the Democratic and Republican parties now have dozens of women elected as representatives in Congress or as governors in the states. Hillary Clinton is not the only smart woman in American politics. For example, Democratic senator Dianne Feinstein of California has had a distinguished career both as a mayor and a senator. She had much more experience as an elected official than either Hillary Clinton or George W. Bush before they ran for President. Why does Hillary Clinton move ahead of a distinguished senator such as Dianne Feinstein who represents the largest state in the nation? The answer seems to be because she was married to Bill Clinton.

Bill Clinton Would Have a Powerful But Undefined Role

An important question for a Hillary Clinton presidency is what role her husband would serve in her administration? In the early part of her presidential campaign in 2007, she said she would use Bill Clinton as a "roaming ambassador" to the world. His job would be to help improve the United States' international reputation.[81] In order to bypass nepotism regulations, Hillary Clinton said she would not give a formal appointment to her husband, but she has made it clear that he would be an important part of her administration.

This response is strikingly familiar and problematic. In 1993, Bill Clinton did not give his wife a formal appointment in his administration, but as noted in chapter 5, she actually became the leader of domestic policy in the White House for much of Mr. Clinton's first term. Presidential advisors had to report to *both* Clintons on certain issues. As a roaming ambassador, Bill Clinton would not have been elected by the American people or confirmed by the U.S. Senate. Would the chaos that occurred in the first two years of the Clinton administration return, when White House aides sometimes were not sure who was really in charge?

Moreover, what happens when the Clintons publicly disagree during a Hillary Clinton presidency? Who would make the final decisions? Would government officials know which Clinton to obey? The Clintons' public disagreements have occurred before during Bill Clinton's presidency. During the health-care reform effort in 1993 and 1994, President Bill Clinton publicly stated that mandatory health insurance coverage for everyone was important but not necessary to pass health-care reform legislation. This removal of mandatory health-care coverage was in direct conflict with the first lady's policy.[82] The first lady who had been chosen by her husband to lead the health-care reform effort forced the president to restate his position that supported her ideas.

Moreover, as noted earlier in the chapter, during the first lady's senatorial run in 1999, she first stated her support for her husband's decision to give clemency to sixteen members of a Puerto Rican nationalist group. After loud criticism from New York's law-enforcement community, she retracted her support three weeks later.

What if a similar policy dispute occurred during one of Bill Clinton's overseas trips during a Hillary Clinton presidency? It is one circumstance to offer conflicting messages to Congress during a domestic-policy dispute, it is quite another circumstance for a presidential spouse to be on a foreign-policy trip and give the wrong message to friends or foes. How would foreign governments react to such a dispute? Would they believe "the most popular person in the world" Bill Clinton or would they follow the words of the president of the United States Hillary Clinton? The military and diplomatic consequences could be severe.

The Clintons' Marriage Could Become a Major Issue Again

As of this writing, the Clintons' marriage remains tightly linked to their political life. Critics of the Clintons' claim that their marriage is simply a political arrangement. Supporters of the Clintons and most of their biographers see the marriage as a volatile but enduring union of love and ambition. The exact nature of their private marital relationship really should not be of consequence as long as it would not impact Hillary Clinton's presidential duties. Numerous presidents including Franklin Roosevelt and John Kennedy did not have close marriages and still performed their duties well. Yet, because of their tumultuous history and the fact that Bill Clinton was impeached because he lied about a sexual affair, their marital relationship must be considered when evaluating a potential Hillary Clinton presidency. With the attention of the media and their political opponents always upon them, both Hillary and Bill Clinton must know that their marital behavior will be examined intensely. Common sense would suggest that no president or presidential spouse would engage an adulterous behavior during their presidency under the glare of the modern press corps. Yet the same argument was made about Bill Clinton before he admitted to his affair with Monica Lewinsky during his presidency.

Since the rumors of other relationships have been a central reality of their marriage, it would be naïve to imagine that these rumors would not persist into a Hillary Clinton presidency. But after the public humiliation of the Monica Lewinsky affair and his recovery from heart surgery in 2004, Bill Clinton would appear to be more chastened about his private conduct. Yet because of his history, every move that he makes and every time he is in a public place with another woman, media speculation would begin on the state of their marriage. With Mr. Clinton traveling the world as a roaming ambassador, he would have numerous opportunities to be in situations that could be misunderstood. The Clinton marriage cannot be a major distraction in another Clinton presidency. With terrorism, Iraq, a Middle East crisis, and other major issues, the nation's attention cannot afford another diversion.

Hillary Clinton's Experience and Competence

The cornerstone of a Hillary Clinton campaign and presidency rests upon her competence and experience in the public arena. Clearly, Hillary Clinton understands political campaigning and partisan politics. She has been a tough and loyal partner in her husband's political career. Her concern for children's issues and other social causes is genuine, and she earned favorable reviews as a senator. Yet, her experience and competence may be overstated. She has never had to manage a large organization. After her move to Arkansas in the 1970s, she became a law professor and a partner in the Rose Law firm. During her time at the Rose Law firm, the firm's reputation suffered greatly under the weight of investigations and indictments. As first lady of Arkansas, she was successful in getting education reforms passed through the legislature, but she did not have to implement these changes. When she asserted herself as a copresident at the beginning of the Clinton presidency, the results were disastrous. The first two years of the Clinton presidency were chaotic and unorganized. Her major piece of legislation, the health-care reform effort, did not make it to the floor of Congress even though Democrats controlled both chambers.

As a senator, she has found success by acting like a typical member of Congress; she attempts to get as much money and support for her home state as possible. She has been an effective but cautious Senator.[83] Yet this parochial legislative experience may not translate well into executive experience. For example, Edward Kennedy, the heir to the Kennedy political mantle, found out that he was a much better legislator than potential president. Moreover, regarding her most important vote as a member of Congress, the Iraq War vote, she now regrets her decision to give authorization for President Bush to go to war. She has only two more years of experience as an elected official than George W. Bush who has been criticized for his brief political resume when he ran for the presidency.

In essence, the experience that Hillary Clinton's campaign highlights is directly related back to her role as political partner and wife to Bill Clinton. This same argument was made for George W. Bush. Although George W. Bush was inexperienced, he could have both his father's counsel and previous advisors to make up for this inexperience. This argument has collapsed as George W. Bush's presidency has continued. Apparently, Bush's father will not offer advice unless asked, and the advisors his father recommended to his son have argued amongst themselves and not served the president well. Presidential experience is not something that can be transferred by simply being in the presence of a president. The Clintons have had their presidency; the Twenty-Second Amendment was put in place to limit individuals from occupying the presidency for more than two terms. Although Hillary Clinton's candidacy does not violate the legal provisions of the Twenty-Second Amendment, her candidacy does subvert the intent of the amendment if her husband is going to be a major force in her administration.

Chapter Eight

The Prince in Waiting

"Dynasty shmnasty."

—Jeb Bush in 2000.[1]

Then governor of Florida Jeb Bush recited these words when asked by a reporter about the Bushes' rise to power in American politics. The second Bush son rejected the idea that his family had engineered some type of plan to take over American politics. Prescott, George H. W., George W., and Jeb had all won tough elections and Jeb Bush did not want their accomplishments diminished by the insinuation that only their name had carried them to political victory.

After the controversial presidential election of 2000, Jeb Bush would find himself in a place where no other American had ever been. He was the governor of the fourth largest state in the country, but he was also known as both a son of a former president and a brother of the sitting president. This unique history would inevitably bring questions about Jeb Bush's political future. He may not have believed in the concept of family dynasties, but his family had put together the most successful political family dynasty in American history.

Before examining Jeb Bush's political career, it is important to ask for the purposes of this book, would Jeb Bush actually run for president? Again the focus of this book is not on political families, it is on *presidential* families. As of this writing, his brother George W. Bush is struggling at the end of his second term. In June 2007, President George W. Bush's approval ratings reached a low of 29 percent.[2] As noted in chapter 6, he has become one of the most divisive presidents in modern American history.[3] Although criticisms from Democrats and the political Left in the nation have been constant and expected, Republicans have also severely criticized President George W. Bush.[4]

A noted historian and vocal Bush critic, Sean Willentz, has advanced the argument that he is "the worst president in American history."[5] Approval ratings can fluctuate and observers often change their views so the president may recover some political ground before the end of his term. The U.S. military surge in Iraq in 2007 has been able to diminish the violence in the country. Yet unless the situation in Iraq greatly improves, President George W. Bush's presidency likely will be viewed as a failure.

Given these conditions, is it possible that another Bush brother would attempt a run at the presidency? Jeb Bush has clearly stated his intentions for 2008. He will not be a candidate for president.[6] Yet even with the current dismal prospects of the George W. Bush presidency, Jeb Bush may be considered as a vice presidential candidate in 2008 (depending upon the Republican presidential nominee). More importantly, he would be given wide consideration as a candidate for president in 2012 or 2016 if he decided to pursue his family legacy.

How could another Bush even consider running for the presidency when voters may be having Bush fatigue? The possibility of Jeb Bush emerging on the national stage illustrates the enduring power of family political legacies in modern American politics. If Hillary Clinton or Barack Obama wins the White House in 2008, Republicans around the country would soon turn to a popular conservative ex-governor of the Florida to consider challenging the Democratic incumbent.

Why would Jeb Bush even be considered for the presidency after two difficult Bush presidencies? First, he left the governor's office in Florida after two successful terms in office. Florida represents a microcosm of the nation's demographics. The northern part of the state is Southern conservative. The central and southeastern parts of the state have large Latino populations. The southwestern part of the state is home to conservative migrants from the Midwestern United States. African-Americans are prominently represented in the large cities in the state and several rural counties. Senior citizens make up a critical voting group in the state's politics, and Florida also continues to grow with younger migrants coming from other parts of the United States. With these political demographics, Jeb Bush governed very conservatively but also was elected by wide margins. If he were to run for president, the state of Florida would be a foundation of both his primary and general election strategy.

Florida is also one of the most critical states for political fundraising.[7] In 1980s, Jeb Bush served as chair of the Dade Republican Party in Miami. He built up a fund-raising structure for his party in Southern Florida and has expanded his financial base to all parts of Florida especially the conservative North. He could combine his Florida network with a national network created by his brother and father. As almost all viable presidential candidates now forgo public financing, the ability to raise funds is obviously critical for presidential candidates.

With both his state contacts and family contacts, Jeb Bush would immediately be one of the strongest fund-raisers in any presidential field.

For Republicans who are looking for a true conservative, Jeb Bush has the credentials after eight years as governor of Florida. During his two terms in office, he was a political force in Florida State government. He led the efforts to pass tax cuts, provide private school vouchers for the families of public schoolchildren, ban most affirmative action programs, and to privatize a new significant portion of Florida State government.

He also has the unique ability to combine both economic conservatives and religious conservatives in the Republican Party—something that the 2008 Republican presidential candidates have been unable to do. He consistently has made it known that his religion is important in his life and his decision making. He is staunchly pro-life on the abortion issue. As governor of Florida, he approved legislation that banned partial-birth abortions. He advocated a widespread expansion of "faith-based" programs included faith-based prisons and faith-based child care.[8] He also helped to lead the effort to pass a law to force medical authorities to reinsert a feeding tube for Terri Schiavo, a woman who had been in a long-term vegetative state. Her cause had been adopted by religious conservative groups who claimed that her husband Michael Schiavo was trying to kill her by ordering the feeding tube removed. The president of the Florida Right to Life organization said this about Jeb Bush, "we have been so well-served by the governor for our agenda."[9]

Moreover, he could engage in an historical outreach to Latino voters across the nation. His wife Columba is a native of Mexico. Jeb Bush once worked in Venezuela. He and all of the members in his immediate family speak fluent Spanish. He also has long-term ties to the Cuban community in Miami. Depending upon the outcome of the immigration reform debate, by 2012 or 2016, Republicans may be looking for a candidate who could expand their voting base. Jeb Bush could provide this opportunity.

Moreover, recent family dynasties have shown an incredible ability for political comebacks. After his father's crushing loss in 1992, few political observers could have imagined that his son would win the presidency eight years later. In 2000, after two terms of Bill Clinton and his family drama that led to his impeachment, having another Clinton run for the presidency would have seemed far-fetched. As of this writing Hillary Clinton is one of two leading candidates for the Democratic nomination in 2008.

Because of familiarity, name recognition, and loyalty, American voters seem to go back to families that they know. George W. Bush's presidency may fall to such a depth that another Bush presidency would be unlikely. Yet, the strong possibility remains that Jeb Bush will one day seek the presidency. Both his brother and his father believe that Jeb Bush would make a good president.[10] Unlike George W. Bush, as president Jeb Bush would have to deal with the legacies of a father *and* a brother. They both have been critical factors in Jeb Bush's political ambitions.

The Father and the Second Son

Jeb Bush's admiration for his father George H. W. Bush is both passionate and clear. In a 2005 interview, Jeb Bush stated, "As far I am concerned, my father is the closest thing to perfection as a human being can be."[11] Yet like his brother George W., he would have to navigate his life between following his father's legacy and striking out on his own. In his father's 1970 senatorial campaign and his father's 1980 presidential campaign for the Republican nomination, Jeb Bush worked tirelessly.[12] When his father lost both these elections, Jeb Bush had a difficult time dealing with the defeats. From these defeats, his political competitiveness was evident, and he understood the pain of losing elections. He also watched, in both the 1970 and 1980 campaigns, as his father was branded a moderate and even a liberal by his political opponents. When he would launch his own political career, he would never be called a moderate or liberal.

After the 1980 campaign where his father became Ronald Reagan's vice presidential nominee, Jeb Bush left Texas with his own family for the state of Florida. He told a reporter that "I left Houston to get out from my father's shadow...it took me about a week to figure out that the shadow a Vice President casts is very large."[13] Ironically by attempting to get out from under in his father's legacy, he was actually repeating it. George H. W. Bush had moved to Texas twenty years earlier to remove himself from his own father's orbit. Jeb Bush also married as a young man just like his father. His wife Columba was a Mexican native whom had met on a high school trip. He married her three years later.

Jeb Bush's decision to move his family to Miami, Florida would have important personal and political consequences for his future. In the 1980s, Miami was almost a modern frontier American city. Miami in southeastern Florida was a combustible mix of long-time immigrants from Cuba and new immigrants from Central and South America. It was becoming a hub for international trade and commerce. It also was a center for illegal drug smuggling and drug cartels.

With the infusion of interest and money from around the world, real estate in Miami became a terrific investment. Armando Condino, a Cuban refugee who had become a successful investor in Florida, offered to make a young Jeb Bush a partner in a real estate development firm in Miami. As the son of the vice president of the United States, Jeb Bush would make a good business partner. The Condino-Bush group did well during the 1990s and by the end of the decade, Jeb Bush was a millionaire.[14] During his real estate years, he encountered and assisted a few Miami residents with questionable histories. One of his clients, Miguel Recarey, would later be indicted for Medicare fraud and bribery. Before his indictment Jeb Bush had called the Federal Department of Health and Human Services on Recarey's behalf to vouch for Recarey's character during a time when his father was vice president.[15] Bush said he was not aware of his client's illegal activities and was not trying to lobby for his company. The Recarey incident highlights how Jeb Bush's business interests and political connections were not always beneficial for his reputation.

His emergence as a force in Florida politics also began in the city of Miami. Just as his father had done, he became chair of the local Republican Party. Republican Party politics in Miami were closely aligned with the Cuban immigrant community. George H. W. Bush had long been a supporter of the Cuban immigrant cause. Most Cuban immigrants in Miami were strongly opposed to the Communist regime on the island they had departed. The strong anti-Communist stand within the Republican Party made the naturalized Cuban-Americans a dependable Republican voting bloc. Jeb Bush's contacts and knowledge of the Cuban community in Miami would pay dividends to his father, his brother, and himself. By drastically increasing registered Republicans in Dade County (Miami), Jeb Bush would be cultivating thousands of more votes for the Republican Party. These votes were needed in southeast Florida for the Republicans because Democrats had a huge advantage in two nearby counties that have large Jewish populations and trend Democratic. His father George H. W. Bush would use Jeb Bush's connections in 1988 and 1992 to win the state of Florida. The 1992 race was especially difficult because Bill Clinton's campaign had targeted Florida. Even though Clinton won the presidency in 1992, he was still upset that he was beaten in the state of Florida and has vowed that his wife will win the state in her presidential bid.[16]

Jeb Bush and His Brother

After his father's loss in the 1992 presidential campaign, Jeb Bush would soon make plans for his own political future. In the mid-1980s, he had considered running for a congressional seat from South Florida. His father advised against it because he wanted him to earn more money for his family before he entered elective politics.[17] By 1993 at the age of forty-one, he felt he was ready to run for governor of the State of Florida. In many ways he had been preparing for a political career for much of his life. Unlike George W., Jeb Bush told his family he was going to be president someday when he was a young child.[18] After working on his father's presidential campaign in 1980, he moved to Miami and established himself as a businessman and a political activist. He had now earned enough money as his father had advised him. He served a brief stint as secretary of commerce for the State of Florida under Republican governor Bob Martinez in 1987 and 1988. In a difficult year for Republicans in 1992, he helped his father win the State of Florida again. He also helped build the Republican Party in southeast Florida and throughout the state.

Thus in 1993, it came as no surprise when Jeb Bush announced that he was running for governor. The Bush family immediately moved in to aid his effort. His father sponsored nine fund-raisers for his son in Houston and in Florida. More than half of the 7million dollars Jeb Bush raised for his 1994 campaign came from fund-raisers held by his parents or by friends of the family.[19] His father was excited and emotionally invested in Jeb Bush's campaign. At one campaign stop in Orlando, his father broke into tears when talking about his son.

Yet another family member would deliver a different type of surprise to Jeb Bush's campaign in 1994. His brother George W. Bush shocked family members and the political establishment in Texas by announcing that he too would to run for governor of a large state. Barbara Bush thought George W. had no chance of winning and most of the other family members shared her view.[20]

George W.'s campaign in 1994 would heavily impact Jeb Bush's effort in Florida. With two Bush sons running for governor, the storyline for Jeb Bush's effort in Florida changed. No longer was Jeb Bush the son who had left Texas to find his own way in Florida. Now he was one of two sons of a former president who thought they were entitled to be governor. According to Bush biographers Peter and Rochelle Schweizer, Jeb Bush was annoyed that his older brother was also running.[21] Jeb Bush said that having two brothers run for governor transformed his campaign from a campaign about issues to a "cover story for *People* magazine."[22] Jeb Bush even said his brother had stolen the best line in this campaign about running for governor not because he was the son of George and Barbara because he was the father of his own children.[23]

The Schweizers have written that this tension between the two brothers was always present in a competitive family. As the second son in the family, Jeb was in constant competition with his older brother George.[24] As he pursued entering his political career, Jeb Bush had to wonder how George W. could run for governor in the same year that he was running. Jeb Bush had been preparing for this opportunity for much of his adult life. He had worked in his father's campaigns; he had found business success in Miami; he served in the executive branch as commerce secretary for a brief time; he had help build the Republican Party in southeastern Florida. Moreover, he liked politics and had made it clear to most of his family members that he would run for office one day.

In contrast, his older brother George W. had struggled for much of his adult life. His oil businesses in Texas had little success, and he lost his 1978 congressional campaign. Until he quit drinking at the age of forty, he was also described as rambunctious and immature. Jeb Bush attempted to do everything in proper order. Now just as he was ready to emerge on his own, the prodigal son George W. came along and made the 1994 election a "two brothers" act.

Jeb Bush also had a major problem in his campaign that George W. would not have to face in his own. He would have a competitive Republican primary. The Republican primary included the Florida Senate president and the Florida secretary of state. With his name recognition and campaign money, Jeb Bush would win the Republican primary by a decisive margin. One of his opponents Republican Jim Smith, had earlier in the campaign said Bush was too inexperienced to be the next governor. When Smith conceded to Bush after the vote in the primary he said about Bush "he is a young man and hasn't had the experience, but he certainly has the energy and the intelligence."[25]

Jeb Bush's general election opponent was the incumbent governor of Florida, Lawton Chiles. Chiles was a legend in Florida politics who had never lost a race. Yet in the early 1990s, he was struggling with a recession and a weak response to Hurricane Andrew that decimated Homestead, Florida. The Chiles campaign would pick up on the criticism that Jeb Bush did not have the experience to be governor and was riding the coattails of his parents. In a speech Chiles said, "in our last debate, Jeb said it is not fair for me to talk about his mom or daddy. It's okay for them to come to Florida and raise 4 million for him, but don't say anything about them, it's not fair."[26]

From his father's failed campaigns, Jeb Bush knew to run as a conservative. Yet in 1994 he went too far to the Right in his campaign. He described himself as a "head-banging conservative."[27] He did not want to reform government; he wanted to reinvent it. His hard Right campaign would turn off some voters in the crucial central part of the state. His lieutenant governor nominee Tom Feeney was controversial and reckless in some of his comments.[28]

During an increase in crime in the State of Florida, the Bush campaign made a campaign ad featuring a mother of a murder victim. She wanted to know why Lawton Chiles had not put her daughter's murderer to death.[29] The ad backfired because Bush was accused of manipulating a mother of a murder victim. With a controversial late appeal to senior citizens in southeastern Florida, Lawton Chiles defeated Jeb Bush by 2 percent. On the same day in Texas, his brother George W. Bush won his election by a convincing margin.

A Second Try

Against the expectations of most of the Bush family, George W. Bush would become governor while Jeb Bush would be the last family member to lose an election. As a competitive man in an ultracompetitive family, Jeb Bush took the defeat personally. Having his brother being inaugurated as governor while he was not must have also been difficult. After George W. Bush's inauguration in Texas, the two Bush brothers reportedly did not speak to each other for half a year. George W. Bush told a family cousin that he was frustrated his brother would not communicate with him.[30] History and their political interests would bring them closer together in a few years.

Even with the loss, Jeb Bush realized that his goal of becoming Florida's governor was far from over. He was only forty-one years old and had almost beaten a Florida political legend. The state was trending more and more Republican, and the Democrats had no strong candidate for the next election. Less than two months after he was beaten in the 1994 election, he signaled that he may run again in four years, "it would be disingenuous of me to say that I am not still interested."[31]

During the four years between gubernatorial elections, Jeb Bush worked on moderating his image. In the 1994 campaign when he was asked what he would do for African-Americans, Jeb Bush replied "probably nothing."[32] This curt response was one that he regretted. As a result of this mistake, he started a charter public school in the poorest area in Miami after the 1994 election. The students were predominantly African-American and the school became popular in the area.[33]

Bush announced early in the 1998 election cycle that he was a candidate for governor. Unlike last time, he had no Republican opposition. He had tremendous name recognition and fund-raising ability. He raised three times the amount that his Democratic opponent, Lieutenant Governor Buddy McKay raised.

McKay tried to make Bush's fund-raising an issue in the campaign by claiming that Texas money was buying Jeb Bush's campaign. The charge did not work.

As in other Southern states, Democrats were losing a large percentage of the white vote to the Republican Party. Moreover, Florida Democrats had their own internal problems and removed an African-American Senate leader from his position. This removal provoked outrage among black elected officials and helped Bush to double his percentage of the black vote in 1998 compared to 1994. The final piece of the victorious campaign was a Jeb Bush commercial that simply said about his opponent, "Hey Buddy, You're Liberal." Bush won in landslide by 12 percent.[34]

Jeb Bush's victory was a triumphant moment for the Bush family. On the same day in Texas, his brother George W. Bush would also win his reelection in a landslide. Two Bush brothers were governors in two of the largest states in the nation. George W. Bush was already looked upon as a presidential candidate. Even in 1998, most observers believed that for George W. Bush to win the presidency, he would have to win his brother's state of Florida.

Jeb Bush the Executive

When Jeb Bush was inaugurated as Florida's governor in 1999, both his father and brother were in attendance. In his inaugural address, he promised to transform the state. He would achieve most of those legislative objectives through sheer force and excellent political timing. Since the Civil War, Florida State government had been known as a weak governor system. The governor shared executive power with other cabinet members. During the 1998 election, constitutional revisions were passed to shrink the size of the cabinet and to give the governor more authority. In the capital city of Tallahassee, the legislature had been known as the powerful branch of state government for years. Even the popular Democratic governor Lawton Chiles had his difficulties with the Florida legislature. Just as Jeb Bush was coming to power in Florida, the term limits provision enacted in 1992 was limiting the power of long-time Florida legislators. Under the new term limits system, legislators could not amass long periods of seniority. Without these senior members, the governor became a much more powerful figure. Jeb Bush also came to power just as Republicans won both the House and Senate in Florida. Accordingly, Florida became the first Southern state since Reconstruction to have a Republican governor serve with a Republican legislature.

All these changes had one important impact; they gave more constitutional and political power to the governor. Jeb Bush used these powers for all they were worth. The Florida legislature only meets three months out of the year. With his domineering personality and his emphasis on personal loyalty, Jeb Bush became the central figure in Florida politics. During his first term, almost all of his priorities were passed by the legislature. Bush's agenda included large tax cuts, the privatization of many state government functions, and a massive overhaul of the state's education system including the use of vouchers to allow public school children to attend private schools. With a compliant legislature, all these conservative reforms were passed without much debate. Jeb Bush had become "the most powerful governor the state had since Andrew Jackson," and Jackson had ruled Florida as a military governor.[35]

Heading to 2000

One of Jeb Bush's bold reforms would almost cost his brother the presidency in the year 2000. Ward Connerly, an activist from California who opposed affirmative action, had targeted the state of Florida as his next battle.

Connerly was going to attempt to put on the ballot a vote that would ban all race-based preferences in state government and state universities. By this time in 1999, it was well-known that George W. Bush would be running for president in the year 2000. Jeb Bush and other Republicans in Florida were concerned that the anti-affirmative-action Constitutional amendment would spur turnout among African-Americans who were overwhelmingly Democratic.

To rebut Connerly's efforts, Jeb Bush quickly put together an anti-affirmative-action plan called "One Florida." Bush and his aides had really not prepared black elected officials in the state about this fundamental shift in Florida government practice. As his brother had done in Texas, Jeb Bush advocated a plan that would cancel all race-based admission policies in Florida's universities and Florida government. As a substitute, the top 20 percent of every public high school in the state would be given admission to a Florida university. Bush had acted too soon; the Supreme Court of Florida blocked Ward Connerly's attempted constitutional amendment.[36] Even after the Florida Supreme Court's actions, Bush continued with his plan to, limit affirmative action.

The One Florida plan attracted passionate opposition among most black elected officials in the state. Other Democrats also joined in opposition to the plan. Two black state legislators sparked a sit-in at the governor's office in Tallahassee. The sit-in was soon followed by a massive civil rights demonstration on the opening day of the Florida legislature in 2000. Hundreds of civil rights protesters came in from out of state. Jesse Jackson led the chant "Stay out of the Bushes." Signs at the march also referred to Jeb Bush as "Jeb Crow."[37] A version of Jeb Bush's plan passed the Florida legislature and thus the issue was carried into the presidential election of 2000.

Jeb Bush and Campaign 2000

Running against an incumbent vice president in a divided nation, the general election between George W. Bush and Al Gore was going to be close. Jeb Bush traveled throughout the state of Florida in support of his brother. Their relationship had been repaired as the family united in his brother's presidential quest. Jeb and his advisers knew the African-American turnout would be large. The election in Florida was going to be close and in the final weeks of the campaign in Florida, Jeb Bush was concerned about the outcome.[38]

The results of the 2000 election in Florida were even closer than Jeb Bush had predicted. In a surreal situation, the presidential election of the world's most prominent constitutional democracy would come down to a recount in the state where a brother of one of the candidates was governor. Fortunately for the Bush family, George W. Bush always stayed slightly ahead of Al Gore in the official state count. To add even more to Democratic suspicions, the highest election authority in the state was Secretary of State Katherine Harris who was cochair of the George W. Bush campaign in Florida. The problems with Florida's county by county election process became evident throughout the nation.

Jeb Bush removed himself from the statewide canvassing election committee but he appointed a political ally in his place. Bush made it clear that he would help his brother where he could, "I recused myself as the chairman... but I was not going to recuse myself as governor or from being my brother's brother."[39] Jeb Bush and his advisors communicated with his brother's recount effort throughout November and December of 2000.[40]

Jeb Bush also showed his disdain for the Florida Supreme Court during much of the process. If George W. Bush was not granted the electoral votes by the judiciary, he supported an effort by his allies to have the Florida legislature declare his brother the winner in Florida. The U.S. Constitution grants state legislatures the right to determine how presidential electors are chosen in the states for the electoral college. Since the 1800s, every state legislature in the United States allowed voters to determine which presidential candidate's electors would represent the state. If the Florida legislature had taken the responsibility of choosing the electors *after* the election, it would effectively have nullified all the votes in the state because the legislature would be choosing the electors. This action would have been legally dubious and politically explosive; Governor Jeb Bush indicated his support for the idea.[41] When word of the possible electoral vote legislation surfaced, a New York tabloid newspaper ran a large headline, "OH BROTHER."[42] George W. Bush could no longer complain that his brother was not communicating with him. His brother almost instigated a constitutional crisis on his behalf. This action became unnecessary after his brother's position prevailed at the U.S Supreme Court in December of 2000.

Democrats had promised revenge against Jeb Bush for the 2000 campaign. Yet once the campaign was over, Jeb Bush again established himself as the most important politician in Florida. He reordered the entire governance structure of the state university system. The new system would give the governor the authority to appoint trustees to all of the state universities. Although he was challenged by a respected Democratic attorney in his reelection bid, he won easily. The revenge for the 2000 election did not occur in the Florida' governor's race in 2002.

Jeb Bush began his second term as governor of Florida with an unprecedented portfolio. He was the son of a former president and the brother of a sitting president. With his reelection victory and allies in the Republican legislature, he had tremendous power in the state. Two series of events would occur in his second term that highlight his relationship with his brother. These events would also show how Jeb

Bush operates when he has unchallenged political power. In the first situation, he used his status to rally the state's citizens in an unprecedented time of crisis. In the second situation, he stubbornly pursued an individual agenda that almost resulted in a state and federal constitutional showdown.

Two Crises

During the presidential election year of 2004, Jeb Bush would have much more to be concerned about that his brother's reelection. In a historical first, the state of Florida was hit by four major hurricanes in the span of two months. During the late summer and fall of 2004, millions of Floridians were without power and thousands were without fresh drinking water. Thousands of homes had been either destroyed or damaged. A year before Hurricane Katrina struck New Orleans, this hurricane period in Florida impacted more citizens than any other natural disaster in recent years. Throughout the summer of hurricanes, Jeb Bush stayed at the emergency operations center in Tallahassee. He helped to coordinate the response between the federal, state, and local governments. He was a confident and comforting presence during his press conferences about the storms. To Florida's Latino residents, he spoke in flawless Spanish about emergency protocol. He worked on the minute details of getting electricity, ice, and other supplies to weary residents.[43]

Compare Jeb Bush's actions with the actions of his brother a year later during Hurricane Katrina. George W. Bush was extremely detached from the Katrina disaster in New Orleans. An American city had been basically destroyed and the Bush administration's response was slow and inconsistent. The state and local government in Louisiana were also inept in trying to deal with the tragedy. Yet, George W. Bush did not step in and fill the leadership vacuum during the crisis. Ironically, Jeb Bush's good management of Florida's hurricane crisis in 2004 helped to secure the state politically for his brother. The last hurricane came ashore less than a month before the 2004 presidential election. George W. Bush won the state by 5 percentage points when most observers thought the race was going to be too close to call in Florida.

As mentioned above, the second incident involved the case of Terri Schiavo. Terri Schiavo was a forty-one-year-old woman who had been in a vegetative state for over a decade. Her husband Michael Schiavo had been seeking to remove her feeding tube for several years because he believed that his wife would not have wanted to continue in her deteriorated medical condition. Terri Schiavo's parents and her siblings objected vehemently to the removal of the feeding tube. They wanted to have custody of her daughter because Michael Schiavo was living with another woman. Her parents and her husband had been in a legal battle for years, and the Florida courts had consistently ruled in favor of Michael Schiavo.

Pro-life groups throughout the country took up the Schiavo case as their cause. Jeb Bush also strongly objected to the removal of the feeding tube. In 2003, Jeb Bush had ordered a state agency to reinsert Terri Schiavo's tube.

By 2005, Michael Schiavo's legal position again had prevailed. The state judge ordered that the tube be removed. Jeb Bush lobbied for the U.S. Congress and his brother President Bush to take up the cause. In an emergency session of Congress, a bill was passed to allow Terri Schiavo's parents to seek relief in federal courts. President Bush returned to Washington from his vacation to sign the bill. Conservative groups and Jeb Bush had elevated a tragic family dispute into a showdown between the executive and judicial branches of government. After the bill was signed into law, Terri Schiavo's parents took their case to the federal courts, but they lost their case again, and the U.S. Supreme Court refused to hear their case.

After the federal courts refused to take action to have the feeding tube reinserted, Jeb Bush would not give up. Bush publicly questioned the medical diagnosis of the experts who had testified in court. He also suggested that the state can take custody of Terri Schiavo if they had evidence that she was being abused or neglected. His legal counsel stated that the state "could take protective custody of the Mrs. Schiavo and I'll leave it at that."[44] Terri Schiavo was in a state-regulated hospice center, and there was no evidence of abuse or neglect. What Jeb Bush and his counsel were suggesting was to ignore the state and federal courts. After another state court issued an injunction against the governor, the case ended when Terri Schiavo died a few days later. Yet, Jeb Bush was not finished with the case. Two months later he ordered the state to investigate Terry Schiavo's husband for the possibility that he intentionally caused his wife's original injury. The investigation found nothing to the allegations.[45]

Jeb Bush's actions during the Schiavo episode were strange. Undoubtedly, he felt passionately about the issue in this difficult situation. Yet when his position did not prevail, he almost provoked a constitutional showdown between the governor's office and state and federal courts. He also instigated a spiteful investigation of Terri Schiavo's husband. Just like his brother, Jeb Bush has strong opinions about the strength of the executive branch of government. Both brothers have consistently talked about activist judges and the damage they have done to American society. Jeb Bush took this idea to a dangerous level; he almost challenged the rule of law set down by the courts. This potential challenge is disturbing coming from a member of a family that has amassed so much political power in the United States.

The Prince in Waiting?

After the negative outcomes of his father's and brother's presidencies, Jeb Bush may decide not to run for president. He would have to consider the strain on his own family. Moreover, his own son George P. Bush is seen as a likely political candidate for the future. George P. Bush is a smart and handsome thirty-two year old attorney in Texas. With the Latino background of his mother Columba, he also could help the Republican Party reach out to more Hispanic voters. The good prospects for his son George P. might convince Jeb Bush to forgo his own future political plans.

Yet the pull for Jeb Bush to continue the Bush political dynasty will be considerable. As noted above, he will have many advantages if he decides to seek the Republican nomination in 2012 or 2016. He can raise money; he can attract economic and religious conservatives; he is a skilled public speaker; and he has been governor of one of the largest and most diverse states in the country.

If he were to become president, he would govern in a conservative and partisan manner. Like his brother, he believes in the supremacy of the executive branch over the judicial and legislative branches. He would be a policy innovator and an unabashed social conservative. Among Republicans, this profile would be a perfect antidote to a Hillary Clinton or Barack Obama presidency. Barack Obama may fight off one family dynasty in 2008, but he may face another in 2012 with another Bush comeback.

Accordingly, the American War of Roses may continue. The most important casualty of this political battle between the Clintons and the Bushes would be the American presidency itself because the presidency would lose its democratic legitimacy as a representative institution for all the people. Moreover, during this familiar–domination, personal family issues have come to dominate presidential policymaking. With serious challenges facing the nation, the Bush-Clinton struggle for power in the United States will leave a lasting mark on American democracy and the presidency itself. The presidency will be transformed from Andrew Jackson's "tribune of the people" to the guardian of family political power. If Hillary Clinton and/or Jeb Bush become president, American democracy will never reach its potential in the first decades of the twenty-first century. Instead of an office that provides energy and leadership in a system of separated powers, the presidency would be transformed to the elective monarchy that George Mason warned about more than 200 years ago.

Notes

Chapter One   Introduction

1. Sheehy 1999, 197.
2. Ibid., 153.
3. Crowley 1994, 1A.
4. Parliament was also unpopular—but the king was still the undisputed head of the government at the time of the revolution.
5. Renshon 2004, 27.
6. Sheehy 1999, 144.
7. DeFrank 2005, 14.
8. Dye 2001.
9. Keen 2000, 15A.
10. Ibid.
11. Pious 1996, 26.
12. Bowen 1966, 561.
13. Pious 1996, 25.
14. Ibid.
15. Ibid.
16. Farrand 1966, vol. 2, 101.
17. Milkis and Nelson 1990, 259.
18. Genovese 1999.
19. Dumbrell 1995, 89.

Chapter Two   American Democracy and Family Presidencies

1. Guerrero 1999, 23; Bernstein 1992, 1.
2. Lawrence 2006, 1A.
3. Hinckley 1980, 642.
4. Bowen 1966, 55.
5. Bendix 1978, 21.
6. Ibid.
7. Wilson 1991, 5.
8. Cohen and Fermon 1996, 258.
9. Pious 1996, 53.
10. Urofsky 1988, 49.
11. Ibid., 50–51.

12. Bowen 1966, 55.
13. Ibid., 57.
14. Ibid., 58.
15. Farrand 1966, 66.
16. Pious 1996, 27.
17. Bowen 1966, 54.
18. Ellis 1999, 100; Storing 1981, 5: 76–77.
19. Hamilton 1788, Federalist 69.
20. Thach 1969.
21. Flexner 1974.
22. Ibid.
23. Ibid., 173.
24. Ibid., 209.
25. Kennedy 2001, 7.
26. Flexner 1974, 172.
27. Maraniss 1995, 19.
28. Sheehy 1999, 123.
29. Balz 1998, A01.
30. Jacobsen 2007.
31. Cohen and Nice 2003, 24.
32. Thach 1969, 169.
33. Milkis and Nelson 1990, 119.
34. Cohen and Nice 2003, 208.
35. Milkis and Nelson 1990, 269.
36. Ibid., 259.
37. Farnsworth and Lichter 2005, 94.
38. Greenstein 2007, 55.
39. Wayne 1996, 93.
40. Cohen and Nice 2003, 203.
41. Pew Global Attitudes Project 2003.
42. Ridenour 2006.

Chapter Three   Families Matter

1. Anthony 2000, 123.
2. Cherlin 2005, 300.
3. Ibid., 302.
4. Ibid.
5. Ibid., 255.
6. Ibid.
7. Flexner 1969, 42.
8. Ibid., 43.
9. Goodwin 2005, 49.
10. Ibid., 179.

11. Ibid.
12. Dallek 1998.
13. Ibid., 234
14. Anthony 2000, 75.
15. Ibid.
16. Ambrose 1987, 75.
17. Anthony 2000, 87.
18. Wead 2003, 1.
19. Ibid.
20. Ibid., 3.
21. Ibid., 74.
22. Anthony 2000, 92.
23. Wead 2003, 2.
24. Troy 2000, 3.
25. Anthony 2000, 142–147.
26. Kellerman 1981, 167.
27. Watson 2000, 28.
28. Ibid., 15.
29. Ibid., 37.
30. Troy 2000, 11.
31. Ibid.
32. Collier and Horowitz 1984, 283.
33. MacPherson and Radcliffe 1978, A5.
34. Cannon 1988, A1.
35. Kellerman 1981, Preface.
36. Troy 2000, Preface.
37. Ibid.
38. Boller 2004, 157.
39. Bumiller 2006, 12.
40. Hess 1966, 16.
41. Ibid., 13.
42. Ibid., 22–23.
43. Ibid., 24.
44. McCullough 2001, 352.
45. Hess 1966, 25.
46. Boller 2004, 6.
47. Ibid., 10.
48. McCullough 2001, 505.
49. Anthony 2000, 26.
50. Ibid.
51. Hess 1966, 16.
52. Anthony 2000, 19.
53. Hess 1966, 17.
54. Ibid., 24–26.
55. Boller 2004, 36.
56. Hess 1966, 31.

57. Boller 2004, 37.
58. Ibid., 45.
59. Ibid.
60. Hess 1966, 19.
61. Wead 2003, 335.
62. Ibid.
63. Burns and Dunn 2001, 133.
64. Ibid., 162.
65. Chafe 1984, 3.
66. Ibid., 8.
67. Burns and Dunn 2001, 99.
68. Watson 2000, 95.
69. Burns and Dunn 2001, 394.
70. Ibid., 502.
71. Ibid., 512.
72. Chafe 1984, 24.
73. Hess 1966, 490–492.
74. Collier and Horowitz 1984, 45.
75. Hess 1966, 481.
76. Collier and Horowitz 1984, 131.
77. Ibid., 134–135.
78. Ibid., 141.
79. Ibid., 146.
80. Ibid., 146.
81. Clinch 1973, 98.
82. Ibid., 323.
83. Ibid., 340.
84. Kellerman 1981, 169.
85. Ibid., 293.
86. Collier and Horowitz 1984, 339.
87. Ibid., 346.
88. Ibid., 348.
89. Ibid., 365.
90. Clinch 1973, 323.
91. Coller and Horowitz 1984, 366.
92. Ibid., 369.
93. Wills 1985.
94. Ibid., 10–11.
95. Bush 1999, 7.

Chapter Four   The Father Begins a Dynasty

1. Schweizer and Schweizer 2004, 150.
2. Parmet 1997, 19.

3. Ibid., 21.
4. Ibid., 30.
5. Ibid., 59–60.
6. Ibid., 67.
7. Ibid., 74–76.
8. Ibid., 77.
9. Ibid., 89.
10. Ibid., 72.
11. Ibid., 82.
12. Ibid., 94.
13. Ibid., 95.
14. Wicker 2004, 17.
15. Ibid.
16. Tilove 2004, 16.
17. Scher 1997, 94.
18. Parmet 1997, 98.
19. Ibid.
20. Schweizer and Schweizer 2004, 163.
21. Wicker 2004, 18.
22. Ibid., 21.
23. Parmet 1997, 132–134.
24. Ibid., 134.
25. Wicker 2004, 23.
26. Schweizer and Schweizer 2004, 202.
27. Ibid., 205.
28. Ibid., 185.
29. Parmet 1997, 148.
30. Ibid., 165.
31. Schweizer and Schweizer 2004, 237.
32. Wicker 2004, 42.
33. Schweizer and Schweizer 2004, 248.
34. Parmet 1997, 216.
35. Ibid., 226.
36. Boller 2004, 358.
37. Parmet 1997, 233.
38. Schweizer and Schweizer 2004, 274.
39. Ibid., 275.
40. Parmet 1997, 245.
41. Ibid., 262.
42. Germond and Witcover 1989, 30.
43. Simon 1990, 1–5.
44. Parmet 1997, 226.
45. Germond and Witcover 1989, 400–413.
46. Boller 2004, 358.
47. *Grand Rapid Press* 2004, A18.
48. Schneider 1989, 14A.

49. Brinkley 1991, A21.
50. Greene 2000, 99.
51. *U.S. News and World Report* 1992, 248.
52. Parmet 1997, 475.
53. Bush and Scowcroft 1998, 484–485.
54. Parmet 1997, 484.
55. Neuman 1991, 1A.
56. Greene 2000, 138.
57. *U.S. News and World Report* 1992, 403.
58. Ibid., 395.
59. Schweizer and Schweizer 2004, 399.

Chapter Five   The Clintons Take Power

1. Brock 1996, 248.
2. Ibid.
3. Morris 1996, 249.
4. Maraniss 1995, 49.
5. Ibid., 37–41.
6. Ibid., 247.
7. Ibid.
8. Ibid.
9. Ibid., 248.
10. Ibid., 249.
11. Lawrence 2007, 1A.
12. Maraniss 1995, 79.
13. Ibid., 81.
14. Ibid., 201–202 A.
15. Brock 1996, 12.
16. Ibid., 21.
17. Ibid., 15.
18. Ibid., 22.
19. Ibid., 36.
20. Ibid., 37.
21. Clinton 2003, 61.
22. Ibid., 54.
23. Ibid., 64.
24. Ibid., 63.
25. Ibid., 69.
26. Ibid.
27. Maraniss 1995, 337.
28. Ibid., 335.
29. Brock 1996, 84.
30. Ibid., 256.
31. Maraniss 1995, 354.

32. Ibid., 361
33. Clinton 2004, 282.
34. Ibid., 284.
35. Ibid., 287.
36. Brock 1996, 153.
37. Ibid., 155.
38. Ibid., 154.
39. Sheehy 1999, 147.
40. Maraniss 1995, 411.
41. Sheehy 1999, 152.
42. Ibid., 153.
43. Ibid.
44. Arkansas Business and Education Alliance 2000.
45. Sheehy 1999, 153
46. Ibid., 155.
47. Maraniss 1995, 443.
48. Ibid., 444.
49. Sheehy 1999, 186.
50. Maraniss 1995, 455.
51. Toobin 1999, 147.
52. Sheehy 1999, 181.
53. Germond and Witcover 1993, 169–170.
54. Sheehy 1999, 198.
55. Ibid., 200.
56. Germond and Witcover 1993, 203.
57. Sheehy 1999, 208.
58. Brock 1996, 260.
59. Ibid., emphasis added.
60. Sheehy 1999, 198.
61. Germond and Witcover 1993, 266.
62. Ibid., 410.
63. Allen-Mills 1998, 14.
64. Marcus 1993, F20.
65. Drew 1994, 24.
66. Ibid.
67. Woodward 1994, 217.
68. Clinton 2003.
69. Gergen 2000, 303.
70. Ibid., 292.
71. Drew 1994, 22.
72. Gergen 2000, 302.
73. Ibid., 309.
74. Sheehy 1999, 246.
75. Achenbach 1994, C1.
76. Ibid., 274.
77. Sheehy 1999, 258.

78. Ibid., 260.
79. Toobin 1999, 80.
80. Ibid.
81. Clinton 2004, 441.
82. Harris 2005, 308.
83. Ibid., 444.
84. Clinton 2004, 803.
85. Harris 2005, 347.
86. Clinton 2004, 800.
87. Harris 2005, 327.
88. Ibid., 346.
89. Ibid., 359.
90. Clinton 2003, 471.
91. O'Brien 1998, A1.
92. Boller 2004, 407.

Chapter Six   The Bush Redemption

1. Minutaglio 1999, 192.
2. Condon 2000, A1.
3. Minutaglio 1999, 69.
4. Renshon 2004.
5. Navarette 2007, G-3. Navarette used the quote in another context.
6. Minutaglio 1999, 77.
7. Ibid., 61.
8. Ibid., 85.
9. Ibid.
10. Ibid., 120.
11. Ibid., 131.
12. Schweizer and Schweizer 2004, 195.
13. Minutaglio 1999, 141.
14. Schweizer and Schweizer 2004, 220.
15. Renshon 2004, 39.
16. Minutaglio 1999, 187.
17. Ibid., 187.
18. Ibid., 188.
19. Ibid.
20. Ibid., 190.
21. Ibid.
22. Bruni 2002, 122.
23. Minutaglio 1999, 190.
24. Ibid., 191, this quote refers to Minutaglio's description of the interview.
25. Ibid.
26. Ibid.
27. Ibid.

28. Bruni 2002, 122.
29. Schweizer and Schweizer 2004, 306.
30. Ibid., 303.
31. Ibid.
32. Reinhold 1986, 1A.
33. Renshon 2004, 27.
34. Schweizer and Schweizer 2004, 303.
35. Ibid., 331.
36. Ibid., 335.
37. Kristof 2000, 1.
38. Ibid.
39. Schweizer and Schweizer 2004, 365.
40. Bush 1999.
41. Moore and Slater 2003, 199.
42. Ibid., 200.
43. Morris 1989, 2A.
44. Moore and Slater 2003, 161.
45. Minutaglio 1999, 263.
46. Ibid., 223.
47. Bruni 1999, 1.
48. Moore and Slater 2003, 197.
49. Minutaglio 1999, 266.
50. Bush 1999, 26.
51. Moore and Slater 2003, 135–136.
52. Ibid., 137.
53. Schweizer and Schweizer 2004, 420.
54. Minutaglio 1999, 274.
55. Ibid.
56. Ibid., 87
57. Moore and Slater 2003, 164.
58. Ibid., 205.
59. Ibid., 167.
60. Ibid., 209.
61. Ibid., 210.
62. Schweizer and Schweizer 2004, 426.
63. McGrory 1995, 1.
64. Robison 1996, 13.
65. Ibid.
66. Keen 1997, 1A.
67. Ibid.
68. Ibid.
69. Kenna 1997, F6.
70. Keen 1997, 1A.
71. Schweizer and Schweizer 2004, 459.
72. Ibid., 460.
73. Ibid.

74. Herman and Greenberger 1999, 1A.
75. McGrory 1995, A3.
76. Schweizer and Schweizer 2004, 476.
77. Moore and Slater 2003, 256.
78. Ibid., 257.
79. Ibid., 263.
80. DeFrank 2000, 7.
81. Orr 2000, S1.
82. Page and Benedetto 2000, 5A.
83. Ibid.
84. Keen 2000a, 1A.
85. Rosenbaum 2000, A28.
86. Ibid.
87. Ibid.
88. Toobin 2001, 45.
89. Woodward 2006, 6.
90. Keen 2000b, 1A.
91. Burke 2004, 132.
92. Ibid., 130.
93. Woodward 2006, 2.
94. Ibid., 12.
95. Ibid.
96. Bookman 2004, 17A.
97. Walsh et al. 2003, 26.
98. Ibid.
99. Woodward 2006, 9.
100. Ibid., 6.
101. Ricks 2006, 6.
102. Ibid., 16.
103. Woodward 2006, xii.
104. Ibid., 28.
105. Ibid., 33.
106. Ibid., 32.
107. Ibid., 78.
108. Gellman and Becker 2007, 1A.
109. Ibid., 77.
110. Gall 2003, 8.
111. Woodward 2006, 78.
112. Pincus 1998, A2.
113. Woodward 2006, 83.
114. Ibid., 419.
115. Ricks 2006, 38.
116. Ibid., 49.
117. Pfiffner 2007.
118. Ricks 2006, 49.
119. Ibid., 90.

120. Ibid., 93.
121. Ibid., 100.
122. Woodward 2006, 129.
123. Ricks 2006, 179.
124. Deans 2007, 3A.
125. Ibid.
126. Abercromie and Ortiz 2007, 9.
127. Ali 2007, 44.
128. Deans 2007, 3A.
129. Butler 2007, A10.
130. Ricks 2006, 3.
131. Baker and Hamilton 2006, 6.
132. Duffy and Allen 2006, 40.
133. Isikoff and Corn 2006, 3.
134. Ibid., 3.
135. Woodward 2006, 114.
136. Ibid., 420.
137. Ibid.

Chapter Seven   From First Lady to President?

1. Kasindorf 2000, 5A.
2. Tomasky 2001, 44.
3. Maraniss 1995, 441.
4. Sheehy 1999, 186.
5. Ibid., 187; Brock 1996, 233
6. Gerth and Van Natta 2007, 105.
7. Burns and Dunn 2001, 502.
8. Chafe 1984, 25.
9. Benedetto 1995, 6A.
10. Davies 1999, A-13 quoting Sheehy.
11. Tomasky 2001, 34.
12. McCarthy 1999, 48.
13. Rauber et al. 1999, 7.
14. Lardner 2000, A6.
15. Tomasky 2001, 47.
16. Dugan 1999, A9.
17. Ibid.
18. Williams 2000, 10A.
19. *New York Post* 1999, 28.
20. Harris 1999, A1.
21. Berke 2000a, 1.
22. Ibid.
23. Fink and Rubin 2000, 19.

24. Deans and Shepard 1999, 1B.
25. Finnegan 1999, 2.
26. Dicker 1999, 2.
27. Ibid.
28. Harris 2000, A8.
29. Ibid.
30. Tomaksy 2001, 53.
31. Usborne 1999, 14.
32. Tomasky 2001, 81.
33. Ibid., 142.
34. Ibid., 143.
35. Ibid., 148.
36. Ibid., 169.
37. Ibid., 172.
38. Ibid.
39. Ibid., 237.
40. Helmore 2000, 10.
41. Ibid.
42. Lardner 2001, A3.
43. Dejevsky 1999, 113.
44. Ibid.
45. Borger 2001, 31.
46. Jakes 2001, 6A.
47. *St. Petersburg Times* 2001, 3A.
48. Green 2006.
49. Fineman 2001, 50.
50. Ibid., 50.
51. *Hobart Mecury* 2001.
52. Ricks 2006, 63.
53. Gerth and Van Natta 2007, 242.
54. Von Drehle 2003, A13.
55. Morris 2002, 4.
56. Standora 2002, 18.
57. Ibid.
58. Meek 2003. 8.
59. Conner 2002, 6.
60. Green 2006, 72.
61. Robison 2003, 35.
62. Halperin and Harris 2006, 14.
63. Green 2006, 68.
64. Harris 2004, A1.
65. Lawrence 2005, 16.
66. Hook 2006, A26.
67. Nagourney 2006, 4.
68. Lehigh 2006, A17.
69. Ibid.

70. Ibid.
71. Dowd 2007, A21.
72. Gerth and Van Natta 2007, 326.
73. Haberman 2007a, 4.
74. Hunter 2007, 17.
75. Marinucci 2007, A1.
76. Haberman 2007b, 4.
77. Healy 200, 22.
78. Tumulty and Carney 2007.
79. Gerth and Van Natta 2007, 218.
80. Ibid., 217.
81. Buncombe 2007.
82. Sheehy 1999, 240.
83. Green 2006.

Chapter Eight   The Prince in Waiting

1. Schweizer and Schweizer 2004, 481.
2. National Broadcasting Company 2007.
3. Jacobsen 2006.
4. Kurtz 2007.
5. National Review 2006.
6. Atkins 2006, 5.
7. House 2007, 1.
8. Salinero 2002, 1.
9. Ibid.
10. UPI 2005; Pickler 2006.
11. Berke 2000, 1.
12. Schweizer and Schweizer 2004, 203.
13. Ibid., 307.
14. Date 2007, 71.
15. Ibid., 96.
16. *St. Petersburg Times* 2007, 3B.
17. Schweizer and Schweizer 2004, 319.
18. Ibid.
19. Ibid., 417
20. Ibid., 413.
21. Ibid., 423.
22. Ibid.
23. Debenport 1994b, 1A.
24. Schweizer and Schweizer 2004, 137.
25. Debenport 1994c, 1A.
26. *New York Times* 1994, A26.
27. Schweizer and Schweizer 2004, 422.
28. Debenport 1994a, 6B.

29. Bakkalagulo 1994, 1.
30. Schweizer and Schweizer 2004, 451.
31. *Houston Chronicle* 1995, A6.
32. Rado 1994, 2B.
33. Schweizer and Schweizer 2004, 451.
34. March 1998, 1.
35. Date 2007, 133.
36. March 2000, 1.
37. Ibid.
38. Becker and Milbank 2000, A29.
39. Date 2007, 120.
40. Ibid., 121; Schweizer and Schweizer 2004, 494.
41. Schweizer and Schweizer 2004, 495.
42. *New York Daily News* 2000, 1.
43. Bousquet 2004, 1A.
44. Ibid.
45. Karp and Tisch 2005, 1B.

Bibliography

Abercrombie, Neil and Ortiz, Solomon. "How to Fuel up the Out-of-Gas US Military Machine." *Christian Science Monitor*, March 19, 2007, 9.

Achenbach, Joel. "The First Lady's Mission Impossible." *Washington Post*, December 14, 1994, C1.

Ali, Lorraine. When Home Becomes Hell: As Its Middle Classes Flee, Iraq Is Losing Skills, Open Minds, and Perhaps the Hope of Renewal. One Family's Story." *Newsweek*, March 19, 2007.

Allen-Mills, Tony. "Team Clinton, a Faustian Fable." *The Australian*, February 2, 1998, 14.

Ambrose, Stephen E. *Nixon*. New York: Simon & Schuster, 1987.

Anthony, Carl Sferrazza. *America's First Families: An Inside View of 200 Years of Private Live in the White House*. New York: Touchstone, 2000.

Arkansas Business and Education Alliance. 2000. *Facing the Facts about Arkansas Education*. Little Rock: Institute for Economic Advancement, University of Arkansas Little Rock.

Atkins, Kimberly. "That's the Ticket: Speculation Swirls over Mitt-Jeb Pairing in 2008." *The Boston Herald*, October 30, 2006, 5.

Baker, James A and Hamilton, Lee H. *The Iraq Study Group Report*. New York: Vintage Books, 2006.

Bakkalapulo, Ann. "Mother Doesn't Regret Bush Ads." *Tampa Tribune*, November 7, 1994, 1.

Balz, Dan. "Bush Derides Talk He Fears a Run in 2000." *Washington Post*, October 15, 1998, A01.

Barber, James D. "The Nixon Brush with Tyranny." *Political Science Quarterly* 92, 4 (1977): 581.

Becker, Jo and Millbank, Dana. "For Jeb Bush, 'Business as Usual': Florida Governor Waits, Works Behind the Scenes as Chaos Reigns over Vote." *Washington Post*, November 17, 2000, A29.

Bendix, Reinhard. *Kings or People: Post and the Mandate to Rule*. Berkeley, CA: University of California Press, 1978.

Benedetto, Richard. "First Lady's Role Take Traditional, Political Turn." *USA Today*, October 16, 1995, 6A.

Berke, Richard L. "The 2000 Campaign: The Florida Governor; Feeling the Burden of a Name, One Bush Focuses on Florida." *New York Times*, July 14, 2000a, A1.

———. "Running for Office? The President Has Some Ideas." *The New York Times*, May 7, 2000b, 1.

Bernstein, Alan. "Convention '92; Hillary Clinton's New Role; She Is Husband's Chief Surrogate." *Houston Chronicle*, July 12, 1992, E1.

Boller, Paul F. *Presidential Campaigns: From George Washington to George W. Bush.* New York: Oxford University Press, 2004.
Bookman, Jay. "Nuance Vital in a Complex Terror War." *The Atlanta Journal-Constitution*, August 19, 2004, 17A.
Borger, Gloria. "Now It's About Her." *U.S. News and World Report*, February 26, 2001, 31.
Bousquet, Steve. "Bush's Newest Mantle: Hurricane Governor." *St. Petersburg Times*, September 15, 2004, 1A.
Bowen, Catherine. *Miracle at Philadelphia.* New York: Little, Brown and Company, 1966.
Brinkley, Alan. "Bush Surrenders at Home." *New York Times*, January 29, 1991, A21.
Brock, David. *The Seduction of Hillary Rodham.* New York: Free Press, 1996.
Bruni, Frank. "Senior Bush's Loss Set Course for Son's Candidacy." *New York Times*, December 26, 1999, 1.
———. *Ambling into History: The Unlikely Odyssey of George W. Bush.* New York: HarperCollins, 2002.
Bumiller, Elisabeth. "A Few Years, and Then Another Bush?" *New York Times*, May 29, 2006, A12.
Buncombe, Andrew. "Hillary to Appoint Bill 'Cheerleader for America.'" *The Independent (London)*, April 23, 2007.
Burke, John P. *Becoming President: The Bush Transition, 2000–2003.* Boulder, CO: Lynne Rienner, 2004.
Burns, James MacGregor and Dunn, Susan. *The Three Roosevelts: Patrician Leaders Who Transformed America.* New York: Atlantic Monthly Press, 2001.
Bush, George H. W. *Looking Forward.* New York: Doubleday, 1987.
Bush, George H. W. and Scowcroft, Brent. *A World Transformed.* New York: Alfred A. Knopf, 1998.
Bush, George W. *A Charge to Keep.* New York: Morrow, 1999.
Butler, Don. "World Opinion of U.S. Drops Sharply, Poll Finds." *Ottawa Citizen*, January 23, 2007, A10.
Cannon, Lou. "Astrologers Used by First Lady, Regan Book Says." *Washington Post*, May 3, 1988, A1.
Caroli, Betty Boyd. *First Ladies.* New York: Oxford University Press, 1995.
Chafe, William H. (n. d.). "Biographical Sketch." In Joan Hoff-Wilson and Marjorie Lightman (eds.), *Without Precedent* (3–27). Bloomington: Indiana University Press, 1984.
Cherlin, Andrew J. *Public and Private Families.* Boston, MA: McGraw Hill, 2005.
Clinch, Nancy Gager. *The Kennedy Neurosis.* New York: Grosset & Dunlap, 1973.
Clinton, Bill. *My Life.* New York: Alfred A. Knopf, 2004.
Clinton, Hillary Rodham. *Living History.* New York: Random House, 2003.

Cohen, Jeffrey and Nice, David. *The Presidency.* New York: McGraw-Hill, 2003.

Cohen, Mitchell and Fermon, Nicole (eds.). *Princeton Readings in Political Thought.* Princeton: Princeton University Press, 1996.

Collier, Peter and Horowitz, David. *The Kennedys: An American Drama.* New York: Summit Books, 1984.

Condon, George E. "Bush Promises 'A New Beginning': Pledges End to 'Scandal...Broken Faith' GOP Rife with Optimism after Upbeat, Amicable Convention." *San Diego Union-Tribune,* August 4, 2000, A-1.

Conner, Tracy. "Strange Bedfellows Bush, Hil Top Most-Admired List." *New York Daily News,* December 29, 2002, News 6.

Crowley, Brian E. "The '80s: A Quick Million for Jeb Bush." *Palm Beach Post,* June 26, 1994, 1A.

Dallek, Robert. *Flawed Giant: Lyndon Johnson and His Times.* New York: Oxford University Press, 1998.

Date, S. V. *Jeb: America's Next Bush; His Florida Years and What They Mean for the Nation.* New York: Jeremy P. Tarcher/Penguin, 2007.

Davies, Frank. "The Book on Hillary and Her Run for Redemption." *Buffalo News,* December 1, 1999, 1D.

Deans, Bob. "War in Iraq: The Costs: 3, 217 American Lives, $351 Billion." *The Atlanta Journal-Constitution,* March 19, 2007.

Deans, Bob and Shepard, Scott. "First Lady, Gore Get Top Billing; Clinton Relishes Aiding Campaigns." *The Atlanta Journal-Constitution,* July 25, 1999, 1B.

Debenport, Ellen. "Bush Running Mate Feeney Is a Man of His Words." *St. Petersburg Times,* August 10, 1994a, 6B.

———. "The Bush Brothers Aren't Twins." *St. Petersburg Times,* October 2, 1994b, 1A.

———. "Smith Throws Support to Bush, Unified GOP." *St. Petersburg Times,* September 13, 1994c, 1A.

DeFrank, Thomas M. "It's Official—It's Cheney—Bush Follows Father's Advice on Veep." *New York Daily News,* July 26, 2000, 7.

———. "Poppy, Bubba Best Buds: Old Rivals Make Odd Couple, but Affection's Real." *New York Daily News,* April 24, 2005, 14.

Dejevsky, Mary. "Clinton Election Gurus Flock to Hillary's Campaign." *The Independent,* June 8, 1999, 13.

Dicker, Fredric U. "Bush Kin Flays Hillary over Lapses in Ethics; Exclusive." *New York Post,* April 12, 1999, 2.

Dowd, Maureen. "Obama's Big Screen Test." *New York Times,* February 21, 2007, A21.

Drew, Elizabeth. *On the Edge: The Clinton Presidency.* New York: Simon & Schuster, 1994.

Duffy, Michael and Allen, Mike. "Advice and Grudging Consent." *Time,* December 18, 2006.

Dugan, Ianthe. "Clinton Supporters Eye $25 Million Campaign for New York Seat." *Washington Post,* July 16, 1999, A09.

Dumbrell, John. *The Carter Presidency: A Re-evaluation.* 2nd edition. Manchester: Manchester University Press, 1995.
Dye, Thomas. *Who's Running America? The Bush Restoration.* Upper Saddle River, NJ: Prentice Hall, 2001.
Ellis, Richard J. *Founding the American Presidency.* Boston, MA: Rowman & Littlefield, 1999.
Farnsworth, Steven and Lichter, Robert. "The Mediated Congress." *The Harvard International Journal of Press/Politics* 10, 2 (2005): 94–107.
Farrand, Max. *The Records of the Federal Convention of 1787*, 4 vols., rev. edition. New Haven, CT: Yale University Press, 1966.
Fineman, H., Gegax T., Rosenberg, D., and Bai, M. "A President Finds His True Voice." *Newsweek,* September 24, 2001, 50.
Fink, Mitchell and Rubin, Lauren. "Hil's Grateful for Own Domestic Policy Advisor." *New York Daily News,* April 7, 2000, 19.
Finnegan, Michael. "Rudy Rips Clintons, Dem Foes." *New York Daily News,* December 23, 1999, 2.
Flexner, James Thomas. *Washington: The Indispensable Man.* Boston, MA: Little, Brown, and Co., 1974.
Gall, Carlotta. "Mixed Views in Pakistan on Amount of U.S. Aid." *New York Times,* June 27, 2003, A8.
Gellman, Barton and Becker, Jo. "A Different Understanding with the President." *Washington Post,* June 24, 2007, A01.
Genovese, Michael A. *The Presidential Dilemma: Leadership in the American System.* New York: Longman Publishing Group, 1999.
Gergen, David. *Eyewitness to Power: The Essence of Leadership Nixon to Clinton.* New York: Simon & Schuster, 2000.
Germond, Jack and Witcover, Jules. *Whose Broad Stripes and Bright Stars? The Trivial Pursuit of the Presidency.* New York: Warner Books, 1989.
———. *Mad as Hell: Revolt at the Ballot Box, 1992.* New York: Warner Books, 1993.
Gerth, Jeff and Van Natta, Don. *Her Way: The Hopes and Ambitions of Hillary Rodham Clinton.* New York: Little, Brown, and Co., 2007.
Goodwin, Doris Kearns. *Team of Rivals: The Political Genius of Abraham Lincoln.* New York: Simon & Schuster, 2005.
Grand Rapids Press "America's First Co-President." October 10, 2004, A18.
Green, Joshua. "Take Two: How Hillary Clinton Turned Herself into the Consummate Washington Player." *The Atlantic,* November, 2006, 56.
Green, Lisa. "The Terri Shiavo Case." *St. Petersburg Times,* March 30, 2005, 11A.
Greene, John Robert. *The Presidency of George Bush.* Lawrence: University of Kansas Press, 2000.
Greenstein, Fred I. "Toward a Modern Presidency." In James P. Pfiffner and Roger H Davidson (eds.), *Understanding the Presidency* (55–58). New York: Pearson Education, 2007.
Guerrero, Lucio. "Ex-first Lady: Kids Need Attention." *Chicago Sun-Times,* October 1, 1999, News 23.

Haberman, Maggie. "Aides Learn Hill Drill; 'How to Talk About Bubba Fatigue & Iraq.'" *New York Post,* February 24, 2007a, 4.

———. "Bubba Has Hil's Back." *New York Post,* February 14, 2007b, 2.

Halperin, Mark and Harris, John. *The Way to Win: Taking the White House in 2008.* New York: Random House, 2006.

Hamilton, Alexander. "The Federalist Papers #69: The Real Character of the Executive from the New York Packet." (1788). *The Avalon Project at Yale Law School.* Retrieved June 25, 2007 from http://www.yale.edu/lawweb/avalon/federal/fed69.htm/.

Harris, John F. "White House Ex-Aides Find 2nd Chance with First Lady." *Washington Post,* September 23, 1999, A01.

———. "For Hillary Clinton, A Heap of Invective." *Washington Post,* July 14, 2000, A08.

———. "At Opening of Clinton Library, Democrats to Talk Strategy." *Washington Post,* November 15, 2004, A01.

———. *The Survivor.* New York: Random House, 2005.

Healy, Patrick. "Obama Disputes Claim of Sharing Clinton's Stance on War." *New York Times,* May 18, 2007, A22.

Helmore, Edward. "U.S. Election 2000: The Clintons: First Family's Next Steps: The Court of Camelot Arrives in New York: Chelsea May Go into Medicine, Bill Has a Library to Build, and Hillary Has a New Job—But Could She Be Tempted to Run for the White House Next Time." *The Observer,* November 12, 2000, 10.

Herman, Ken and Greenberger, Scott. "Big Win for Bush in Iowa; Margin Encourages Runner-Up Forbes." *The Atlanta Journal-Constitution,* August 15, 1999, 1A.

Hess, Stephen. *America's Political Dynasties.* New York: Doubleday, 1966.

Hinckley, Barbara. "House Re-elections and Senate Defeats: The Role of the Challenger." *British Journal of Political Science* 10 (October, 1980): 441–460.

Hobart Mercury. "Clinton Tells of Kill Plan." September 15, 2001.

Hook, Janet. "The Nation; Bayh Says Bye to '08 Bid; Up against Big-Name Potential Candidates like Clinton and Obama, the Democrat Decides Not to Run for President." *Los Angeles Times,* December 17, 2006, A26.

House, Billy. "Florida Is Cash Cow for Contenders." *Tampa Tribune,* April 17, 2007, 1.

Houston Chronicle. "Jeb Bush Gets Back to Work; May Run Again." January 8, 1956, A6.

Hunter, Jennifer. "Why Hillary? 'She Doesn't Need a Tour of the White House.'" *Chicago Sun Times,* February 20, 2007, 17.

Isikoff, Michael and Corn, David. *Hubris: The Inside Story of Spin, Scandal, and the Selling of the Iraq War.* New York: Crown Publishers, 2006.

Jacobson, Gary C. *A Divider, Not a Uniter: George W. Bush and the American People.* New York: Pearson Education, 2007.

Jakes, Lara. "Clinton Wins Praise from Colleagues, If Not from Voters." *Milwaukee Journal Sentinel,* April 15, 2001, 6A.
Karp, David and Tisch, Chris. "Governor Bush to Close Schiavo Inquiry." *St. Petersburg Times,* July 8, 2005, 1B. Kasindorf, Martin. "Clintons Ride Separate Waves at Convention." *USA Today,* August 15, 2000, 5A.
Keen, Judy. "Like Father, Like Son: Pedigree Is Presidential, but Are Bush's Ambitions?" *USA Today,* December 4, 1997, A1.
———. "Bush Embraces Legacy." *USA Today,* July 28, 2000a, 1A.
———. "Risks Taken, Lessons Learned along the Way Bush, Certain He Could Do Better Than Clinton, Learned from Missteps." *USA Today,* November 8, 2000b, 15A.
Kellerman, Barbara. *All the President's Kin.* New York: Free Press, 1981.
Kenna, Kathleen. "He's the Other George Bush for Now, He's the Texas Governor. But Many Believe He'll Retrace His Father's Steps to the White House." *The Toronto Star,* July 6, 1997, F6.
Kennedy, Helen. "GOP Donors Spend $24m to Visit Prez." *New York Daily News.* May 23, 2001, News 7.
Kristof, Nicholas. "The 2000 Campaign: The 1988 Campaign, For Bush, Thrill Was in Father's Chase. *New York Times,* August 29, 2000, A1.
Kurtz, Howard. "Bailing on Bush." *Washington Post,* June 5, 2007, opinion.
Lardner, George Jr. "GOP Report Raps 'Air Hillary' Costs; Clintons Travel Bill Tops $182,000." *Washington Post,* March 24, 2000, A06.
———. "Gifts Were Not Meant for Clintons, Some Donors Say." *Washington Post,* February 5, 2001, A03.
Lawrence, Jill. "N. Y. Republicans Suggest Pirro Try Something Else; Support Slumps for Her Challenge to Sen. Clinton." *USA Today,* December 16, 2005, 10A.
———. "Congress Full of Fortunate Sons and Daughters." *USA Today* August 8, 2006, 1A.
———. "Big Question for Hillary: What Will Bill's Impact Be?; Some Democrats Worry, but Most Americans Polled Say He's a Plus. *USA Today,* March 29, 2007, 1A.
Lehigh, Scot. "Obama Bandwagon Is Filling up Fast." *Boston Globe,* December 12, 2006, A17.
MacPherson, Myra and Radcliffe, Donnie. "Betty Ford Says She Is Addicted to Alcohol." *Washington Post,* April 22, 1978, A5.
Maraniss, David. *First in His Class: A Biography of Bill Clinton.* New York: Simon & Schuster, 1995.
March, William. "The Governor's Race; Bush vs. MacKay; Democrat Buddy MacKay Makes His Play for the Job He Has Pondered for More Than a Decade." *Tampa Tribune,* October 18, 1998, Nation/World 1.
———. "Fla. Controversies Plague Bushes." *Tampa Tribune,* March 13, 2000, Florida/Metro 1.
Marcus, Ruth. "Now, 'A Different Kind of First Lady.'" *Washington Post,* January 20, 1993, F20.

Marinucci, Carla. "Clinton Sees Role for Husband." *San Francisco Chronicle*, February 24, 2007, A1.
McCarthy, Robert J. "Campaign Low-Key While First Lady Decides." *Buffalo News*, April 25, 1999, 4B.
McCullough, David. *John Adams*. New York: Simon and Schuster, 2001.
McGrory, Brian. "Gov. George Bush Makes a Name for Himself in Texas. *Boston Globe*, June 21, 1995, 1.
Meek, James Gordon. "Hillary Diplomatically Mum on Prez's Failure at the UN." *New York Daily News*, March 20, 2003, News 8.
Milkis, Sidney and Nelson, Michael. *The American Presidency: Origins and Development 1776–1990*. Washington, DC: Congressional Quarterly, 1990.
Minutaglio, Bill. *First Son: George W. Bush and the Bush Family Dynasty*. New York: Random House, 1999.
Moore, James and Slater, Wayne. *Bush's Brain: How Karl Rove Made George W. Bush President*. Hoboken: John Wiley & Sons, Inc., 2003.
Morris, Julie. "Bush's Son Eyes Texas' Top Job; Weighs Run for Governor." *USA Today*, May 31, 1989, 2A.
Morris, Roger. *Partners in Power*. New York: Henry Holt and Co., 1996.
Morris, Vincent. "State's Pols on the Fence over Bush's Plan of Action." *New York Post*, September 16, 2002, 4.
Nagourney, Adam. "Early 'Maybe' from Obama Jolts '08 Field." *New York Times*, December 4, 2006, A1.
National Broadcasting Corporation (NBC). "New Poll Shows President Bush's Approval Rating at 29 Percent." *Today Show*, June 14, 2007.
National Review. "The Week." May 22, 2006.
Navarrette Jr., Ruben. "Being a Dad Is One Tough Job." *San Diego Union-Tribune*, March 11, 2007, G-3.
Neuman, Johanna. "Baker Visits Iraqi Refugee Camp." *USA Today*, April 9, 1991, 1A.
New York Daily News. "Oh Brother! Gov. Jeb Bush Says He'd Sign Bill Giving Florida's 25 Electoral Votes to W." November 30, 2000, 1.
New York Post. "What Hillary Learned from Bill." July 9, 1999, 28.
New York Times. "In their Own Words: Standard Stump Speeches of Chiles and Bush." October 28, 1994, A26.
O'Brien, Ellen. "A More Popular Clinton, on the Defense." *Philadelphia Inquirer*, December 20, 1998, A1.
Orr, J. Scott. "The Bush Clan Descends on Philly." *The Star-Ledger (Newark, New Jersey)*, August 3, 2000, News 1.
Page, Susan and Benedetto, Richard. "Race Resembles a Family Feud, Observers Say. Some Suggest George W. May Be after Payback for Father's Loss." *USA Today*, August 2, 2000, 5A.
Parmet, Herbert. *George Bush: The Life of a Lone Star Yankee*. New York: Scribner, 1997.

Pew Global Attitudes Project. *Views of a Changing World 2003: War with Iraq Further Divides Global Publics.* (June 3, 2003). Retrieved October 3, 2006, from http://people-press.org/reports/display.php3?ReportID=185/.
Pfiffner, James P. *George W. Bush and the Abuse of Executive Power.* Presented at the Annual Meeting of the American Political Science Association, Chicago, IL. August 30, 2007.
Pickler, Nedra. "Another President Bush? George Thinks Brother Jeb Would Be a Great One." *Associated Press Worldstream,* May 10, 2006.
Pincus, Walter. "Bush Says He Hoped Saddam Would Flee Iraq; Capturing Leader at Gulf War's End Was Ruled Out." *Washington Post,* September 2, 1998, A02.
Pious, Richard. *The Presidency.* Needham Heights, MA: Simon & Schuster, 1996.
Rado, Diane. "Bush Alienates Black Lawmakers." *St. Petersburg Times,* October 28, 1994, 2B.
Rauber, M., Birnbaum, G., and Dicker, F. "Hillary Bills Taxpayers for Trips to Apple." *New York Post,* June 15, 1999, 7.
Reagan, Ronald. *The Reagan Diaries.* New York: HarperCollins, 2007.
Reinhold, Robert. "In Troubled Oil Business, It Matters Little If Your Name Is Bush, Sons Find." *New York Times,* April 30, 1986, A14.
Renshon, Stanley A. *In His Father's Shadow: The Transformations of George W. Bush.* New York: Palgrave MacMillan, 2004.
Ricks, Thomas. *Fiasco: The American Military Adventure in Iraq.* New York: Penguin Press, 2006.
Ridenour, Ron. "1m March against US Assassins." *Morning Star,* January 27, 2006.
Robison, Clay. "Republican National Convention; Though He Has High-Profile Role, Gov. Bush Low-Key about Future." *The Houston Chronicle,* August 12, 1996, A13.
———. "Clinton Criticizes Bush on Tour Stop." *The Houston Chronicle,* December 6, 2003, A35.
Rosenbaum, David. "The 2000 Campaign: The Florida Race; A Bush Rally Becomes a Family Affair." *New York Times,* November 1, 2000, A28.
Salinero, Mike. "Bush's Agenda Emerges." *Tampa Tribune,* November 13, 2002, 1.
Scher, Richard K. *Politics in the New South: Republicanism, Race, and Leadership in the Twentieth Century.* Armonk, NY: M. E. Sharpe, 1997.
Schneider, William. "President's Deal-Maker Style Could Cost Him." *St. Petersburg Times,* April 28, 1989, 19A.
Schweizer, Peter and Schweizer, Rochelle. *The Bushes: Portrait of a Dynasty.* New York: Doubleday, 2004.
Sheehy, Gail. *Hillary's Choice.* New York: Random House, 1999.
Simon, Roger. *Road Show.* New York: Farrar, Straus and Giroux, 1990.
St. Petersburg Times. "Sen. Clinton: Presidency Not My Goal." April 7, 2001, 3A.

———. "Bill Still Burns over Loss, So Hillary Will Be Here." February 25, 2007, 3B.
Standora, Leo. "Hil Says Bush too Eager to Fight Saddam." *The New York Daily News,* November 21, 2002, News 18.
Storing, Herbert J. (ed.). *The Complete Anti-Federalist.* Volume 5 Chicago, IL: University of Chicago Press, 1981.
Thach, Charles. *The Creation of the Presidency 1775–1789: A Study in Constitutional History.* Baltimore, MD: Johns Hopkins Press, 1969.
Tilove, Jonathan. "Black Support Proves Crucial to Bush Win." *Times-Picayune (New Orleans),* November 7, 2004, 16.
Tomasky, Michael. *Hillary's Turn: Inside Her Improbable, Victorious Senate Campaign.* New York: Free Press, 2001.
Toobin, Jeffrey. *A Vast Conspiracy.* New York: Random House, 1999.
———. *Too Close to Call: The Thirty-Six Day Battle to Decide the 2000 Election.* New York: Random House, 2001.
Troy, Gil. *Mr. and Mrs. President: From the Trumans to the Clintons.* Lawrence: University Press of Kansas, 2000.
Tumulty, Karen and Carney, James. "Inside Hillary's Obama Counter Attack." *Time,* April 26, 2007.
United Press International (UPI). "Dad Says Jeb Bush Would Be a Good President." June 1, 2005.
Urofsky, Melvin I. *A March of Liberty.* New York: Alfred A. Knopf, 1988.
U.S. News and World Report. *Triumph Without Victory: the Unreported History of the Persian Gulf War.* New York: Times Books. 1992.
Usborne, David. "Clintons Clash over Puerto Ricans." *The Independent (London),* September 6, 1999, 14.
Von Drehle, David. "Clinton Diverges from Bush on Iraq; Democrat Supports Relaxed Deadline." *Washington Post,* March 13, 2003, A13.
Walsh, K., Whitelaw, K., Marek, A., and Stanford, J. "The Man behind the Curtain." *U.S. News and World Report,* October 13, 2003, 26.
Watson, Robert P. *The Presidents' Wives: Reassessing the Office of First Lady.* Boulder, CO: Lynne Rienner, 2000.
Wayne, Stephen. *The Road to the White House 1996.* New York: St. Martin's Press, 1996.
Wead, Doug. *All the President's Children.* New York: Atria Books, 2003.
Wicker, Tom. *George Herbert Walker Bush.* New York: Penguin Group, 2004.
Williams, Jeannie. "Stars Pack Farewell Lovefest for the Clintons." *USA Today,* August 14, 2000, 10A.
Wills, Gary. *The Kennedy Imprisonment: A Meditation on Power.* Boston, MA: Little, Brown and Co., 1985.
Wilson, Harold A. *European Thought from Locke to Lenin.* New York: McGraw-Hill, 1991.
Woodward, Bob. *The Agenda.* New York: Simon & Schuster, 1994.
———. *State of Denial: Bush at War, Part III.* New York: Simon & Schuster, 2006.

Index

abortion, 36, 63, 68, 69, 97, 132, 181
Adams, Abigail, 40, 43
Adams, Charles (son of John and Abigail Adams), 41
Adams, Charles (son of John Quincy Adams), 43
Adams, George Washington, 43
Adams, John (father), 22, 38, 39–40, 41, 42, 43, 44, 71
Adams, John (grandson), 43
Adams, John Quincy (son), 34, 38, 40–43, 44, 112
Adams, Luisa, 43
Adams, Nabby, 41
Adams, Samuel, 38
Adams, Thomas, 41
Adams family, 3, 12, 37, 38, 43–44
affirmative action, 2, 181, 188–89
Afghanistan, 108, 142–43, 144, 145
Africa, 107, 141
African-Americans
  and Bush family, 61
  and civil rights, 24, 61
  and crime, 71, 162
  and Democratic party, 188
  in Florida, 180, 186–87, 188–89
  and Hillary Rodham Clinton, 172
  and Jimmy Carter, 8
  and poverty, 80
  and Republican Party, 81
Ailes, Roger, 70
Al Qaeda, 142, 144
  see also Terrorism
Alaska, 52
Alexander, Lamar, 130
Alinsky, Saul, 81

All the President's Children: Triumph and Tragedy in the Lives of America's First Families (Wead), 33
Ambrose, Stephen, 32
American Civil Liberties Union (ACLU), 120
American Medical Association, 101
American Revolution, 3, 14–15, 18, 19, 20, 38, 39, 41
Andover Academy, 55, 113
Aniston, Jennifer, 158, 159
anti-Federalists, 17, 39, 40
Arafat, Mrs. Yasser, 162
Arbusto (business owned by George W. Bush), 115
Arizona, 55, 58
Arkansas
  conservatism in, 84, 87, 88
  Cubans in, 4, 87
  and economy, 91
  education in, 88, 89, 91, 154, 156, 177
  legal aid in, 156
  legislature of, 86–87, 89, 154, 177
  and Paula Jones scandal, 104, 107
  political importance of, 156, 157
  political power in, 80, 86
  poverty in, 80, 156
  race relations in, 80
  Republicans in, 94
  road system in, 87
  taxes in, 89
  and U.S. Senate, 86
  and Whitewater scandal, 96, 99, 102, 104, 105, 154, 164

Arkansas—*continued*
 see also Clinton, Bill; Clinton, Bill and Hillary Rodham, as couple; Clinton, Hillary Rodham
Arkansas Savings and Loans, 102
Arlington, Tex., 121
Arlington Stadium (Tex.), 121
Armitage, Richard, 139
Army, British, 31, 39
Army, U.S., 75, 147
Articles of Confederation, 5, 12, 15, 16, 39
assassinations, attempts, and plots
 George H. W. Bush and, 150
 Gerald Ford and, 36
 John F. Kennedy and, 7, 24, 38, 50, 51
 Robert Kennedy and, 51, 52
 Ronald Reagan and, 36, 69
Atlanta, Ga., 91
Atwater, Lee, 70, 120
Austin, Tex., 130
A World Transformed (Bush and Scowcroft), 141

baby boom generation, 77, 79, 124, 128, 130
Baghdad, Iraq, 75, 143, 147, 150
 see also Gulf Wars
Baker, James, 74, 135–36, 145, 148, 149–50
Bandar Bin Sultan, 138, 141
Barber, James, ix
Beirut, Lebanon, 69
Bentsen, Lloyd, 64
Berlin Wall, 73
bin Laden, Osama, 107–8, 118, 142, 166
Birth Control League, 58
Blair House (Washington, DC), 97
Blythe, William, 78, 99
Bob Jones University, 132
Bosnia, 109
Boston, Mass., 14–15, 38, 39
Bremer, Paul, 147

Brock, David, 84
Brokaw, Tom, 95
Brooke, Edward, 81, 82
Brown, Jerry, 95, 96
Browning, Dolly Kyle, 93
Buchanan, Pat, 44, 97, 125
Bush, Barbara
 and 1980 presidential election, 68
 and Bill Clinton inauguration, 97
 children of, 59
 and husband's 1964 Senate election, 62
 marriage of, 57
 and move to Texas, 57, 59
 and son George, 11, 21, 57, 115, 122, 123, 135, 151, 184, 185
 and son Jeb, 11, 135, 184–85
Bush, Columba, 181, 182, 193
Bush, Dorothy, 59
Bush, George H. W. (father)
 and 1964 presidential election, 60
 and 1964 U.S. Senate election, 55, 60–62, 63, 64, 70, 111, 113, 114
 and 1966 congressional election, 61, 63
 and 1970 U.S. Senate election, 55, 64, 65, 66, 70, 111, 114–15, 182
 and 1976 Republican Convention, 67
 and 1980 presidential election, 55, 67–69, 70, 111, 116, 135, 184
 and 1988 presidential election, 17, 25, 33, 55, 69–71, 72, 91, 119–20, 132, 183
 and 1992 presidential election, 2, 5, 26, 44, 78, 95, 96, 97, 109, 111, 122, 123, 124, 125, 127, 134, 135, 144, 181, 183, 184
 and 2000 presidential election, 128, 131, 132, 133, 134, 138, 139, 151
 assassination plot against, 150

Index   221

as author, 141
and Bill Clinton, 4, 97, 193
brother of, 160
as businessman, 57, 59, 61, 64, 67, 113, 115–16
characteristics of, 44, 64, 120
children of, 1, 53, 54, 57, 59, 112, 115, 118
as CIA director, 4, 65, 66, 67, 73
as congressman, 4, 63, 64
and conservatives, 55, 58, 59, 62, 67–68, 69, 70, 71, 72, 111, 125, 128, 186
as diplomat, 4, 44, 60, 65, 66, 73, 137
education of, 56, 57, 113
and fall of Soviet Union, 142
and family legacy, 179
and father, 57, 59, 60, 182
and First Gulf War, 3, 26, 65, 73–76, 77, 111, 122, 133, 143, 144, 146, 148, 150, 168
and Ford administration, 65–66
foreign policy team of, 72, 74, 112–13, 135, 136, 139, 140, 141, 145, 146, 150, 151
and fund-raising, 56, 65, 117, 125, 131, 149
and James Baker, 135, 148, 149–50
and Karl Rove, 124
and liberals, 70, 71, 120, 182
marriage of, 120, 182
military service of, 4, 57, 113, 114
and moderates, 63, 66, 68, 182
and move to Texas, 57, 59, 64, 116
political network of, 56, 65, 67, 72, 116, 120, 121, 125, 131, 149, 151
popularity of, 76, 77
positions of, on political issues, 60, 61, 63, 64, 68, 70, 144, 183
post-presidential career of, 4, 19

and presidency, 11, 20, 71–72, 99, 127, 131, 137
and religion, 119
and Republican Party, 4, 57, 59–60, 62–63, 65, 66, 68, 116, 124, 131
and Richard Nixon, 63–64, 65
scholarship on, 57
as vice president, 4, 44, 55, 69, 118, 131, 137, 182, 183
see also Bush, George W. (son): and father; Bush, Jeb: and father; Bush, Prescott
Bush, George P., 134, 193
Bush, George W. (son)
and 1978 congressional election, 21, 44, 68, 116–18, 134, 185
and 1980 presidential election, 68
and 1988 presidential election, 25, 33, 70, 71, 119–21, 122
and 1990 gubernatorial election, 122
and 1992 presidential election, 122–23, 125
and 1994 gubernatorial election, 21, 118, 123–27, 149, 157–58, 184–85, 186
and 1996 presidential election, 127
and 1998 gubernatorial election, 129, 170, 187
and 2000 presidential election, 5, 21, 26, 55, 109–10, 118, 125, 128, 129, 130–36, 137, 139, 143, 148, 149–50, 175, 181, 188, 189–90
and 2004 presidential election, 144, 169, 170, 191
and 2008 presidential election, 111–13
and alcohol dependency, 44, 54, 115, 118, 119, 135, 149, 185
autobiography of, 53, 120, 123
and Bill Clinton, 123, 193
biographies of, 131, 132, 184–85
birth of, 57

Bush, George W. (son)—*continued*
  and brother Jeb, 38, 54, 119, 149–50, 179, 182, 183, 184–85, 186, 187, 189–90, 192
  as businessman, 25, 44, 114, 118–19, 121, 128, 136, 149, 185
  campaign style of, 62, 70, 71, 133, 144
  characteristics of, 62, 114, 116, 118, 119, 120, 130–31, 185
  children of, 33, 118, 185
  and Congress, 142
  and conservatives, 58, 69, 114, 127, 132, 137
  critics of, 179
  and Dick Cheney, 3, 72, 133–34, 139
  education of, 44, 56, 113–14, 115, 117, 125–26
  and family legacy, 129, 134, 135, 136, 174, 179, 182
  and father, 3, 34, 44, 53, 55, 57, 62, 64, 65, 71, 72, 76, 111, 112–13, 114–15, 116–17, 118–24, 125, 126–27, 128, 131, 132, 133, 134, 135, 136, 137, 138, 139, 140, 141, 148–51, 168, 174, 178, 184, 185
  and First Gulf War, 76
  and foreign policy, 27, 112–13, 117–18, 133, 136–37, 138–48, 150, 167
  and fund-raising, 125, 126, 131, 132
  governing style of, 70, 73, 122, 127, 137, 138–39, 144, 150
  as governor of Texas, 44, 71, 72–73, 111, 127, 128, 129, 137
  and Hurricane Katrina, 191
  and independents, 21
  and intellectuals, 114, 115
  and judicial branch, 193
  and liberals, 55, 68, 114
  marriage of, 116, 128
  and media, 119, 120, 121, 122, 125, 128, 132, 137, 141
  media adviser to, 171
  and moderates, 55
  and morality, 127, 129–30
  and mother, 11, 21, 115, 122, 123, 135, 151, 184, 185
  and Northeasterners, 114, 115
  as polarizing agent, 21, 179
  and policy issues, 121, 125, 126, 127, 137
  political network of, 119
  popularity of, 2, 146, 168, 169, 170, 179
  as president, 1, 3–4, 17, 26–27, 71, 72–73, 74, 112, 116, 120, 137, 170, 173, 178, 179–80, 182
  qualifications of, 7, 133, 178
  relatives of, 160
  and religion, 119–20, 128
  and Republican Party, 127, 128, 133, 179
  scholarship on, 34
  and Second Gulf War, 24–25, 26, 74, 76, 113, 117–18, 150, 167, 168, 169, 178, 179–80
  and Sept. 11, 2001, terrorist attacks, 142, 166
  and Terri Schiavo case, 192
  and Vietnam War, 114
Bush, Herbie, 59
Bush, Jeb
  and 1964 U.S. Senate election, 62
  and 1970 U.S. Senate election, 64, 182
  and 1980 presidential election, 68, 182, 184
  and 1988 presidential election, 70, 71
  and 1992 presidential election, 123
  and 1994 gubernatorial election, 126–27, 184–86, 187
  and 1998 gubernatorial election, 129, 186–87

and 2000 presidential election, 179, 189–90
and 2002 gubernatorial election, 190
and 2004 presidential election, 191
and 2008 presidential election, 180
and African-Americans, 186–87
and brother George, 38, 54, 119, 149–50, 179, 182, 183, 184–85, 186, 187, 189–90, 192
as businessman, 2, 183, 184, 185
campaign style of, 62, 70, 71, 182
characteristics of, 62, 185, 186, 187, 188, 193
children of, 193
and conservatives, 69, 181, 186, 193
and education, 187, 188
and family legacy, 179, 180, 182
and father, 44, 55, 57, 59, 62, 64, 65, 70, 71, 72, 126–27, 135, 179, 182, 183, 184, 185, 186, 190
as Florida secretary of commerce, 2, 119, 184, 185
and fund-raising, 131, 180–81, 187, 193, 197
governing style of, 70, 73, 191, 193
as governor of Florida, 1, 2–3, 26, 38, 71, 72–73, 135, 136, 149, 150, 179, 180, 181, 187–89, 190–93
and judicial branch, 193
and liberals, 68
marriage of, 2, 181, 182
mentioned, 134
and mother, 11, 59, 135, 185
and move to Florida, 2, 182, 184
and name recognition, 185
political network of, 181, 183
and post-2008 presidential elections, 180
and presidency, 1, 38, 179, 180–82, 184, 193, 194

qualifications of, 184, 185
and religion, 181, 193
and Republican Party, 180, 183, 184, 185
as Spanish speaker, 181, 191
wealth of, 183
Bush, Jonathan, 160
Bush, Laura Welch, 116, 119, 128
Bush, Marvin, 59, 115
Bush, Neil, 54, 59
Bush, Prescott
as businessman, 56, 57
as candidate for U.S. Senate, 57–58, 179
children of, 53, 57, 182
education of, 56
and father, 56
grandchildren of, 111
and ideology, 60, 62, 69
mentioned, 133
military service of, 56
as Republican, 56, 57–58, 60
and Richard Nixon, 63
as U.S. senator, 56, 58, 59, 60, 111
Bush, Robin, 59
Bush, Samuel, 56
Bush Bluebonnet Belles, 113
Bush family
competitiveness in, 185, 186
and conservatives, 156
as dynasty, 37, 43–44, 53–54
and foreign policy, 28
and fund-raising, 20, 112
and gubernatorial elections, 127, 129
and ideology, 58
legacy of, 180
and morals, 123
and New England, 156
offices held by, 4–5, 11
personal issues of, 3–4
political discourse of, 21
political network of, 122, 131, 180–81
political power of, 193

Bush family—*continued*
political successes of, 179
and presidency, 1, 3, 6, 11, 13, 16, 18, 20
and presidential elections, 5, 60, 69–71, 123, 130, 131, 135, 172, 189
and Republican Party, 55
social status of, 78
and vice presidency, 1, 20
Byrd, Robert, 166

California, 8, 51, 95, 175, 188
Canada, 14, 51
Capitol, U.S., 53
Card, Andy, 137
Carson, Johnny, 91
Carter, Billy, 35
Carter, Jimmy, 8, 24, 35, 52, 66, 67, 68, 87
Carville, James, 96, 159
Castro, Fidel, 60
Catholics, 58
caucuses, 24, 55, 67, 130, 132
see also Iowa: caucuses in
Central America, 183
Central Intelligence Agency (CIA), U.S., 4, 65, 66, 67, 141–42, 143, 146
Chappaquiddick, Mass., 52
character, 5, 70–71, 109–10, 133, 135, 149
Cheney, Dick
and Bush transition team, 137
as congressman, 72
as conservative, 133
and Don Rumsfeld, 140
and First Gulf War, 145
and George H. W. Bush, 137, 146, 150
and George W. Bush, 133–34, 140, 150
and presidential elections, 133, 139
and Second Gulf War, 145–46, 150

as secretary of defense, 3, 72, 74, 75, 133, 140
and Sept. 11, 2001, terrorist attacks, 142
as vice president, 3, 72, 112, 134, 139, 140, 142, 145–46
Cher, 158
Cherlin, Andrew, 29, 30
Chicago, Ill., 11, 24, 52, 55, 78, 81
Children's Defense Fund, 77, 82
Chiles, Lawton, 2, 185–86, 188
China, 8, 66, 137, 141, 156
Christians, 68, 117, 119–20
civil rights, 24, 36, 46, 47, 51, 58, 60, 61, 71
Civil War, U.S., 23, 32, 33, 43, 128, 187
Clay, Henry, 42
Cleland, Max, 167
Clinton, Bill
and 1974 congressional election, 85, 86
and 1976 attorney general election, 86
and 1980 gubernatorial election, 87, 88
and 1982 gubernatorial election, 88, 91
and 1982 presidential election, 96
and 1988 presidential election, 90–91, 93, 154
and 1990 gubernatorial election, 91, 92
and 1992 presidential election, 2, 5, 11, 21, 26, 47, 76, 77, 78, 81, 84, 86, 92–97, 101, 183
and 1994 mid-term elections, 104, 149
and 1996 presidential election, 103, 127, 128
and 2000 presidential election, 134, 149, 159
and 2008 presidential election, 3, 79
as attorney general of Arkansas, 2, 86

autobiography of, 79, 107
biographies of, 78, 80, 84, 86, 90–91
brothers of, 35, 99
characteristics of, 76, 78, 79–80, 91, 159
and conservatives, 96
and Democratic Party, 167
early life of, 77–78, 80
early political career of, 20, 80–81
education of, 78, 80, 83
and George H. W. Bush, 4, 193
and George W. Bush, 111–12, 123, 193
as governor of Arkansas, 2, 4, 5, 26, 47, 76, 86–87, 94, 96, 154
health of, 177
and Hillary Rodham Clinton's 2000 Senate campaign, 158, 159
and Hillary Rodham Clinton's 2008 presidential campaign, 174
impeachment of, 3, 5, 7, 36, 102, 107, 108, 109, 110, 130, 133, 149, 153, 154, 155, 157, 176, 181, 193
and media, 91, 93, 94, 98, 99, 100, 102, 105
and Monica Lewinsky scandal, 3, 5, 36, 105–6, 107, 108–9, 130, 153, 177
and New York State, 156
and Newt Gingrich, 127
and parents, 77–78, 84, 86, 99
and Paula Jones scandal, 92–93, 99
and policy issues, 99, 109
political network of, 126
popularity of, 169–70, 176
and post-presidential career, 4, 19, 169–70
as president, 3, 26, 27, 37, 79, 83, 93, 98–110, 124, 135, 138, 142, 150, 161–62, 165, 166, 169–70, 172, 175–76, 177
and presidential nomination system, 24
and Republican Party, 21, 128, 129, 130, 134
and Second Gulf War, 168
and Vietnam War, 80–81, 94
and Whitewater scandal, 5, 96, 99
see also Clinton, Bill and Hillary Rodham, as couple

Clinton, Bill and Hillary Rodham, as couple
and 1992 presidential election, 47, 77, 92, 93–96, 98, 154, 173
and 1994 mid-term elections, 103
and 2008 presidential election, 172–74, 183
in Arkansas, 83, 84, 85–86, 87–92, 93, 154
and Bill Clinton's first term as president, 175–76, 177
and conservatives, 124
and Daniel Patrick Moynihan, 161
and Democratic Party, 164, 170
and departure from White House, 165, 169, 170
financial support for, 20
and foreign policy, 175, 176
and fund-raising, 158, 159, 170
and Gennifer Flowers affair, 154
and health care reform, 101–2, 154, 161, 175–76, 177
and a Hillary Rodham Clinton presidency, 167, 168, 171–73, 175–77
and Hillary Rodham Clinton's 2000 Senate campaign, 159, 164
and Hillary Rodham Clinton's political aspirations, 157, 170
and impeachment of Bill Clinton, 153

Clinton, Bill and Hillary Rodham,
as couple—*continued*
and infidelity, 79, 85–86, 87, 90–91,
93–94, 96, 154, 176–77
marriage of, 77, 79, 83, 84, 85,
86, 90, 93, 94, 107, 108–9,
154, 164, 170, 176–77
and media, 176–77
and Monica Lewinsky scandal, 3,
105–6, 107, 108–9, 155, 164
in New York, 157
offices held by, 4–5
political discourse of, 21
political network of, 86, 124,
158, 174
political partnership of, 47, 77,
78, 79, 81, 82–83, 84, 86,
87, 88–90, 93, 95–96, 97, 98,
100–2, 103, 104, 105, 124,
153–55, 159, 162, 164,
175–76, 178
and Rudolph Giuliani, 160
and Second Gulf War, 167–68
and U.S. presidency, 1, 3, 6, 13, 16
and Whitewater, 154–55, 164
at Yale Law School, 78–79, 82, 83
Clinton, Chelsea, 87, 91, 94, 107, 166
Clinton, Hillary Rodham
and 1964 presidential election, 81
and 1974 congressional election,
85, 86
and 1980 gubernatorial election,
87, 88
and 1982 gubernatorial election,
88, 91, 96, 154
and 1988 presidential election, 91
and 1990 gubernatorial election,
91–92
and 1992 presidential election,
2, 11, 21, 36, 47, 77, 84, 86,
92, 93–94, 95–96, 98
and 1994 elections, 103
and 2000 U.S. Senate election, 153,
154, 155, 156–64, 170, 176
and 2004 presidential election,
166, 169

and 2006 elections, 169, 170
and 2008 presidential election,
1, 3, 20, 38, 77, 79, 162, 163,
168, 170–75, 180, 181
advisers to, 46
in Arkansas, 2, 4, 25–26, 47, 83,
85, 86, 87–90, 91–92, 96,
154, 156, 177
autobiography of, 79, 83, 84,
108–9, 165
and Bill Clinton's first term as
president, 175–76, 177
biographies of, 84, 89, 103, 154,
157
brother of, 165
characteristics of, 78, 79, 94, 155
childhood of, 156
and conservatives, 87, 88, 96, 97
and daughter's birth, 87
and Democratic Party, 153, 156,
169–70
early political career of, 2, 25, 79,
81–82, 83–84, 154
education of, 78, 81–82, 83, 88,
154, 156
Eleanor Roosevelt as role model
for, 38, 45, 155, 156
and fund-raising, 158–59, 169,
170, 174
and impeachment of Bill Clinton,
155, 157
as liberal, 82–83, 84
and media, 82, 87, 88, 94, 95, 98,
99, 100, 102, 103, 105–6,
154, 164
and Monica Lewinsky scandal,
3, 5, 36, 163, 164
and New York State, 156–57
and parents, 99
political network of, 83, 174
popularity of, 109, 165–66, 168,
172
positions of, on political issues,
88, 156, 177
and Puerto Rican nationalists,
161–62, 176

qualifications of, 177–78
and Republican Party, 21, 81, 82, 103, 106, 156, 160–61, 193
and Second Gulf War, 167–69, 173, 178
and Sept. 11, 2001, terrorist attacks, 166
and U.S. presidency, 18, 20–21, 48, 84, 96, 101, 110, 157, 193, 194
and U.S. Senate, 2, 5, 46, 47–48, 109, 153, 156, 164–66, 177, 178
as U.S. first lady, 2, 3, 4–5, 36, 37, 38, 45, 47, 79, 83, 93, 98, 99, 100–2, 103, 138, 154, 155, 156, 157, 158, 162, 172, 176, 177
and Whitewater scandal, 96, 99, 103, 104, 105, 154–55, 157
see also Clinton, Bill and Hillary Rodham, as couple
Clinton, Roger (father), 78
Clinton, Roger (son), 35
Clinton, Virginia, *see* Kelley, Virginia Dell Cassidy Clinton
Coalition Provisional Authority, 147
Codino, Armando, 2, 183
College Republications, 124
Colorado, 90
Communism, 8, 59, 69, 183
Confederate States of America, 43
Congress, U.S.
and 1994 comprehensive crime bill, 99
and 1994 elections, 99
Andrew Jackson and, 42
Bill Clinton and, 102
and CIA, 66
and Constitutional Convention, 5, 6
and deficit reduction, 98
Democrats and, 72, 103, 106, 128, 177
family connections in, 11
and First Gulf War, 74, 146

Franklin Roosevelt and, 46
and gays in military, 99
George W. Bush and, 142
and health-care reform, 101, 102, 176
and Hillary Rodham Clinton, 102
and John Adams's presidency, 40
and John F. Kennedy's presidency, 50
and John Tower, 72
Kennedy family and, 53
media coverage of, 24
and Monica Lewinsky scandal, 105, 106
and North American Free Trade Agreement, 99
powers of, 17, 24–25
Republicans and, 6–7, 85, 99, 102–3, 105, 106, 131
Richard Nixon and, 63
and Second Gulf War, 146, 148, 168
and taxes, 98
and Terri Schiavo case, 192
and Watergate, 25
women in, 175
see also House of Representatives, U.S.; Senate, U.S.
Connecticut, 56, 57–58, 60, 61, 62, 111, 113
Connecticut National Guard, 56
Connerly, Ward, 188–89
Conrad, Kent, 108
conservatives
during 1970s and 1980s, 78
and 1980 presidential election, 67–68, 70
and 1988 presidential election, 119–20
and 1992 presidential election, 44, 96
and 2000 presidential election, 132
Bill Clinton and, 96, 124
Bush family and, 156

conservatives—*continued*
  Democratic Party and, 63, 113, 127, 128, 157, 169
  Dick Cheney and, 133
  in Florida, 180, 186
  George H. W. Bush and, 55, 63, 71, 72, 111, 113, 128, 186
  George W. Bush and, 127, 128, 137
  Hillary Rodham Clinton and, 87, 88, 96, 97
  Jeb Bush and, 186, 193
  and John Birch Society, 59
  Lloyd Bentsen and, 64
  Michael Medved and, 82
  Newt Gingrich and, 102
  Pat Buchanan and, 97, 125
  political positions of, 58, 63, 68, 69, 72, 126
  and religion, 68, 119–20, 181, 193
  Republican Party and, 55, 58, 67, 68, 102, 132, 133, 137, 181
  Ronald Reagan and, 63, 67, 71
  Ted Kennedy and, 53
  and Terri Schiavo, 181, 192
  in Texas, 57, 59
Constitution, U.S.
  amendments to, 6–7, 36, 40, 90, 178
  anti-Federalists and, 17
  articles of, 18
  and pardons, 165
  and presidency, 14, 16, 17–18, 19
  and presidential elections, 190
  ratification of, 17–18
  signers of, 17
Constitutional Convention, 5–6, 12, 15–17, 19, 20, 100
Continental Congress, 18, 39
  see also American Revolution; Congress, U.S.
crime and criminal justice, 125, 126, 127, 183, 186, 193
Croft, Steve, 94
Cuba, 2, 28, 60, 87, 182–83
Cubans and Cuban-Americans, 4, 87, 181, 182–83
Cuomo, Andrew, 160
Cuomo, Kerry Kennedy, 160
Cuomo, Mario, 160
Custis, John, 33
Custis, Martha, *see* Washington, Martha Dandridge Custis

Dade County, Fla., 183
Dade Republican Party, 180, 183
Daley family, 11
Dallek, Robert, 32
Declaration of Independence, 3, 15, 16, 18, 40
democracy
  in Iraq, 147
  leaders of, 30
  in Middle East, 27
  opportunities presented by, 78
  and political families, 77, 173, 174
  U.S., 1–2, 3, 13, 25, 26, 27, 28, 129, 136
Democratic National Conventions, 24, 52, 91, 123, 130, 158, 171
Democrats and Democratic Party
  and 1928 presidential election, 61
  and 1968 presidential election, 51
  and 1970 election for U.S. Senate, 64
  and 1988 Florida gubernatorial election, 187
  and 1988 presidential election, 90, 91, 120
  and 1990 Arkansas gubernatorial election, 92
  and 1992 presidential election, 21, 80, 96, 97
  and 1994 mid-term elections, 102–3
  and 1994 Texas gubernatorial election, 126
  and 2000 presidential election, 133, 153, 164, 189
  and 2002 Florida gubernatorial election, 190
  and 2008 presidential election, 171, 172, 173, 181
  in Arkansas, 80

and assassination of John
  Kennedy, 60
Bill Clinton and, 86, 164, 167,
  170
and conservatives, 63, 113, 127,
  128, 157, 169
Eleanor Roosevelt and, 46, 47,
  155
and First Gulf War, 146, 167
in Florida, 183, 186, 188
and foreign policy, 167, 169
Franklin Roosevelt and, 56, 169
and fund-raising, 169
George H. W. Bush and, 127
George W. Bush and, 21, 128,
  179
Hillary Rodham Clinton and, 86,
  153, 156, 164, 169–71
leaders of, 4
moderates and, 170
and Monica Lewinsky scandal,
  108, 109
and New Deal, 155
and New York, 160, 164
Nita Lowery and, 157
and Northeast, 156
and poverty, 32
and presidency, 169
and presidential nomination
  system, 24
and race, 61, 187, 189
Samuel Bush and, 56
in South, 187
Ted Kennedy and, 52, 53
in Texas, 57, 126, 127, 128
and U.S. Congress, 72, 103, 128,
  177
and U.S. Senate, 146
and Vietnam War, 167
and Watergate, 85
women and, 175
Department of Commerce, U.S.,
  119
Department of Defense, U.S., 140,
  147
  see also Pentagon

Department of Health and Human
  Services, U.S., 106, 107, 183
Department of State, U.S., 140, 143,
  146, 147
Department of Transportation, U.S.,
  130
Detroit, Mich., 69
Dixon, Ill., 8
Dole, Elizabeth, 130
Dole, Robert, 70, 103, 127–28
Douglas, Stephen, 31
Dowd, Maureen, 172
Drew, Elizabeth, 100
Dukakis, Michael, 70–71, 91, 120
Duke University, 8

economy, U.S.
  and 1988 presidential election, 70
  in 1990s, 149
  and 2000 presidential election,
    111
  Bill Clinton and, 109
  and Clinton administration, 172
  George H. W. Bush and, 71–72,
    77
  Great Depression, 8, 23, 46, 56
  and health care, 101
  and Sept. 11, 2001, terrorist
    attacks, 142, 166
  and stock market, 6
Edelman, Marian Wright, 82, 83
education
  in Arkansas, 91, 154, 156, 177
  Bill Clinton and, 88, 91
  and civil rights, 58
  in Florida, 2, 181, 188, 190
  George W. Bush and, 125, 126,
    127, 137
  Hillary Rodham Clinton and,
    2, 88, 89, 91
  Jeb Bush and, 187
  Republican Party and, 97
  in Texas, 126
Education Standards Committee, 89
Edwards, John, 167
Egypt, 75

Eisenhower, Dwight D., 7, 8, 47
electoral college, 20, 21, 23, 39, 40
embassies, U.S., 107, 141
Enron, 126
Equal Rights Amendment, 36, 68
Europe, 2, 12, 13, 83
Evans, Don, 119

Federalist Papers, 17–18
Federalists, 39, 40, 41, 44
Feeney, Tom, 186
Feinstein, Diane, 175
Ferraro, Geraldine, 160
First Amendment, 40
First Baptist Church (Orlando, Fla.), 135
First Gulf War, *see* Gulf Wars: First
first ladies, 35–38, 79
   see also Clinton, Hillary: as U.S. first lady; Roosevelt, Eleanor: as U.S. first lady
Flexner, James, 18, 19, 30, 31
Florida
   and 1980 presidential election, 68
   and 1992 presidential election, 183, 184
   and 2000 presidential election, 26, 130, 135, 136, 148, 149–50, 189–90
   and 2004 presidential election, 191
   and 2008 presidential election, 183
   abortion in, 181
   affirmative action in, 2, 181, 188–89
   African-Americans in, 180, 188–89
   conservatives in, 180, 186
   courts in, 192
   crime in, 186
   and Cuba, 60
   Democratic Party and, 183, 186, 187, 188
   demography of, 180
   economy of, 185
   education in, 2, 181, 187, 188, 190
   fund-raising in, 180
   George W. Bush in, 142
   gubernatorial elections in, 2, 126–27, 129, 184, 186–87, 190
   and hurricanes, 185, 191
   Latinos in, 87, 180, 191
   legislature of, 2, 185, 187–88, 189, 190
   officials of, 2, 185, 187, 189
   race in, 187, 188–89
   Republican Party and, 2, 180, 183, 184, 185, 186, 187, 188, 190
   state government of, 119, 181, 187–88
   taxes in, 181, 188
   and Terri Schiavo case, 181
   see also Bush, Jeb
Florida Supreme Court, 136, 189, 190
Flowers, Gennifer, 94, 154
Foley, Tom, 101
Forbes, Steve, 130
Ford, Betty, 36
Ford, Gerald, 4, 36, 66, 67, 69
foreign policy, U.S.
   and 1979 Iran hostage crisis, 144
   and 2000 presidential election, 111, 143
   and Bay of Pigs, 50, 60
   Bill Clinton and, 107–8, 109, 176, 177
   challenges in, 25
   and cold war, 8, 58, 70, 73, 142
   credibility of, 26
   and Cuban missile crisis, 50
   Democratic Party and, 167, 169
   Dick Cheney and, 72, 150
   and fall of Berlin Wall, 73
   George H. W. Bush and, 65, 66, 73, 138, 139, 142, 151
   George W. Bush and, 112–13, 117–18, 136–37, 138–48, 150, 167

Hillary Rodham Clinton
   presidency and, 176, 177
   and ideology, 74
   and preemption, 167
   presidency and, 23, 25
   Republican Party and, 167
   Richard Nixon and, 8
   see also Gulf Wars; Vietnam War
Fort Chafee (Ark.), 87
Foster, Vince, 99
France, 39, 40, 41, 56
Fulbright, William, 80

Gallup Poll, 168
Gates, Robert, 74
Geffen, David, 172
Genovese, Michael, 7
George III, king of England, 3, 15, 39
Georgetown University, 78, 80
Georgia, 8, 95, 102, 167
Gergen, David, 100, 101, 103
Germany, 48
Gibson, Charlies, 141
Gingrich, Newt, 102, 103, 127
Giuliani, Rudolph, 160, 161, 162–63
Goldwater, Barry, 8, 58, 60, 61, 63, 67, 69, 81
Goodwin, Doris Kearns, 31
Gore, Al
   and 1992 presidential election, 97
   and 2000 presidential election, 5, 26, 111, 118, 133, 134, 135, 136, 149, 159, 164, 189
   and Bill Clinton, 159
   media coverage of, 98
   and Rudolph Giuliani, 160
   and Terry McAullife, 159
   as U.S. senator, 133
   as vice president, 98, 100, 133
Gow, Robert, 115
Graham, Billy, 119
Grant, Ulysses ("Buck"), Jr. (son), 33
Grant, Ulysses (father), 33

Great Britain, 14, 15, 22, 39, 41, 43, 48, 108
   see also Monarchies: British
Greenwich, Conn., 57
Grunwald, Mandy, 159
Gulf Wars
   First, 3, 26, 65, 73–76, 77, 111, 122, 133, 139, 140, 143, 144, 146, 150, 167
   Second, 3, 25, 26, 72, 113, 114, 117–18, 134, 143–48, 150, 167–69, 171, 173, 178, 179–80

Hamilton, Alexander, 17–18, 19, 20, 21–22, 40, 44
Hamptons (N.Y.), 158
Hance, Kent, 116–17, 118
Hanover, Donna, 163
Hardball, 168
Harken Energy, 118
Harris County, Tex., 59, 62
Harris, John, 160
Harris, Katherine, 189
Harrison, Benjamin, 37
Harrison, William Henry, 37
Hart, Gary, 90, 120
Harvard Business School, 115
Harvard University, 43, 50, 120, 125–26
Havana, Cuba, 28
health care
   and economy, 101
   and Medicaid and Medicare, 103, 126, 137, 183
   reform of, 2, 99–100, 101, 102, 103, 154, 157, 161, 175–76, 177
Henry VIII, king of England, 26
Hillary's Choice (Sheehy), 84
Hiroshima, Japan, 144
Hispanics, *see* Latinos
Holland, 41
Hollywood, Calif., 8, 172
Holt, Frank, 80
Homestead, Fla., 185

Horton, Willie, 71
House of Representatives, U.S.
   and 1824 presidential election, 42
   and 2002 elections, 146
   Adams family members in, 43
   Democratic majority in, 72
   George H. W. Bush and, 4
   and health-care reform, 101
   and impeachment of Bill Clinton, 106, 108, 153
   Judiciary Committee of, 83
   Kennedy family members and, 49, 53
   mentioned, 82
   speakers of, 42, 101, 102, 103, 127
Houston Post, 126
Houston, Tex., 59, 62, 63, 68, 97, 123, 182, 184
Hubbell, Webb, 104
Hurricane Andrew, 185
Hurricane Katrina, 191
Hussein, Qusay, 27
Hussein, Saddam
   and Al Qaeda, 144
   children of, 27
   Dick Cheney and, 146
   and First Gulf War, 26, 73, 74, 75, 140, 143, 144, 145
   George H. W. Bush and, 150
   George W. Bush and, 76, 150
   and inspections of nuclear facilities, 107, 108
   and Kurds, 75
   and Republican Guard, 75
   and Second Gulf War, 144, 147
   and Shiites, 75
   as U.S. ally, 73
Hussein, Uday, 27
Hyannis Port, Mass., 53
Hyde Park, N.Y., 45

Ickes, Harold, Jr., 46, 153, 155, 159
Ickes, Harold, Sr., 46, 155
Illinois, 95, 156, 171
   see also Chicago, Ill

immigrants and immigration, 40, 55, 181, 182–83
impeachment
   Bill Clinton and, 3, 5, 7, 36, 93, 102, 106, 107, 108, 109, 110, 130, 133, 149, 153, 154, 155, 157, 176, 181, 193
   Richard Nixon and, 83
independents, 21, 132
Iowa
   and 2000 presidential election, 131–32
   caucuses in, 52, 67, 70, 132, 171, 173
   Republican Party in, 131–32
   straw polls in, 131–32
Iran, 73, 144, 145, 148
Iran-Contra Scandal, 69
Iraq
   Bill Clinton and, 108, 150
   and Iran, 145
   Kurds in, 75, 147
   as political issue, 177
   rebuilding of, 72
   refugees from, 140
   Shiites in, 75
   UN inspections of, 108
   see also Gulf Wars
Iraq Study Group, 148
Iraqi Army, 74, 75
Ireland, 109
Islam, 156
Israel, 26, 74, 75, 162
Ivy League, 4, 64, 70, 111, 114, 115

Jackson, Andrew, Jr. (son), 33
Jackson, Andrew (father), 13, 23, 33, 42–43, 188, 194
Jackson, Darrell, 172
Jackson, Jesse, 189
Jacobsen, Gary, 21
Jay, John, 17
Jefferson, Thomas, 15, 19, 20, 26, 40
Jews, 162, 165, 183
John Birch Society, 59

Johnson, Claudia ("Lady Bird"), 32
Johnson, Lyndon B., 7, 32, 35, 51, 60, 61, 63
Johnson, Sam, 35
Joint Chiefs of Staff, U.S., 74
Jones, Don, 164
Jones, Paula, *see* scandals: Paula Jones affair
Jordan, 26

Kabul, Afghanistan, 143
Kellerman, Barbara, 37
Kelley, Virginia Dell Cassidy Clinton, 77–78, 84, 86, 99
Kennedy, David, 53
Kennedy, Edward ("Ted"), 38, 49, 50, 51–53, 178
Kennedy, Jacqueline, 36
Kennedy, John F. (father)
　and 1960 presidential election, 8, 50
　assassination of, 7, 24, 38, 50, 51, 60
　and Bill Clinton, 20, 80
　and brother Bobby, 35, 50, 51
　characteristics of, 49, 51
　congressional campaigns of, 49–50, 51
　and Eleanor Roosevelt's funeral, 47
　and entry into politics, 29
　and father, 49
　George H. W. Bush compared to, 64
　marriage of, 36, 85, 176
　media coverage of, 37, 85
　popularity of, 36
　Prescott Bush and, 58
　as president, 50, 58, 97
　scholarship on, 49
　and World War II, 49
Kennedy, John F., Jr. (son), 53, 157
Kennedy, Joseph, Jr. (son), 48–49, 51
Kennedy, Joseph P. (father), 29, 38, 48, 49, 50, 51, 53, 112
Kennedy, Patrick (father of Joseph P. Kennedy, Sr.), 48
Kennedy, Patrick (son of Ted Kennedy), 53
Kennedy, Robert (father), 35, 38, 49, 50–51, 52, 53, 54
Kennedy, Robert, Jr. (son), 160
Kennedy family
　and 1968 presidential election, 51
　as dynasty, 3, 12, 37, 38, 48
　and fund-raising, 56
　mentioned, 129
　political network of, 56
　and presidency, 48
　and Rudolph Giuliani, 160
　scholarship on, 53
　social status of, 78
　and World War II, 49
　younger generations of, 53
Kennedy, Ted, *see* Kennedy, Edward ("Ted")
Kentucky, 42
Kerry, John, 169, 170
Kim Jung II, 27
Kopechne, Mary Jo, 52
Korea, *see* North Korea; South Korea
Kuhn, Bowie, 117
Kurds, 75
Kuwait, 26, 28, 61, 73, 74, 75, 150
　see also Gulf Wars: First

Laden, Osama bin, *see* bin Laden, Osama
Latinos, 129, 180, 181, 191, 193
Lay, Ken, 126
Lazio, Rick, 163–64
League of Nations, 45
League of Women Voters, 45, 82
legislation
　Alien and Sedition Acts (U.S., 1798), 40
　in Arkansas, 154
　Brady Bill (U.S., 1993), 98–99
　Civil Rights Act (U.S., 1964), 60, 61
　Civil Rights Act (U.S., 1968), 63
　deficit reduction (U.S., 1993), 98

legislation—*continued*
  Family Medical Leave Act (U.S., 1993), 98
  on funding Nicaraguan anti-Communists, 69
  Highway Beautification Act (U.S.), 32
  for open housing (U.S.), 61, 63
  Stamp Act (British, 1765), 14
  Tea Act (British, 1773), 14
  on Terri Schiavo case (U.S., 2005), 192
  Townshend Duties (British, 1767), 14
  Voting Rights Act (U.S., 1965), 13
Lewinsky, Monica, *see* scandals: Monica Lewinsky affair
liberals
  and 1988 presidential election, 120
  George H. W. Bush and, 70, 113, 120, 182
  George W. Bush and, 114, 179
  Hillary Rodham Clinton as, 83, 84
  Jeb Bush and, 187
  Michael Dukakis and, 71
  Republican Party and, 68
  Tom McRae as, 92
Libya, 35
Lieberman, Joe, 164
Life magazine, 82
Lincoln, Abraham, 23, 31–32, 58
Lincoln, Mary Todd, 31–32
Lincoln, Nancy, 31
Lincoln, Sarah, 31
Lincoln, Thomas, 31
Little Rock, Ark., 87, 92, 93
Locke, John, 13
London, Eng., 46
Lone Star Rising (Dallek), 32
Long Island, N.Y., 163
Los Angeles, Calif., 158
Louisiana, 191
Lowery, Nita, 157, 158–59
Lubbock Press Club, 117

MacArthur, Mrs. Douglas, 117
Madison, Dolly, 35–36
Madison, James, 6, 17, 35–36
Maraniss, David, 78, 80, 86, 90
Maritime Commission, U.S., 48
Martinez, Bob, 184
Mason, George, 6, 16, 17, 23, 194
Massachusetts
  constitution of, 39
  Kennedy family in, 48, 50
  legislature of, 41, 43
  Michael Dukakis and, 70, 91
  Paul Tsongas and, 95
  Shay's Rebellion in, 12
  U.S. senators from, 81
  Willie Horton case in, 71
Matthews, Chris, 168
McAullife, Terry, 159
McCaffery, Barry, 75
McCain, Cindy, 132
McCain, John, 55, 130, 132–33, 144, 149
McCall, Carl, 158
McCarthy, Eugene, 51
McCarthy, Joseph, 47
McDougal, Jim, 96, 102, 104
McGovern commission, 24
McKay, Buddy, 187
McKinnon, Mark, 171
McLarty, Mack, 87, 100
McRae, Tom, 92
Medicaid, *see under* health care
Medicare, *see under* health care
Medved, Michael, 82
Mercer, Lucy, 45
Mexico, 56, 181
Miami, Fla., 2, 180, 181, 182–83, 184, 185, 187
Middle East, 27, 28, 74, 78, 144, 146, 148, 162, 177
Midland, Tex., 115, 123
Milkis, Sydney, 23
moderates, 67, 160, 170, 182
monarchies
  British, 5, 14, 15, 16, 18
  elective, 6

Enlightenment and, 13
European, 2, 12
and inequality, 12
in Kuwait, 28
in Saudi Arabia, 28
U.S. founders and, ix, 3, 5, 6, 11, 15, 16–17, 18, 194
Monroe, James, 35, 41
Monroe, Joseph, 35
Morris, Dick, 88, 92, 103
Morris, Gouverneur, 6
Mosbacher, Rob, 125
Moynihan, Daniel Patrick, 161
Mt. Kennedy, 51
Musharraf, Pervez, 143
Muslims, 27

Nagasaki, Japan, 144
name recognition, ix, 1, 11, 182, 185, 187
Nassar (Syrian leader), 27
National Association for the Advancement of Colored People (NAACP), 47, 59
National Bank, 40
National Guard, 56, 87, 114, 147
National Rifle Association (NRA), 98
National Security Council, 74, 136, 140
  see also foreign policy, U.S.
Nebraska, 134
Nelson, Michael, 23
New Deal, 35, 37, 155
New England, 42, 59, 64, 67, 156
New Hampshire
  newspapers in, 70
  presidential primaries in, 51, 52, 55, 67, 70, 93, 94, 95, 132, 133, 154, 173
New Orleans, La., 42, 78, 191
Newsweek, 69–70
New York, N.Y.
  1992 Democratic National Convention in, 97
  and 2000 U.S. Senate election, 153, 158
  African-Americans in, 162
  George Washington in, 19
  homelessness in, 160
  Jewish voters in, 162, 165
  Latino community in, 162
  law-enforcement community in, 162–63, 176
  mayor of, 160, 161, 162–63
  media in, 163, 170, 190
  New Square in, 165
  political machines in, 55
  Puerto Ricans in, 161
  and Sept. 11, 2001, terrorist attacks, 142, 166
  teachers union in, 158
New York Attorney's Office, 165
New York Democratic Convention, 164
New York Police Department (NYPD), 162
New York Republican Party, 160–61
New York State
  African-American officials in, 158
  Bill and Hillary Clinton in, 138
  congressional representatives from, 157, 163
  Democratic Party and, 160, 164, 170
  Dick Morris and, 88
  and economy, 157
  elites in, 158
  governors of, 58, 160
  Jewish voters in, 162
  Republican Party and, 162
  Robert Kennedy and, 51
  size of, 157
  see also Clinton, Hillary Rodham
New York Times, 50, 102, 172
Nicaragua, 69
9/11, *see* Terrorism: and Sept. 11, 2001, attacks
Nixon, Patricia, 36
Nixon, Richard M.
  background of, 8
  and California gubernatorial election, 8

Nixon, Richard M.—*continued*
  and Communism, 8
  and Congress, 63
  and executive power, 145
  and foreign policy, 8, 66, 82
  and George H. W. Bush, 63–64, 65
  marriage of, 36
  as moderate, 67
  and Pat Buchanan, 97
  personality of, 32
  and Prescott Bush, 63
  as president, 7, 8, 32, 83
  and presidential elections, 8, 50, 63, 65, 81
  resignation of, 65, 83, 85
  scholarship on, 32
  as vice president, 8
  and Watergate, 8, 32, 65
North American Free Trade Agreement (NAFTA), 99, 109
North Korea, 2, 27, 138, 145
nuclear test ban treaties, 60
Nussbaum, Bernard, 102, 105

Obama, Barack, 171–72, 173, 174, 180, 193
Odessa, Tex., 59, 116, 117
Office of Independent Counsel, 104, 105, 106, 107, 164
Oklahoma City bombing, 103
O'Neill, Joe, 123
On the Edge (Drew), 100
Orlando, Fla., 135, 184
Oyster Bay, N.Y., 45

Pakistan, 143
Palestine, 162
Parliament (Great Britain), 14, 15, 195n. 4 (chap. 1)
Parmet, Herbert, 57
Peck, Gregory, 158
Penn, Mark, 159, 170
Pennsylvania, 5, 16, 42
Pentagon, 140, 142, 143, 147
People magazine, 185
Perle, Richard, 143

Perot, Ross, 67, 96–97, 122
Pew Research Center, 27
Philadelphia, Pa., 5–6, 133
Pierce, Barbara, *see* Bush, Barbara
Pirro, Albert, 170
Pirro, Jeanne, 170
Pitt, Brad, 158, 159
Planned Parenthood, 58, 63
Pledge of Allegiance, 71
Podesta, John, 105
poverty, 7, 32, 46, 51, 63, 80, 155, 156
Powell, Colin, 74, 75, 112–13, 139–40, 141, 145, 146
Powell doctrine, 139
presidency, U.S.
  access to, 20
  democratization of, 22–24
  and diversity, 9
  expectations for, 173
  and family relationships, ix, 2, 3, 7, 12, 13–14, 77, 109, 149, 150, 153, 173, 180, 182, 193–94
  founders and, ix, 5, 7, 9, 11, 12, 13–14, 15–18, 22–23, 90, 100, 136, 173
  and fund-raising, 180–81
  and gender, 25, 174–75
  limits on, 17
  media coverage of, 22, 23–24, 37
  and name recognition, 182
  and race, 25
  responsibilities of, ix, 17, 22, 23, 24–25, 34
  scholarship on, 18, 31, 32, 37
  and secretary of state, 41
  and security, 20
  state electors for, 13
  and Twenty-Fifth Amendment, 36
  and veto power, 17
primaries
  and 1968 presidential election, 51
  and 1980 presidential election, 52–53, 111
  and 1992 presidential election, 11

and 2000 presidential election, 55, 132–33
and 2008 presidential election, 171, 172
in Arkansas, 85, 88
in California, 51
congressional, 64, 85
Democratic Party and, 51, 52–53, 64, 85, 130
in Florida, 185
in Georgia, 95
in Illinois, 95
Republican Party and, 24, 52, 55, 130
and Super Tuesday, 95
in Texas, 64, 116, 118
see also New Hampshire: presidential primaries in
Protestants, 25
Puerto Ricans, 161–62, 176
Puerto Rico, 161

Quayle, Dan, 97, 120, 130, 131

race, 8, 36, 58, 60, 61, 63, 119, 187, 188–89
Ramallah, Palestine, 162
Randolph, Edmund, 16
Reagan, Nancy, 36, 37
Reagan, Ronald
  and 1964 presidential election, 8
  and 1976 Republican Convention, 66, 67
  and 1978 Texas congressional election, 116
  and 1980 presidential election, 4, 55, 66, 67, 68–69, 70, 116, 119
  attempted assassination of, 69
  background of, 8
  children of, 34
  and conservatives, 63, 67, 71
  and George W. Bush, 144
  and Gerald Ford, 69
  as governor of California, 8
  health of, 7
  and James Baker, 135
  marriage of, 36
  political network of, 67
  popularity of, 69, 71
  as president, 8, 24, 44, 69, 72
  and presidential nomination system, 24
  and Republican Party, 66
Recarey, Miguel, 183
Reconstruction, 61, 129, 188
Reese, Jim, 116
refugees, 4, 46, 75, 87, 140, 147, 155, 183
religion, 119–20, 128, 156, 181, 193
Reno, Janet, 102, 105
Renshon, Stanley, 84
Republican Guard, Iraqi, 75
  see also Iraqi Army
Republican National Committee, 65, 124, 158
Republican National Conventions, 66, 81, 111, 129, 130
Republicans and Republican Party
  and 1964 presidential election, 60, 61
  and 1980 presidential election, 67–69, 111
  and 1992 presidential election, 94, 97, 124, 134
  and 1994 elections, 99, 102–3
  and 1996 presidential election, 103, 127–28
  and 1998 Florida gubernatorial election, 187
  and 2000 presidential election, 130–33, 149
  and 2004 presidential election, 169
  and 2006 New York election for U.S. Senate, 170
  and 2008 presidential election, 180
  and abortion, 132
  African-Americans and, 81
  in Arkansas, 85

Republicans and Republican
    Party—*continued*
  Barack Obama and, 193
  Bill Clinton and, 129, 130, 134
  Bush family and, 55, 56
  and Communism, 183
  and Congress, 6–7, 85, 106, 131
  conservatives and, 59, 67, 68, 72,
    102, 132, 133, 137, 181
  divisions in, 59, 63, 66
  and elections for U.S Senate, 161
  in Florida, 2, 180, 183, 184, 185,
    186, 188, 190
  and foreign policy, 167
  George H. W. Bush and, 4, 57,
    62, 65, 66, 68, 131
  George W. Bush and, 127, 128,
    179
  Hillary Rodham Clinton and, 81,
    103, 106, 156, 160–61, 193
  and ideology, 58, 66
  Jeb Bush and, 2, 183, 184
  Latinos and, 183, 193
  liberals and, 68
  moderates and, 160
  in New York State, 162
  and nominating process, 130
  and North American Free Trade
    Agreement, 99
  and post-2008 presidential
    elections, 181
  Prescott Bush and, 57, 58
  and presidential nomination
    system, 24
  and race, 61, 187
  and religion, 119–20, 181
  Rockefellers and, 58
  Ronald Reagan and, 66
  and South, 156–57, 187
  in Texas, 57, 59, 116, 118, 123,
    124
  and Watergate, 66
  women and, 175
Revolutionary War, *see* American
    Revolution
Rhode Island, 6, 53

Rice, Condoleezza, 74, 113, 136,
    137, 140, 141, 147
Rich, Marc, 165
Richards, Ann, 21, 118, 123, 124,
    125, 126
Rockefeller family, 78
Rockefeller, Nelson, 58, 66, 81
Rodham, Hillary, *see* Clinton, Bill
    and Hillary Rodham, as
    couple; Clinton, Hillary
    Rodham
Rodham, Hugh Ellsworth (father), 99
Rodham, Hugh (son), 165
Roe v. Wade, 63
Roosevelt, Anna, 46
Roosevelt, Eleanor
  characteristics of, 45
  children of, 45, 46
  death of, 47
  and Democratic Party, 46, 47,
    155
  and elective office, 46, 47, 155,
    156
  as first lady of New York, 45–46
  issues championed by, 45, 46–47,
    155
  legacy of, 48
  marriage of, 37–38, 45, 46, 47
  and McCarthyism, 47
  and parents' deaths, 45
  as political presence, 45–46
  as role model for Hillary Rodham
    Clinton, 38, 45, 155, 156
  scholarship on, 36, 95
  and Theodore Roosevelt, 37–38, 45
  and United Nations, 46, 155
  as U.S. first lady, 35, 36, 45, 46,
    47, 95
Roosevelt family, 37, 44, 45
Roosevelt, Franklin Delano
  advisers to, 46
  and American people, 23
  children of, 32, 34, 46
  death of, 155
  as Democrat, 104, 169
  as governor of New York, 45

health of, 45, 46
and Joseph P. Kennedy, 48
marriage of, 37–38, 45, 46, 95, 176
mother of, 45
popularity of, 71
as president, 46, 47, 56
and presidential elections, 45, 46
scholarship on, 23
and term limits, 6
and Theodore Roosevelt, 37–38, 44–45
Roosevelt, Sara, 45
Roosevelt, Theodore (father), 23, 37–38, 44–45
Roosevelt, Theodore, Jr. (son), 45
Rose Law firm, 87, 88, 96, 177
Ross, Diana, 158
Rove, Karl, 122, 124–25, 129, 130, 131, 132, 133
Rumsfeld, Donald, 140, 144, 146, 147
Russert, Tim, 164
Russia, 41, 43
Ryan, Nolan, 121

San Diego, Calif., 127
San Francisco, Calif., 172
Saudi Arabia, 28, 73, 74, 75, 107, 138
scandals
  and 2000 presidential election, 110, 135
  Chappaquiddick, 52
  Clintons' departure from White House, 165
  Gennifer Flowers affair, 94, 154
  Hillary Rodham Clinton's book deal, 165
  Iran-Contra, 69
  Monica Lewinsky affair, 5, 83, 93, 105–6, 107, 108–9, 130, 153, 155, 163, 164, 177
  NYPD shooting, 162–63
  pardons by Bill Clinton, 138, 161–62, 165, 176
  Paula Jones affair, 92–93, 99, 102, 104–5, 107
  Rudolph Giuliani and, 163
  Watergate, 2, 8, 25, 32, 65, 66, 70, 85, 124
  Whitewater, 5, 93, 96, 99, 102, 103, 104, 105, 154–55, 157, 164
Schiavo, Michael, 181, 191–93
Schiavo, Terri, 181, 191–93
Schumer, Chuck, 166
Schweizer, Peter, 131, 132, 184–85
Schweizer, Rochelle, 131, 132, 184–85
Scowcroft, Brent, 141, 145, 151
Second Gulf War, *see* Gulf War: Second
Second Treatise of Government (Locke), 13
Secret Service, U.S., 35, 158
Securities and Exchange Commission (SEC), U.S., 48
Seduction of Hillary Rodham, The (Brock), 84
Senate, U.S.
  and 2002 elections, 146
  Appropriations Committee of, 166
  Arkansas and, 86
  Barack Obama and, 171
  and civil rights, 58
  Daniel Patrick Moynihan and, 161
  Democratic Party and, 72, 146
  Finance Committee of, 161
  and health-care reform, 101
  and impeachment of Bill Clinton, 109, 153, 154
  John Adams's son-in-law and, 41
  John Kennedy and, 49
  John Tower and, 72
  majority leaders of, 127
  mentioned, 82
  Prescott Bush and, 57, 58
  Republicans and, 99, 102
  Robert Kennedy and, 51

Senate, U.S.—*continued*
  Ted Kennedy and, 50, 52, 53
  see also Clinton, Hillary Rodham
September 11, *see* Terrorism: and Sept. 11, 2001, attacks
Shalala, Donna, 106, 107
Shay's Rebellion, 12
Sheehy, Gail, 84, 89, 95, 157
Shiites, 75, 140, 144
60 Minutes, 94
Smith, Adam, 13
Smith, Al, 61
Smith, Jim, 185
Social Security, 137
Somalia, 99
South
  and 1828 presidential election, 42
  and 1964 presidential election, 61
  and 1980 presidential election, 68
  and 1988 presidential election, 71
  and 1992 presidential election, 95
  and civil rights, 58, 60, 61
  conservatives and, 180
  Democratic Party and, 57, 59, 61, 62, 63, 91, 128, 187
  education in, 88
  and Hillary Rodham Clinton presidential campaign, 157
  Jimmy Carter in, 8
  liberals and, 64
  political issues in, 64
  poverty in, 32, 80
  Republican Party and, 57, 58, 61, 62, 113, 156–57, 188
  state governments in, 129
South America, 183
South Carolina, 132–33, 172
South Dakota, 108
South Korea, 138
Soviet Union, 8, 58, 73, 142
Specter, Arlen, 108
Star (newspaper), 94
Starr, Kenneth, 93, 102, 104, 106, 109
Stephanopoulus, George, 96
Stewart, Potter, 18

Sudan, 108
Sultan, Bandar Bin, *see* Bandar Bin Sultan
Sununu, John, 72
Supreme Court, U.S., 18, 93, 97, 136, 190, 192
Syria, 74, 144, 148

Taiwan, 141
Taliban, 142
Talla*has*see, Fla., 187, 189, 191
taxes
  Bill Clinton and, 98
  Bob Dole and, 70
  cuts in, 68, 69, 71, 72, 137, 138, 139, 181, 188
  George H. W. Bush and, 144
  George W. Bush and, 137
Tenet, George, 141–42, 146
Tenne*s*see, 42, 130
terrorism
  and 1993 World Trade Center bombing, 107
  and 1996 Khobar Towers bombing, 107
  and 1998 U.S. embassy bombings, 107, 108, 141
  Clinton administration and, 107, 108, 142, 166
  Democratic Party and, 167
  Iran and, 144
  Islamic groups and, 107–8
  Osama bin Laden and, 107–8
  as political issue, 177
  Puerto Rican nationalists and, 161–62, 176
  and Second Gulf War, 144, 145, 148
  and Sept. 11, 2001, attacks, 21, 108, 142–43, 144, 146, 163, 166, 167
  Syria and, 27, 144
  and weapons of mass destruction, 143
  and year 2000 celebrations, 141

Texas
- affirmative action in, 189
- Ann Richards and, 123, 126
- Bush family in, 57, 61
- business and businessmen in, 26, 118, 124, 125
- campaign contribution limits in, 125
- conservatives in, 57, 59, 60, 63, 64, 113, 117, 126, 127, 128
- criminal justice in, 127
- Democratic Party in, 57, 59, 60, 62, 63, 64, 113, 126, 127, 128, 129
- George H. W. Bush in, 55, 57, 58, 59, 60–65, 68, 70, 72, 111, 113, 114, 116, 117, 120, 125, 128, 182
- George P. Bush in, 193
- George W. Bush in, 21, 44, 55, 61, 62, 68, 70, 72, 73, 111, 113, 114, 115, 116–18, 120, 121, 122, 123–27, 128, 129, 130, 131, 136, 137, 149, 150, 157–58, 184–85, 186, 187, 189
- government structure in, 128–29
- gubernatorial elections in, 21, 118, 122, 123–27, 129, 149, 157–58, 170, 184–85, 186, 187
- Jeb Bush and, 2, 68, 182, 184
- John Tower and, 60, 72
- Karl Rove and, 124, 129
- legislative districts in, 62–63
- legislature of, 127, 128, 129
- Lyndon Johnson and, 7, 32, 60, 61
- mentioned, 56, 150
- political issues in, 126
- poverty in, 7
- presidential elections in, 68
- and race relations, 59, 60, 61, 63
- Republican Party in, 57, 59, 62–63, 113, 116, 123, 124, 125
- Ross Perot and, 67, 122
- state senators in, 116–17, 126

U.S. House of Representatives
- elections in, 21, 44, 63, 68, 116–18, 134, 185

U.S. Senate elections in, 60–62, 63, 64, 65, 66, 70, 113, 114

Texas Air National Guard, 114

Texas Rangers baseball organization, 25, 121, 128

Texas Tech, 117

Thach, Charles, 18

Today show, 105–6, 164

Todd, Mary, *see* Lincoln, Mary Todd

Tonight Show, 91

Tower, John, 60, 72

Travolta, John, 158

Tripp, Linda, 109

Troy, Gil, 36

Truman, Harry, 6, 46, 47, 58, 101, 155

Tsongas, Paul, 95

Tucker, Jim Guy, 104

Turkey, 75

Twenty-Second Amendment, 6–7, 90, 178

Ueberroth, Peter, 121

Uhrman, Sarah, 84

UN Conference on Women, 156

United Nations
- and Afghanistan, 143
- Eleanor Roosevelt and, 46–47, 155
- and First Gulf War, 74, 75
- George H. W. Bush and, 60, 65, 137
- and inspection of Iraqi nuclear facilities, 108
- Prescott Bush and, 58
- and Second Gulf War, 146, 168

United States Military Academy (West Point), 145

Universal Declaration of Human Rights (UDHR), 47

University of Arkansas, 80, 85

University of Arkansas Law School, 84

University of Texas, 113
University of Virginia, 50
Utilities Board (Tex.), 126

Venezuela, 181
Vietnam War
  assessments of, 100, 113, 117
  Bill Clinton and, 80–81, 94
  Democratic Party and, 167
  George H. W. Bush and, 63
  George W. Bush and, 114
  Hillary Rodham Clinton and, 81
  Lyndon Johnson and, 32
  Richard Nixon and, 82
  Robert Kennedy and, 51
  and Tet offensive, 81
  veterans of, 132
Villa, Pancho, 56
Virginia, 6, 16, 170

Waldorf Astoria (New York, N.Y.), 65
Wallace, Henry, 46
Wall Street, 56, 57, 115
Wall Street Journal, 145
Wang, Vera, 158
Warner, Mark, 170
War of 1812, 41
War on Poverty, 7, 63
War Room, The (film), 96
Washington, DC
  Bill Clinton in, 80, 93–94, 104
  Clinton supporters in, 86
  Democratic Party in, 127, 128, 169
  Dick Cheney in, 134
  Dolly Madison in, 36
  Federal Courthouse in, 104
  George H. W. Bush in, 115, 127
  George W. Bush in, 115, 117, 119, 121, 124, 127, 128, 137, 138, 192
  Harry Truman in, 101
  Hillary Rodham Clinton in, 26, 79, 83, 85, 87, 93–94, 104, 154, 169
  journalists in, 100, 119, 137
  legal community in, 26, 86, 104
  Lyndon Johnson in, 32
  mentioned, 62, 87, 119
  and Second Gulf War, 146
  and Sept. 11, 2001, terrorist attacks, 21, 142
  Vince Foster in, 99
Washington, George
  and Alexander Hamilton, 19, 20, 21–22
  and American Revolution, 18–20
  and Constitutional Convention, 6, 19, 20
  death of, 40
  early life of, 30–31
  finances of, 31, 35
  as icon and unifying figure, 20, 21, 23, 39
  and John Adams, 39, 41, 71
  marriage of, 31, 35
  and presidency, 6, 18–20, 21–22, 39, 44
  scholarship on, 18, 19, 30, 31
  stepson of, 33
  and Thomas Jefferson, 19
Washington, Lawrence, 30–31
Washington, Martha Dandridge Custis, 31, 35
Washington Post, 102
Watson, Robert, 35
Wead, Douglas, 32, 34, 120
Wealth of Nations (Smith), 13
weapons of mass destruction (WMD), 143, 144, 145–46, 147, 148
Welch, Laura, *see* Bush, Laura Welch
welfare, 58, 92, 109, 125, 126, 127
welfare state, 6, 23
Wellesley College, 81, 82
Westchester County, N.Y., 170
West Point, 145
West Virginia, 166
White, Frank, 87, 88

White House
  Al Gore and, 133
  Barack Obama and, 180
  and Blair House, 98
  Bush family and, 29, 98, 109, 112, 116, 122, 128, 134, 135, 149, 150, 173
  Clintons and, 48, 83, 86, 89, 96, 98, 99, 100, 101, 102, 103, 105, 134, 138, 158, 162, 165, 169, 170, 172, 173, 175, 180
  Dick Cheney and, 98, 100, 142
  Eleanor Roosevelt and, 48
  James Monroe and, 35
  Jimmy Carter and, 8
  Lincoln bedroom in, 158
  and Monica Lewinsky scandal, 3, 83, 105, 153, 155
  Richard Nixon and, 63, 64
  and Sept. 11, 2001, terrorist attacks, 142
  Ted Kennedy and, 38
  and Whitewater scandal, 102, 104, 105
Whitewater, *see* scandals: Whitewater
Willentz, Sean, 179
Williams, Maggie, 98
Wills, Garry, 52, 53
Wilson, Edith, 36
Wilson, James, 5, 12, 16–17
Wilson, Woodrow, 23, 36

Wolfowitz, Paul, 140, 143
women, 13, 24, 97, 156, 174–75
women's issues, 45, 46, 47, 83, 86, 87, 156
Women's Trade Union, 45
Woodward, Bob, 98, 138, 139, 140
World Trade Center (New York, N.Y.), 21, 107
World War I, 45, 56
World War II
  Bill Clinton's father and, 78
  Bush family after, 56
  Eleanor Roosevelt and, 46
  federal government and, 37
  George H. W. Bush and, 4, 57
  Kennedy family and, 48, 49
  Lyndon Johnson and, 32
  refugees from, 155
  Ronald Reagan and, 8
  and U.S. national security policy, 142
Wright, Betsy, 88, 89, 90–91
Wright, Marian, *see* Edelman, Marian Wright
Wyoming, 72, 133

Yale Law School, 78, 82, 83, 154
Yale University, 44, 56, 57, 113–14, 115, 125–26
Yarborough, Ralph, 60, 61–62, 63, 64
Yonkers, N.Y., 170
Young Republicans, 81